Aid Dependence in Cambodia

SOPHAL EAR

AID

How Foreign Assistance

DEPENDENCE

Undermines Democracy

IN CAMBODIA

COLUMBIA UNIVERSITY PRESS   NEW YORK

Columbia University Press

Publishers Since 1893

New York Chichester, West Sussex

CUP.COLUMBIA.EDU

Chapter 1 is based on two articles that were previously published in the *International Public Management Journal*, 2007 © Taylor and Francis, and the *Asian Journal of Political Science*, 2007 © Taylor and Francis.

Library of Congress Cataloging-in-Publication Data

Ear, Sophal.

Aid dependence in Cambodia : how foreign assistance undermines democracy / Sophal Ear.

p. cm.

Includes bibliographical references and index.

ISBN 978-0-231-16112-1 (cloth : alk. paper) — ISBN 978-0-231-53092-7 (electronic)

1. Cambodia—Politics and government—1979. 2. Democracy—Cambodia. 3. Cambodia—Economic conditions. 4. Economic assistance—Political aspects—Cambodia. 5. Technical assistance—Political aspects—Cambodia. I. Title.

DS554.8.E25 2013

320.9596--dc23

2012006792

Columbia University Press books are printed on permanent and durable acid-free paper.

This book is printed on paper with recycled content.

Printed in the United States of America

c 10 9 8 7 6 5 4 3 2

References to Internet Web sites (URLs) were accurate at the time of writing. Neither the author nor Columbia University Press is responsible for URLs that may have expired or changed since the manuscript was prepared.

For my late mother, the twenty-one lives she saved, and the people of Cambodia

CONTENTS

FIGURES AND TABLES

Figures

Tables

PREFACE

AMONG THE MORE than 1.7 million Cambodians killed by Pol Pot's Khmer Rouge were my father and eldest brother. When the peasant army marched into Phnom Penh on April 17, 1975, my parents lived in a three-story villa near the airport. My father, an army captain who owned a drugstore, was precisely the type of bourgeois the revolution intended to cull from the Cambodian population once and for all.

My mother actually owned the villa because her first husband had built it for her. It was so grand that Ly Bun Yim, one of Cambodia's most famous film directors, shot his first feature, *Ronteah Krousar* (Thunder in the family), in the house. Mom had moved to Phnom Penh as a girl to live with her oldest sister, whose husband had been a government minister. He was also a congenital philanderer who began molesting my mother at age ten and forced her to marry him and become his "second wife" (concubine) when she was eighteen. He was at least twice her age, and she found other husbands elsewhere. One of them was my father.

The city buzzed with excitement that Thursday morning when the Khmer Rouge arrived in Phnom Penh. The bloody five-year civil war was over! Uncertain about what to expect, those who remained in the city hoped peace had arrived. What could possibly be worse than the American bombings? After all, more bombs had fallen on Cambodia since 1965 (2,756,941 tons) than were dropped during all of

World War II by the Allies (just over two million tons of bombs). People cheered as sullen Khmer Rouge soldiers marched down the main boulevards in ragged black uniforms with rifles in hand. My family had planned to escape to Thailand, purchasing a fishing trawler for transport, but my father ultimately decided we would stay and take our chances.

As soon as the peasant army secured the capital's choke points, loudspeakers began to blare orders of an immediate evacuation. Soldiers went door to door and forced the entire city of 2 million to depart, telling citizens they had to leave because the Americans were about to bomb.

We left our Tuol Kuork neighborhood on foot, while my eldest brother went with our aunt and her husband, the former government minister, in their sleek Citroën DS. We all spent the night in front of the airport because car traffic was terrible. The next morning, we were ordered to continue on foot to Kandal province; by then, my aunt's family, which had claimed my eldest brother as their only child, went their separate way, never to be seen again. A week later, we were on a Khmer Rouge boat headed upriver to Tuol Prik in Pursat province, where my parents toiled in rice fields like human water buffalo. Because they were wealthy urban dwellers, they were labeled "new people," the bottom rung of the Khmer Rouge's new social order.

One day, my mother returned from plowing the fields when the commune leaders called a meeting to announce that Vietnamese nationals would be allowed to return home. When Mom heard this, she could only think of survival. She had already seen so many die from illness and exhaustion. "I have to lie, I have to tell them I'm Vietnamese, to get away from this place," she thought. She decided to put our name on the list. When the others warned her, "Auntie, they're lying, they'll kill you when you go back there," she replied, "To stay is to die, to go is to die, so I might as well go."

It was several weeks before the repatriation process began, and safe passage would require not travel documents but mastery of the difficult Vietnamese language. Although my mother had grown up speaking Vietnamese with the servants, she had no way to know if it was enough.

We traveled on foot for three days to a place where trucks waited for us. The group's fear was palpable—although some were Vietnamese, most were pretending, and many thought it was a trap. There was no way to know, and we were exhausted from the trip. In fact, my father resembled the walking stick he propped himself up on. Suffering from diarrhea and bedbug bites, he could barely move, and on the third night, he died. Ironically, his death saved us, because he spoke no Vietnamese and would have given us away. The next morning, the trucks took us to a locomotive that brought us to the train station in Phnom Penh, where Chinese four-wheel-drive vehicles transported us to Kandal province.

Mom passed her first interview easily. A Vietnamese woman she met at the site of the first test helped out, coaching her in the language and giving us all gender-appropriate Vietnamese names. The second interview was conducted by a Vietnamese official. My mother wrapped us in blankets and told us to act sick so we would not be questioned. When the cadre asked, "Sister, what is your name?" she answered in her best Saigon accent, "My name is Nguyen Thi Lan," a name she had made up. After a rigorous interrogation, she and her five surviving children received permission to leave Cambodia for Vietnam.

On the boat trip to Vietnam, we ate rice and drank so much canned milk I became bloated and sick. Mom had no money because it had been banned by the Khmer Rouge, so she traded her last gold ring for a pot and some three-layered pork fat and cooked us our first real meal in six months.

As had happened earlier, our subsequent survival became possible through the kindness of good Samaritans. Once in Vietnam, we were told that if relatives didn't come to retrieve us within a week, we'd be sent to a collective farm, only a small step up from Tuol Prik. A maternal aunt lived in Saigon, but her address had been buried with my father in his shirt pocket. An acquaintance sent word to my aunt, and her husband made it to the camp on the final night, bribed the guards, and got us out.

Because the United States had no diplomatic relations with Vietnam after the war, France was our best option for asylum. We had no immediate family to sponsor us, but a distant cousin studied in Paris as a foreign student. He, in turn, befriended a Frenchman for help, who found a random lady probably in a phonebook with the same last name as my mother's. The Frenchman somehow convinced her to sign sponsorship papers. We left Saigon for France in 1978.

My first impression was of decrepitude; the floors of our small apartment in an eastern suburb of Paris were dirty, and dried-up chewing gum caulked the window frames. We got by on very little. Although I started kindergarten like every other French boy, I wore no underwear. The teacher sent notes home in my backpack, but Mom did not address *le problème*. The exasperated teacher confronted her, only to discover that we were too poor to buy winter coats, much less underwear. Shortly thereafter, bags of clothes appeared at our door. I will never forget the generosity French people showed us.

Europe may be the cradle of the modern welfare state, but in 1980 the French government viewed work as the solution to posttraumatic stress disorder (PTSD). My mother embroidered tiny flowers onto fancy tablecloths and napkins. I would take the train with her on weekends to 19 Avenue Victor Hugo, where she dropped off her piecework and picked up new assignments. Mom suffered from malaria and PTSD; she was offered psychotropic drugs. The end result was nervous breakdowns and long sojourns at mental institutions.

It was a hardscrabble life for my sister Sophie and me, who had to live with French families due to our situation at home. But the setup could not have been more informal, nor better. Our surrogate families were good-hearted people who wanted to help refugee children. There were no papers signed, and no money changed hands. Far better than foster care or adoption, this arrangement allowed us to have the best of both worlds, because every other weekend we spent at home with Mom.

We left France in 1985 to start a new life in the United States, where we stayed at another maternal aunt's home, in Richmond, California. She did not enroll us in school until my mom began screaming and demanded it. We borrowed an address in Berkeley, and I began seventh grade at Willard, one of two junior high schools in the city. Although we moved later to Oakland, I continued to attend Berkeley schools. Mom taught us that we would make sacrifices for education, even if it meant waking up two hours before our classmates and spending much of our time on trains and buses.

A pivotal moment came just before my freshman year at Berkeley High School when a Willard tutor checked my class schedule and saw that I was slated to take English as a second language (ESL). She put her foot down and insisted that I take college preparatory courses so I could get into a decent university. Passing freshman English was painful and required extra tutoring, but it was well worth it. By my senior year, I discovered an ESL netherworld that opened my eyes to the dangers of creating a school within a school and a culture of dependence.

Mom worked as a seamstress in Oakland's Chinatown, where she made designer Jessica McClintock's wedding gowns. Her only goal in life was for her kids to go to college. In her mind, there was no such thing as quick riches; cutting school short was out of the question. Education, for her, was not about making money, it was about learning how to think.

During my junior year, a visit to the University of California (UC), Berkeley, organized by the Society of Women Engineers (yes, men like me were thankfully allowed on the field trip), made a big impression. We dropped carefully protected eggs from the campus rooftops to test engineering principles. I was smitten, but how could I get in? A chance encounter with a UC Berkeley administrator who worked in admissions became another defining moment. Although I gained admission to all the other top schools in the UC system, Berkeley rejected me, and it was a crushing blow. The administrator and I hatched a plan: I'd appeal the rejection with a carefully written letter he vetted. It worked, and I was admitted on appeal.

Going anywhere else, even UCLA, would have been impossible. We could not afford it, and I was only sixteen—too young to live alone. Berkeley was possible only because means-tested Cal grants and Pell grants paid for my tuition, books, and incidentals. Food and housing would be courtesy of Mom. In that enabling environment, I buried myself in books and developed a passion for economics and political science. As former UC president Clark Kerr said, "If you're bored with Berkeley, you're bored with life." Never bored with Berkeley, I penned two honors theses for the challenge of doing it—one on Cambodia's economic history and development, the other on Western academic supporters of the Khmer Rouge taking aim at apologists like Noam Chomsky and others. On the eve of my graduation in 1995, I wrote that Berkeley taught to me not *what* to think but *how* to think.

From Berkeley, I went on to Princeton on a full fellowship for a master's degree in public affairs. After a few years working at the World Bank, I landed back at Berkeley for a PhD program in political science, which I received in 2006. My brother, Sam, graduated from San Francisco State University with a computer science degree. Sophie received a doctorate in pharmacy from UC San Francisco. Mom never missed a single one of our graduations.

Mom died in 2009, six months after the birth of my first a child, a son, her fourteenth grandchild. If nothing else, my mother was a survivor who taught us the values of hard work and self-sufficiency. My family's experience was very different from those of most of my countrymen who survived "Pol Pot time." Unlike Mom, who took our fate in her hands the day she claimed to be Vietnamese, most Cambodians who survived the Khmer Rouge kept their heads down and took no chances. A traditional Cambodian proverb (*cheh mauk pi rean, mean mauk pi rauk*) states that knowledge comes from learning, and wealth comes from searching. My mom had a very limited education, but she knew enough to never stop searching.

The lesson of my mother's story and her life's work is by no means that aid is unnecessary. We could not have survived without welfare after my mom could no longer work in the sweatshops of Chinatown. She didn't get herself and five kids to Vietnam and France on her wits alone or simply by picking herself up by her own bootstraps. At every turn, strangers and family helped. But she had to meet them halfway. In contrast, the handout mentality is ever present in Cambodia, the legacy of a colonial past in which the French told Cambodians what to do, how to speak, and what to think—they even made becoming a civil servant every college-educated Cambodian's dream. The educational system emphasized the creation of *fonctionnaires* (functionaries), not agronomists, economists, or entrepreneurs (Prud'homme 1969). The past lives on in a place like Cambodia, and that past influences Cambodians' dependence on foreign aid and donors. Some might ask: Why return to a place that nearly killed me? Why return to the scene of the crime? Because that's where I am from, and because helping Cambodia has to be part of my life's work. Mom understood. I had survived for a reason; with privilege comes responsibility. Cambodia was a different place by the time I returned, but it was also the same place she had left.

ACKNOWLEDGMENTS

ANYONE WHO HAS written a book knows that you can't get here on your own. This book was made possible because of my late mother. She played the role of both mom and dad throughout my life after my father's passing under the Khmer Rouge when I was less than a year old. My family's escape from Cambodia, thanks to mom's cunning and will to survive, made possible my education in France and the United States. It is with great pleasure that this book is dedicated to my late mother, the twenty-one lives she saved, and the people of Cambodia.

For how this book could finally come to fruition, I cannot but acknowledge the tireless efforts of professor David Leonard. I found David's Web site at UC Berkeley on a spring day in 2001. He was then Dean of International and Area Studies, and as often happens with me, I had the temerity to drop him an e-mail—sight unseen. Little did I know then that I would find the single most important advisor for my doctoral studies. He immediately took an interest in me, sending for my feedback a monograph he had written with Scott Straus, which would become the book *Africa's Stalled Development: International Causes and Cures* (Lynne Rienner Publishers, 2003). I instantly understood that I had found someone who appreciated my sometimes inexplicable interest in development and its discontents, having worked several years for the World Bank and, while doing my PhD in political science, the United Nations Development Programme.

For funding my advanced Khmer-language studies from 2003 to 2004, which enabled the start of three wonderful years in Cambodia, I thank the Blakemore Foundation; for research funding to get the ball rolling on actual research, I thank the University of California, Berkeley, for its generous fellowships and a Council of American Overseas Research Centers-funded Center for Khmer Studies grant. Chapter 2 could not have been possible without World Bank-Netherlands Partnership Program funding, which commissioned research through a consultancy. Chapter 3 was made possible by financial assistance via the Social, Technological and Environmental Pathways to Sustainability Centre of the University of Sussex from the Food and Agriculture Organization Pro-Poor Livestock Policy Initiative; the UK Department for International Development-funded Pro-Poor Risk Reduction project; and the Livestock-Sector Governance in Developing Countries project coordinated by Chatham House, London, with support from the UK Department for International Development and the World Bank. Chapter 4 was made possible through a U.S. Agency for International Development-funded grantee, Pact Cambodia. Neither the views of my employer, the U.S. Department of Defense, nor any of these organizations or agencies are represented in this book. All views are my own.

I am also grateful for comments, suggestions, and help from Peter Maguire, whose encouragement was indispensable, and to Teh-Wei Hu, Federico Podesta, Clay Wescott, Bruce Cain, Jim Robinson, Ken Leonard, Tomoki Fujii, Howard White, Sanja Samirana Pattnayak, Daniel Edelstein, Gabriel Kaplan, David Greenberg, Akira Shibanuma, Steve Golub, Direk Patamasiriwat, Mack Ramachandran, Mridul Saggar, Richard Bourgon, David Freedman, Daniel Butler, Steve Knack, Eric Neumayer, Arthur Brooks, John McPeak, Len Lopoo, Larry Schroeder, Stuart Bretschneider, Doug Wolf, Steve Kelman, Jon S. T. Quah, Ian Scoones and Sigfrido "Ziggy" Burgos, Kurt MacLeod, Karen Knight, Putsata Reang, Paul Randolph, Laura McGrew, Verena Fritz, Stephane Guimbert, Kai Kaiser, Pak Kimchoeun, Chan Sophal, Socheata Vong, Alison Alexanian, Marc Johnston, Ruth Homrigraus, Fayre Makeig, Leslie Kriesel, my editor Anne Routon, and anonymous reviewers. For research assistance, I thank Pete "Sophorl" Pin, Linda "Serei" Zekovitch, Vannarith Chheang, Sopheary Ou, and Chhorvivoinn Sumsethi, among many others. Most of all, I thank the hundreds of informants and respondents who adorn these pages with their wisdom and knowledge and who have given of themselves far more than I deserved.

To Om Radsady and Om Sumita—rest in peace.

Last, but not least, for bearing with me since first meeting me on July 4, 1997, as I strolled into her sister's house (without taking off my shoes!), for foolishly marrying me on July 8, 2006 (in that same house), for delivering our beautiful son, Steven Sophal Ear, in 2009 and our gorgeous daughter, Caitlyn Lim Ear, in 2011, I thank my indefatigable wife, Chamnan Lim. After my mom passed away on October 5, 2009, it was Chamnan who held down the fort, giving me the opportunity to make my own delivery in the form of this book.

NOTE ON CONFIDENTIALITY

INFORMANTS AND SURVEY respondents are, for brevity's sake and more importantly for the protection of personally identifiable information, anonymously coded (1-1, 1-2..., 2-1, 2-2..., 3-1, 3-2..., 4-1, 4-2, etc.), with the first digit associated with the chapter number and the second digit randomly assigned. See the appendix for a complete list of descriptors and other details without personally identifiable information. Today's Cambodia is not a place one wants to name names for reasons of personal safety and freedom of expression.

Aid Dependence in Cambodia

INTRODUCTION

WHEN I CAME to America in 1986, aged ten, starting seventh grade at Willard Junior High School in Berkeley, California, and not speaking a word of English, one of the first things I did was write a letter to President Ronald Reagan to thank him for fighting Communism. It was in Ms. Morrison's English as a second language class that I took pen to paper. Of course I didn't tell her about it. We were in Berkeley, after all. The People's Republic of Berkeley was the last place to admire anti-Communism, which in large part drove my thinking, but I understood that Communism had destroyed my family, killed my father, and made us refugees. As far as I can remember, politics has always held sway over me.

When I was in my mid-teens, I discovered an international newsletter called *Khmer Conscience* (*KC*) that had interesting articles focused on what the Reagan White House called "The Kampuchean Problem,"[1] written from a Cambodian expatriate perspective. Soon thereafter, I started exchanging letters with Mr. Hann So, *KC*'s editor. Using my white Brother electric typewriter, I cranked out diatribe-like streams of consciousness that Hann would later—to my amazement—adapt into short articles. One of these rants became "Are We Ready for Democracy?" and was republished on May 23, 1991, in the Southern California Vietnamese language newspaper *Nguoi Viet Weekly*.

Though I shamelessly framed the article and hung it on my bedroom wall, for years I refused to read it, embarrassed by the poor writing, the idealism, and naïveté. The essay questioned Cambodia's readiness for democracy in anticipation of the Paris Peace Agreement of October 23, 1991, which laid the foundation for Cambodia's first and only internationally organized elections in 1993. "Are the people living in Cambodia ready to accept democracy when it passes by?" I asked. "Because experiences are the events that shape a people. And the experiences have been traumatic." I asserted: "All roads eventually lead to democracy; some take a little longer than others, but there are no shortcuts to the state of democracy. There are only experiences along the way." Young as I was, I had the prescience to recognize that the events that had shaped Cambodia's past made an easy path to democracy unlikely. "Can everything return to normal or business as usual with only a pinch of democracy?" I asked. The answer, I felt certain, was no.

Two years later, the United Nations Transitional Authority in Cambodia (UNTAC)—at the time the United Nation's (UN) largest and most expensive mission ever—held elections in Cambodia (see table I.1). UNTAC had operated in Cambodia with an incredibly broad mandate, spanning civil administration and military functions, elections, and human rights. Yasushi Akashi was appointed the head of UNTAC as the special representative of the secretary general (SRSG). Akashi had the unprecedented power to break deadlocks in the ruling Supreme National Council in the absence of action by then-Prince Sihanouk, the council's chairman. But UNTAC's power was largely theoretical. In addition to failing to disarm the Khmer Rouge, UNTAC failed to control Cambodia's preexisting civil administrative structures, enabling the Cambodian People's Party (CPP) to maintain the upper hand. Despite these failings, Cambodians turned out on May 23–28, 1993, and voted for the royalist Funcinpec party, which won 58 seats compared to the 51 seats won by the CPP. The remainder of the 120-seat National Assembly went to parties with ties to Funcinpec.

To increase pressure on the victors, associates of CPP leader Hun Sen began to secede in three eastern provinces: Kompong Cham, Prey Veng, and Svay Rieng. According to the UN's own account, "As tension increased in those provinces, there were anti-UNTAC demonstrations and a number of attacks against UNTAC personnel and property. This led UNTAC to withdraw its non-essential civilian personnel on 12 and 13 June."[2] Hun Sen had already warned of violence at a June 3, 1993, meeting with Sihanouk. The threats and recriminations worked; even after losing the election, the Cambodian People's Party intimidated the winners into a power-sharing deal in which a world's first took place. Two prime ministers shared power equally—a recipe for disaster, to be sure. The UN saw its job as completed with the

Table I.1 Transition of legal, political, and economic systems in Cambodia

Period	Legal system	Political system	Political power	Economic system
Before 1953	French-based civil code and judiciary	Under French protectorate	Held by the French	Colonial
1953–1970 (The Kingdom of Cambodia)	French-based civil code and judiciary	Constitutional monarchy	Held by King Norodom Sihanouk (until he abdicated in 1955) then as Prince Norodom Sihanouk alternately as prime minister or head of state of an elected government known as the Sangkum Reastr Niyum or People's Socialist Community (1955–1970)	Market and then nationalization
1970–1975 (The Khmer Republic)	French-based civil code and judiciary	Republic	Held by Lon Nol and Sirik Matak with U.S. support	Market, war economy
1975–1979 (Democratic Kampuchea)	Legal system destroyed	All previous systems abolished, extreme Maoist agro-communism	Held by Pol Pot and the Khmer Rouge with Chinese and North Korean support	Agrarian, centrally planned
1979–1989 (The People's Republic of Kampuchea)	Vietnamese communist model	Communist party central committee and local committees	Held by the Kampuchean People's Revolutionary Party, which picks Hun Sen as prime minister beginning in 1985 (Vietnamese backed with 100,000 troops; Soviet support)	Soviet-style central planning
1989–1993 (The State of Cambodia)	Greater economic rights	Communist party central committee and local committees	Held by Cambodian People's Party (renamed from KPRP) with Hun Sen as prime minister (Vietnamese backed, all troops withdrawn) and shared with UNTAC, led by SRSG Yasushi Akashi, in 1992–1993	Liberalized central planning
1993–1998 (The Kingdom of Cambodia) *First mandate*	French-based civil code combined with common law in certain sectors	Constitutional monarchy in which the king reigns but does not rule	Shared between Ranariddh (Funcinpec) and Hun Sen (CPP) in a unique arrangement of co-prime ministers with required two-thirds supermajority for governing coalition	Transition to a market economy
1998–present *Second, third, and fourth mandates*	As above	As above	Held by Hun Sen as prime minister in a CPP-Funcinpec coalition government that required a two-thirds supermajority until 2006 when the constitution was changed to allow 50%+1	Market economy

Source: Adapted from Wescott (2001) and based on Chandler (1991) and MLG and DFDL (1999).

Note: The 1993–1998 period is often seen as an emergency phase, whereas the 1998–present period is seen as a development phase. Pol Pot died in 1998; the Khmer Rouge disbanded completely in 1999.

election, packed its bags, and left in September 1993—and none too soon—Hun Sen had allegedly threatened before the election that tanks would be in the streets should his party lose and that the UN would be kicked out the next day.

It was far from the first time that UNTAC had backed down in the face of a threat of violence. Indeed, Akashi has been criticized for avoiding confrontation at all costs, which Khmer Rouge guerrillas and the government in Phnom Penh alike perceived as a weakness in the leader. He coupled public relations gaffes—most famously saying, "Boys will be boys," in response to aid workers' complaints that a brothel district had grown up on the outskirts of Phnom Penh and was being frequented by UN employees—with an unwillingness to use or even threaten force. In the early days of his mandate, when the Khmer Rouge seemed inclined to back out of the peace agreement, Akashi attempted to visit guerrilla headquarters and was turned back by a single soldier guarding a makeshift roadblock with a bamboo pole. Many UN officials believed there had been no real risk of violence and that Akashi should have insisted upon the meeting (*The Independent* 1994). French generals Lorridan and Rideaux both resigned over UNTAC military policy, claiming that the UN's no-reprisals policy toward Khmer Rouge attacks made it impossible to implement the UN mandate (Maguire 2005:80–81, 93).

Whereas Cambodia's gross domestic product in 1991 was $2 billion, UNTAC's budget swelled to $1.5 billion over a period of eighteen to twenty-four months. (All dollar [$] figures are in U.S. dollars.) Only a small portion of these funds was spent in Cambodia, however, perhaps 10–20 percent. The UN gave its civilian staff generous salaries but added $140 per day for a "daily subsistence allowance" for housing, food, and incidentals. Cambodian per capita income, meanwhile, was but $240 per year (Doyle and Sambanis 2006:222). This contributed enormously to 75 percent inflation in 1992 and 114 percent inflation in 1993.

Despite UNTAC's shortcomings, Cambodia became a UN poster child of peacekeeping magic in the grand new era of the "Responsibility to Protect," an international norm also known by the acronym R2P, which was based on the idea that sovereignty is not a privilege but a responsibility to prevent and halt genocide, war crimes, crimes against humanity, and ethnic cleansing. Hun Sen, never a fan of UNTAC, which he regarded as an entity that had come to interfere with his decade-long *droit du seigneur*, derisively said that "The most UNTAC left in the [*sic*] Cambodia was the AIDS disease,"[3] a reference to a widely observed negative consequence of the massive presence of foreign troops. In 2001, Yasushi Akashi called the claim an "exaggeration" (Kyodo 2001). According to Osborne (1994), Sihanouk himself had many reservations about UNTAC because the massive presence of foreign troops had negative consequences, chiefly the denigration of women, the tripling of prostitution (from 6,000 prostitutes in 1991 to 20,000 in 1992), and, yes, the introduction of AIDS. The late Richard Holbrooke once said of HIV/AIDS: "My first personal observation was in Cambodia in 1992, when I went there as a private citizen and I saw the peacekeepers from the U.N. . . . and they were doing a good job. But at night I saw them wandering around the street drunk and going into whorehouses and so on and so forth, and I was quite upset about this. So I wrote a letter to the head of the U.N. in Cambodia saying, 'You've really got to do something about this,' and I never got a reply" (qtd. in *FRONTLINE* 1996). By 1995, there were 50,000–90,000 Cambodians affected by AIDS, according to a World Health Organization estimate. According to the U.S. State Department's 2011 *Trafficking in Persons Report*, larger entertainment establishments in Cambodia exploit as many as 200 women and children in a given night, and the Cambodian authorities do little to identify or protect trafficking victims (U.S. Department of State 2011:109).

The damage UNTAC did to Cambodia went well beyond this, however. Far from "laying a sound foundation for the people of Cambodia to build a stable and peaceful future,"[4] as one UN document claims, UNTAC sowed the seeds of failure for democracy in Cambodia. What the UN seems not to have understood was that an election alone did not a democracy make. The golden age of Wilsonian interventionism had arrived, courtesy of the UN, but it was merely fool's gold. Underneath the rhetorical terrain was a vacuum of resolve and credibility.

In March 1996, while I was in graduate school at Princeton, Akashi (who had recently ended a stint as head of the UN's Bosnia mission, in which he was accused of failing to prevent the genocide at Srebrenica, and had since been promoted) came to campus to give a talk. By then it had become apparent that it was his leadership (or lack thereof) that had led the UN to kowtow to the Cambodian People's Party. I asked Akashi if, in retrospect, he had any regrets with respect to UNTAC. To be sure, he had come to speak about Bosnia, and he probably had no idea that the twenty-one year old sitting in the back of the room was from Cambodia. Akashi gave a standard, dismissive diplomatic line: no, not really. And so, I thought, the UN's head honcho in Cambodia washed his hands of any responsibility for what UNTAC had done or failed to do there. Yet the only standard by which UNTAC—and indeed most of the international interventions in Cambodia that have followed—can honestly be judged a success is in comparison to 1.7 million deaths under the Khmer Rouge, a comparison hardly worth making. And while Cambodians complain, when push comes to shove, the game of chicken that the international community half-heartedly plays with the Cambodian People's Party will always be won by the CPP. Lacking credibility and fortitude to stand up to abuses and misdeeds, the UN showed the international community's cards to the ruling party.

Unfortunately, this is not unusual behavior for the UN, and it had even more tragic results in the former Yugoslavia in 1995. Two years earlier, the UN had declared Srebrenica a "safe zone" under UN protection, only to see 8,000 men and boys massacred in the first genocide committed in Europe since World War II. "Srebrenica has ... become a symbol ... of the United Nations' failure to stand up to genocide—especially given the fact the 'safe zone' created by the United Nations was not defended but simply allowed to be taken over by the Serbs" (Totten and Bartrop 2008:405). More than 200,000 died in Bosnia alone. Then in Rwanda in 1994, when the UN left, the Don Bosco Technical School was filled with 2,000 Tutsis (Larson 2009), who were then massacred by Hutu militants waiting outside. Rwanda's death toll from the genocide was between 800,000 and 1 million. Because of the heroic acts of UN force commander Canadian Lt. Gen. Romeo Dallaire, whose request for 5,000 UN peacekeeping troops was denied by the Security Council, tens of thousands of Tutsis were saved—a small percentage compared to the numbers killed.

In Cambodia, the damage is less obvious—the carnage having been committed long before the UN showed up. But the pattern of failure by the UN is still the same. This pattern is repeated during every yearly donor-government meeting. In an annual exercise in cognitive dissonance, donors chastise the government while pledging even more money than it has requested. In doing so, they permit the Cambodian government to remain unaccountable, corrupt, and lacking the political will to solve the nation's problems and create a truly firm foundation for democratic governance.

Less than four years after UNTAC had left and a year after I attended Akashi's lecture, the 1997 coup, which the Cambodian government euphemistically named "the events of 5–6 July 1997," shattered the UN's erstwhile sound foundation for the people of Cambodia to build a stable and peaceful future. The coup—the first outbreak of open warfare within the coalition government parties following the signing of the Paris Peace Accords in 1991—reconfirmed Cambodia's problem child status. On July 5–6, 1997, then-First Prime Minister Norodom Ranariddh was ousted from power by Second Prime Minister Hun Sen. This resulted in more than seventy extrajudicial killings of mostly Funcinpec civilian loyalists. Although the precise details may never come to light, the general story line is that in the lead-up to the events, a power struggle between Funcinpec and the CPP emerged in recruiting senior Khmer Rouge defectors. To the victor would go the Khmer Rouge, whose forces were still wreaking havoc in Cambodia and whose leaders controlled swaths of the countryside.

Forces loyal to Hun Sen launched violent and sustained attacks against forces loyal to Ranariddh, claiming that Hun Sen was ready to take sole power (Amnesty International 1997). To preserve some semblance of normalcy, the minister of foreign affairs and international cooperation, who belonged to Funcinpec, was named first prime minister. Yet in the aftermath of 1997, there was no doubt who called the shots, and the entire military landscape has shifted as a result—Hun Sen has consolidated military power, using the armed forces to completely usurp democratic rule. Hun Sen trounced Ranariddh and the opposition in subsequent elections. He proved that if he did not win by the ballot, he would resort to the bullet. Few modern political actors have been able to navigate such troubled political waters as successfully as Prime Minister Hun Sen (who has held the post since 1985), with his long history of political intimidation (culminating with the 1997 coup) and his long view of history. While the prime minister deserves criticism for stealing elections and killing political opponents, this must be balanced against his success in defeating the Khmer Rouge and successfully reintegrating them back into Cambodian society. Above all, the Cambodian leader succeeded where the UN failed miserably. Since then, he's gained a powerful incumbency advantage—by controlling the government, he's able to use his power and wealth to control the entire democratic process. Despite his well-known corruption, moreover, Hun Sen remains the West's go-to man in Cambodia. Nongovernmental organizations (NGOs) and international organizations work with him because they can't get anything done without him.

In January 2003, anti-Thai riots fueled by false rumors that fanned old grievances between Cambodia and Thailand resulted in the burning of the Thai Embassy, along with the Royal Phnom Penh Hotel and other Thai businesses. The authorities took the opportunity to accuse opposition leader Sam Rainsy of inciting the riots (Rainsy asserts he had been trying to prevent them), and they arrested Cambodia's leading independent radio talk show host, Mom Sonando. This roundup of the opposition culminated in the assassination in broad daylight of Om Radsady, a former parliamentarian and friend of mine who was alleged to have been looking at ways to force Hun Sen to answer questions about the rioting. While Hun Sen may not have masterminded the 2003 anti-Thai riots, he accidentally burned down the house while playing with matches by making inflammatory anti-Thai speeches in the preceding days. He responded by calling in the fire trucks and further consolidating power, exploiting the riots to his advantage.

The anti-Thai riots caused at least $47 million in damage. Hun Sen offered unconditional compensation, but he used a Western checkbook to pay. "Cambodia gave a non-specific but blanket assurance [it would pay for anything]," said a Western diplomat. "Since donors pay for about 50 percent of the national budget, my question is, What account is this going to come from? They don't have the money" (qtd. in Coren 2003).

Did it really matter? Money is fungible and can be taken from Peter to pay Paul. Foreign aid for one purpose offsets the need to spend, freeing up money to be moved elsewhere.

It's not a new story in Cambodia. For nearly two decades, the country has depended on the largesse of international donors, as well as on the hundreds of nongovernmental organizations (NGOs) that have operated there since the United Nations–sponsored elections in 1993. But ultimately, what has this money bought? According to the best publicly available data from the World Bank, the world development indicators (as of February 24, 2012), the maternal mortality ratio (national estimate per 100,000 live births) increased from 440 deaths in 2000 to 472 in 2005 before dropping to 460.8 in 2008 (although notably still higher than in 2000). Moreover, inequality has increased dramatically from a Gini coefficient of 0.38 in 1994 to 0.42 in 2004 and 0.44 in 2007. (A Gini coefficient is an index that ranges between 1, the most inequitable possible outcome, and 0, the most equitable possible outcome.) Cambodia is tied with the Philippines and on par with the Democratic Republic of the Congo in terms of inequality. These outcomes are disturbing, particularly considering how much foreign aid Cambodia received over this period. Circumstantial evidence suggests that increased corruption siphoned resources from the health sector at the delivery end; increasing income inequality undoubtedly exacerbated the problem. Unbridled inequality rose from 1994 to 2007, a fact that even the World Bank conceded was "somewhat unusual"—diplomatic-econ speak for "Something's rotten in the Kingdom of Cambodia." Land grabbing, an acute problem in rural areas, has crept into the heart of Phnom Penh, at Boeung Kak Lake, where thousands of families have been left homeless thanks to Chinese investors in cahoots with Cambodian authorities and World Bank complacency.

Political and press freedoms have simultaneously been curtailed. Newspaper editors are perennially arrested, if not assassinated. A United Nations World Food Programme security guard served six months for printing (mind you, *not* writing) a blog entry critical of the government and sharing it with two colleagues.

Along with foreign aid by the C130-load, a new utilitarianism has taken root. There was a time when Cambodians took on the task of civic improvement for their pagodas, but after food-for-work programs began to dot the landscape, they started to ask their abbot, "What's in it for me?"[5]

But if something *is* rotten in the Kingdom of Cambodia, where do we assign the blame for it? Until recently, it has been both fair and convenient to attribute all the country's woes to the Khmer Rouge and call it a day. To do so in 2012 is a copout— modern Cambodia is a kleptocracy *cum* thugocracy, and the international community, led by the UN, is its enabler. Today, there is abject poverty amidst plenty, and despite an economy that has had near double-digit growth each year of the first decade of the new millennium, net aid received equaled, on average, 94.3 percent of central government spending between 2002 and 2010. A donor culture views aid dependence as a fact of life.

Speak to any Cambodian who survived the time of Pol Pot, and you will hear a recurring theme: the absence of food (Sanders 2006). The Khmer Rouge did not mince words; one of their better-remembered maxims was the deceptively simple "hunger is the most effective disease."[6] Although contemporary Cambodia bears little resemblance to Democratic Kampuchea, after decades of foreign aid, physical hunger has been replaced by a hunger for solutions to urgent problems. During most of the 1990s and 2000s, foreign aid dwarfed Cambodian government spending, yet basic measures of change—like inequality and maternal mortality—grew worse. Today, Cambodia ranks among the world's leaders when it comes to inequality, unbalanced growth, and dodgy development.

At the same time, the country has developed from a regional—indeed global—basket case into one of the world's fastest-growing economies. The past decade has witnessed a remarkable transformation: average economic growth near double digits; property prices skyrocketing and then plummeting; the birth of Cambodia's first internationally managed private equity fund, Leopard Capital (for which I served as an advisor from its founding in 2008 until December 2009); and an explosion of private university education of dubious quality. Yet these transformations, positive on the surface, mask severe ongoing governance problems that affect almost every aspect of Cambodian daily life. Cambodia faces difficult years ahead, with both the garment industry and tourism—the twin engines of Cambodia's recent economic transformation—hurting. The coming decade will witness further challenges to Cambodia's economy if good governance is not achieved. Since the creation of the Association of Southeast Asian Nations (ASEAN) Free Trade Area on January 1, 2010, a trade bloc supporting local manufacturing in ASEAN member countries, it will no longer suffice for Cambodia to do the bare minimum—by which I mean passing laws without implementation or with selective implementation. There are two roads ahead for Cambodia. One values loyalty above all else, even more than competence or merit; the other values competence at least as much as loyalty. The right road must be chosen to turn bread and circuses into wealth and prosperity.

Cambodia's problems are the world's problems, and they are intractable. The current international environment strives to reduce global poverty and prevent state failure, in no small part to remove breeding grounds for terrorism. The threat of a global flu pandemic also stresses the need for international cooperation and for the international community—however problematic this "community" may be as a concept—to be able to effect changes in weak states.[7] At the same time, scholars and policy makers emphasize the difficulty of accomplishing democratic state formation. The single most important tool the international community can bring to bear on these problems is aid. Over the more than six decades that international development has been practiced, however, precious few lessons have been learned. Someone once said that development is a field more akin to gardening than engineering. But even gardeners know more and learn more from one year to the next than development consultants, who seem caught in a perpetual vortex of trial and error from which few learning effects spill over from one generation to the next or from one consultant to another.

Foreign aid—a voluntary transfer of resources from one country to another, given at least partly with the objective of benefiting the recipient country—has poured into Cambodia since the ceasefire in 1991. The best collected measure of this aid, however imperfect, is Official Development Assistance (ODA). ODA is a standardized set of statistics collected by the Organization for Economic Cooperation and Development (OECD) and defined as the "Flows of official financing administered with the promotion of the economic development and welfare of developing countries as the main objective." ODA is both multilateral and bilateral money that is for the economic development and welfare of a developing country. It is concessional—based on a specific formula—which is to say that the loan is made at the market interest rate, for which a developing country might not even be eligible because it is at war or is not creditworthy. Such a loan is effectively "subprime" but subsidized. Not all foreign aid is purely government to government. While foreign aid originates from governments, it can pass through NGOs when it is spent. Corruption makes it impossible for donor governments to trust some developing country governments with foreign aid; thus, arrangements are sometimes made to hand the money to third-party NGOs. This does not usually happen with multilateral aid because the consent of the receiving country is required.

Cambodia has become a laboratory for donor trial-and-error experiments. (I would include, incidentally, the current UN-backed Khmer Rouge tribunal now taking place in Cambodia; one to which I am recognized as a civil party. The tribunal, with a history of corruption and mismanagement, has been so politicized that it is on the verge of collapse—with two back-to-back resignations of international judges claiming Cambodian government pressure and obstruction—as I write these words.) As a postconflict state that had no choice but to accept aid, Cambodia is a forced experiment in aid dependence. The experiment has shown—as have similar experiments elsewhere—that foreign aid has a number of unintended consequences in postconflict environments. A consensus has emerged among those who study aid that even though aid is meant to encourage development, aid dependence results in bad governance, stunting development. As the essay I wrote as a teenager on Cambodia and democracy suggests, a postconflict country like Cambodia may be hungry for aid, but it does not accept it empty handed; rather, it carries with it its traumatic experiences of conflict, those "events that shape a people."

Corruption is one outcome of Cambodia's past, and aid dependence has exacerbated it. Corruption became a problem in Cambodia in the 1960s and began spiraling out of control in the 1970s. The spouse of Lon Non, the brother of former Cambodian head of state Lon Nol, fled the Khmer Rouge and arrived in 1975 at Washington Dulles International Airport with suitcases full of American dollars. To date, Cambodia still owes more than $400 million to the United States for debts incurred under Lon Nol's regime. In 2004, when I asked a cousin in his fifties whether corruption was as bad as or worse than it had been in the 1970s, he said it was worse, without question. Indicators of corruption—which do not date back to the 1970s for Cambodia, or for that matter much of the rest of the world—cannot verify this perception. But it is clear that corruption is entrenched as a political system in today's Cambodia, and aid is either blind to it or is inadvertently fueling the problem. Examining Ghana, LeVine argued that "the development of an incipient culture of political corruption was accompanied by an evolving structure of values that had the effect of rationalizing, if not legitimizing, corrupt behavior" (1989:363). In much the same way, Cambodia values and rationalizes corruption as a standard operating procedure, whereas foreign donors tend to identify it as an evil without making serious efforts to replace the political culture of corruption with a new one.

What is lacking, of course, is political will to change the culture of corruption. The incentives to do so are not present. According to Post et al. (2008:114), "political will can be thought of as support from political leaders that results in policy change." Hammergren (1998:12) characterized political will as "the slipperiest concept in the policy lexicon," calling it "the sine qua non of policy success which is never defined except by its absence." Indeed, when I wrote an inaugural article in the *Cambodian Economic Review*, lack of political will was my primary explanatory variable for why certain policy reforms (such as an anticorruption law that met international standards) had failed while others (like control of inflation) have succeeded (Ear 2005).

The chapters that follow use the case of Cambodia to investigate the by no means simple relationship between aid dependence and governance. My personal history makes Cambodia an obvious choice for such a study, but the case selection makes sense for other reasons. In many ways, Cambodia is both special and mundane—having suffered terribly in the 1970s and been "punished" in the 1980s, it had its slate wiped clean in the 1990s with massive international intervention. It was the first major peacekeeping operation for the UN in the 1990s, costing $1.5 billion, and it was held up as a shining example of the new world order. In many ways, Cambodia in the early 1990s embodied the Wilsonian idealism that the international community could make everything better. Today, however, Cambodia has the typical problems of a developing nation: urbanization, poverty, inequality, aid dependence, corruption, and lack of transparency and accountability. It is atypical only insofar as it suffered a genocide that destroyed trust, or social capital, both among individuals and between the people and their government.

I am convinced that, on balance, the long-term effects of aid dependence have made it difficult, if not impossible, for Cambodia to take ownership of its own development. Foreign aid has crippled the government's political will to tax, and without taxation, the link between government accountability and popular elections is broken. Corruption is the logical outcome. What authorities will not tax officially for the treasury, they can collect privately for the ruling Cambodian People's Party or their pockets. It is by weakening accountability that foreign aid most harms governance, by increasing the incentive for corruption and diluting political will. Few would disagree that poor governance is a scourge on development.

I begin by asking, in chapter 1, whether aid dependence in fact worsens governance. This chapter reinvestigates this relationship with current data and a robust methodology. The answer seems to be that it does so only to a limited degree, and only with respect to rule of law. Findings suggest that aid can play a positive role when the effects of its components are considered and that the causal link between aid dependence and worsening quality of governance may be tenuous at best and sensitive to alternative specifications—that is, the results can change depending on what model is used. Next, I take a qualitative look at the case of Cambodia to consider the consequences of massive and long-term aid infusion on governance. I find that not only has development not happened, but aid also distorts incentives for good governance, influences government spending, and weakens taxation and accountability. There has been a trade-off of voice and accountability, and indeed democracy, for stability. Donors have failed to improve rule of law, though in their own reports of results they tie aid to improvements in governance quality, meritocratic bureaucracy, and independent courts. It is a bit like the all-too-familiar American feeling of loving your congressman but hating Congress.

If aid is bad for Cambodian governance, which is in turn bad for development, I then ask in chapter 2 how are we to explain recent economic growth in Cambodia? I look at the governance consequences of aid dependence in three economic sectors to show that not only is the recent growth not a product of good governance, but poor governance (as distorted by the effects of aid) is also stifling potential for growth in the agricultural sector of the economy. The "ideal" is growth that is equitable, inclusive, and environmentally sustainable. This requires a government committed to providing appropriate laws, institutions, and enforcement of rule of law (a "service delivery model"). Cambodia's case shows the opposite problem of government not encouraging, and sometimes actively discouraging, growth through corruption and bad policies.

When Cambodia's first death from Highly Pathogenic Avian Influenza (HPAI) was discovered *not* in Cambodia but in a hospital in Vietnam in January 2005, the developed world was alarmed. Here was this hapless nation-state, so fragile and incapable that it had failed to protect—indeed had murdered—its own citizens in the mid-1970s that could now be the potential breeding ground for the next global killer pandemic. To add insult to injury, this happened after more than a decade of donor intervention and billions of dollars to rebuild and develop the country. Large new infusions of donated funds went into Cambodia, and huge initiatives were taken to combat HPAI's spread. These issues are explored in chapter 3. The case of HPAI offers a very contemporary and very critical opportunity to assess the effectiveness of aid and the effects of aid dependence. Cambodia's HPAI response demonstrates pervasive weakness in the Cambodian policy process. Evidence of lack of good governance and political will as shown in repeated institutional failures, unwillingness to commit state funds, and failure to protect the livelihood of the poor is explored. But there is also evidence of distortions of aid dependence in donors' uncoordinated plans, failure to take steps to protect and educate the poor appropriately, and excessive emphasis on preventing the spread of HPAI to the developed world.

The ways in which Cambodia remains a shallow democracy are too many to count; in 2009 alone, several opposition figures were sued for defamation, newspaper editors were killed, and yet nothing happened to stop any of this. Chapter 4 goes back to 2005–2006 and looks at indigenous human rights activism that drew on international media and international diplomatic ties to curb the excesses of the state and the ruling Cambodian People's Party. This required direct international pressure, and it resulted in the release of political prisoners. In many ways, this example shows the positive side of international involvement in the realm of voice and accountability. Cambodia's experience with freedom of expression was backed by an internal movement and got important results that probably would not have been delivered without international pressure. The international community helped to fund organizations that are working to make Cambodian democracy more liberal. But this continuous funding has not been targeted to build up civil society beyond elections, and pressure on government to reform has been weak.

Taken together, these four chapters create a portrait of a country plagued by bad governance. Neither the "pinch of democracy" introduced by UNTAC nor the ongoing influx of foreign aid into Cambodia seems likely to feed the country's hunger for representative democratic government without corruption, or for stable and sustainable economic growth. As this volume's concluding chapter suggests, however, certain steps forward emerge out of a close examination of the governance-aid relationship in Cambodia. The first step is to wean Cambodia from foreign aid sooner rather than later, to strengthen tax collection, and to reestablish the link between representation and taxation, an essential—and missing— ingredient for ownership of national development. Cambodia's dependence on foreign aid—or, increasingly, Chinese investment and largesse—is desperately at odds with its desire to graduate from its problem child status and to escape the stifling embrace of the international community.

Cambodia makes an interesting case study of the effects of aid dependence, in part because it had little choice in whether to engage donors or, in a wider sense, how to relate to the overall global political economy. The country was a pariah state for the duration of the 1980s in the aftermath of the Khmer Rouge period and the invasion by Vietnam, and it fervently sought to establish normalized international relations and acceptance. Following the Cold War, the Paris Peace Agreement signed on October 23, 1991, signaled the cessation of open warfare in Cambodia, although not the end of conflict itself. After the country's $1.5 billion United Nations (UN)-organized elections in 1993, Cambodia received $5 billion in official development assistance (ODA),[2] turning it into one of the most aid-dependent countries in the world, with net ODA received equivalent to 94.3 percent of central government spending between 2002 and 2010.

Cambodia's lack of choice has not been without consequences, however. Although aid dependence seems to have only limited negative effects in the aggregate, it creates significant distortions in the Cambodian political economy, with predictably bad consequences for the nation's governance.

Does Foreign Aid Worsen Governance?

Foreign aid has long been justified as essential for development in countries in which investment is missing, and aid helps complete missing or imperfect markets.[3] Peter Boone was the first to consider, empirically, a country's political system in determining aid effectiveness. He found that aid neither significantly increases investment nor benefits the poor as measured by improvements in human development indicators—but it does increase the size of government. According to Boone, "Poverty is not caused by capital shortage, and it is not optimal for politicians to adjust distortionary policies when they receive aid flows" (1996:322).

Boone's study is credited with having singlehandedly motivated World Bank economists Craig Burnside and David Dollar to perform their own analysis in an attempt to rescue aid from policy irrelevance. Burnside and Dollar (1997) substituted Boone's political system proxy with a quality-of-policy proxy and found that money matters in a good policy environment. In their study of the relationships among aid, policies, and growth in fifty-six countries over six four-year periods, they demonstrated that a linear relationship exists between the quality of governance and development outcome and that aid spurs growth and poverty reduction only in a good policy environment. In the presence of poor policies, aid has no positive effect on growth. For example, under weak economic management in developing countries, there is no relationship between aid and change in infant mortality, but in countries where economic management is stronger, there is a favorable relationship.

However, subsequent scrutiny of Burnside and Dollar's analysis has revealed a number of weaknesses. Several scholars have noted that the addition of another four-year period (1994–1997) and some more recent observations to Burnside and Dollar's data set changes the results (Harms and Lutz 2004:20). Henrik Hansen and Finn Tarp (2000) argued that Burnside and Dollar's findings were the result of diminishing returns to aid. Analyzing the same set of countries and using the same basic model specification, they concluded that aid does have a positive impact on growth even in countries with a *poor* policy environment. In a veiled reference to the World Bank's 1998 study *Assessing Aid: What Works, What Doesn't, and Why*, Hansen and Tarp maintained that "the unresolved issue in assessing aid effectiveness is not whether aid works, but how and whether we can make the different kinds of aid instruments at hand work better in varying country circumstances" (2000:394).

Beyond questions of aid effectiveness, concerns emerged that aid dependence degrades the quality of governance. Bräutigam and Botchwey (1999) used data for thirty-one African countries from 1990 to argue that preexisting quality of governance determined the extent to which aid undermines institutions (cited in Knack 2001:314n5). Jakob Svensson (2000) found that, when instrumented with income, terms of trade, and population size, aid expectation increases graft in ethnically fractionalized countries. Using geographic and cultural proximity as instrumental variables for aid, on the other hand, José Tavares (2003) countered that aid does not corrupt. For those who believe in the intrinsic differences in countries, Tavares's method is more appealing.

Discussing empirical findings that aid dependence is associated with corruption—only one of several elements of governance—Paul Collier and David Dollar note that aid changes the relative price of good versus bad governance, making it cheaper and more likely that the former will be substituted for the latter. On the other hand, aid also "directly augments public resources and reduces the need for the government to fund its expenditures through taxation, thereby reducing domestic pressure for accountability" (2004:F263). They conclude that the "net effect" of aid on corruption and thus governance "could be favourable or unfavourable, the question only being resolvable empirically" (F263). Arthur Goldsmith, too, notes that "more work clearly needs to be done to ascertain the extent to which aid has a destructive effect on the state" (2001:128).

The cross-sectional analysis performed by Stephen Knack (2001) finds a negative relationship between aid dependence and quality of governance. According to Knack, aid dependence hurts governance by weakening institutional capacity,

Table 1.1   The more aid-dependent a country, the lower the quality of governance

Independent variable	Intervening variable	Dependent variable
Aid dependence as measured by aid/GDP, aid/government budget	• Weakening institutional capacity • Siphoning off scarce talent from the public sector • Weakening accountability • Encouraging rent-seeking and corruption • Fomenting conflict over control of aid funds • Alleviating pressures to reform inefficient policies and institutions	• Quality of governance as measured by International Country Risk Guide

Source: Adapted from Knack (2001:310).

siphoning off scarce talent from the bureaucracy, undermining accountability, encouraging rent-seeking and corruption, fomenting conflict over control of aid funds, and alleviating pressures to reform inefficient policies and institutions (see table 1.1). The implication is that, through intervening variables, aid dependence causes the quality of governance to worsen over time. Drawing on the Freedom House Index in a more recent empirical study, Knack (2004) finds that little if any of the progress toward democratization between 1975 and 1996 can be attributed to foreign aid. Heckelman and Knack (2005), using Economic Freedom data (and its components) as their dependent variable, find that aid harms market-liberalizing reform.

If verified, Knack's 2001 findings would pose a serious problem for international development. The drive by international financial institutions to assess aid itself (and to pin the blame for its ineffectiveness on poor governance) suggests that they have long since perceived this problem and begun to take stock in an act of self-preservation. Worldwide aid levels tumbled after peaking in 1992. The World Bank was moved to appeal directly to donor countries to essentially hang in there and continue funding. Its *Assessing Aid* report (1998) found that the impact of aid on growth and infant mortality depends on "sound economic management," as measured by an index of economic policies and institutional quality. If good governance is needed for aid to work effectively but aid dependence leads to bad governance, then where does that leave developing countries and the donors trying to help them?

Few would deny that aid dependence can have a pernicious effect on governance. What remains subject to debate is the significance of this effect and which dimensions of governance are affected. Knack's three studies all use cross-sectional analysis, which does not control for potentially omitted variables affecting both aid flows and changes in governance; moreover, Knack's choice of instrumental variables for aid—a statistical procedure that counteracts endogeneity in aid—is at best imperfect. Aid could be endogenous if donors systematically disbursed more or less resources to those countries that had good or bad governance as a reward or punishment.[4] Knack concedes this potential, noting that "aid ... [could] reflect endogeneity bias: if donors direct aid toward countries experiencing deteriorations in the quality of governance, OLS [Ordinary Least Squares] estimates will overstate the adverse impact of aid on governance" (2001:319). Knack's solution is to engage nearly identical exogenous instruments to those used by Burnside and Dollar (1997, 2000)—infant mortality in 1980 and (log of) initial gross domestic product (GDP) per capita as indicators of recipient need, along with initial population (log), a Franc zone dummy, and a Central America dummy as measures of donor interest.[5] A good instrumental variable is one that is highly correlated with the regressor—aid—but is uncorrelated (except through aid) with the dependent variable—governance. Knack cites infant mortality as "easily the most important predictor of aid" (2000:14), and his *Southern Economic Journal* article drawn from his working paper adds population and per capita income as "the most significant predictors of aid" (2001:319). Although unelaborated beyond "good indicator of recipient need," the presumed logic of this instrument is that infant mortality is a basis for why aid is given *regardless* of governance. Of course, infant mortality is unlikely to be purely exogenous—it is likely affected by poor governance, although in the long term it is unlikely to affect governance.

Derek Headey argues eloquently against the use of instruments for aid—which he calls "fundamentally flawed in ways which are largely ignored by the literature to date"—in favor of using lagged aid only to control for endogeneity (2005:4–5). He concludes, "Lagging aid means that we are more likely to test the effects of aid over the medium term, which is probably all the data are capable of doing" (13). In Ear (2007a), I followed a similar design, repeating Knack's use of infant mortality as an instrumental variable for aid, but with the above caveat and the introduction of a lag in aid. Beyond this, I used a more extensive data set. From 2005, it covers 209 countries and territories for five specific years: 1996, 1998, 2000, 2002, and 2004. The data assign up to 352 individual measures of governance to categories that capture key dimensions of governance. I also introduced pooled time-series cross-sectional (TSCS) analysis with fixed effect to control for potential omitted variable bias, and I examined different elements of aid. I reported both instrumented and uninstrumented findings and showed that they are generally consistent.

Table 1.2   Six dimensions of governance

Governance is defined as "the traditions and institutions by which authority in a country is exercised"		
Process by which governments are selected, monitored, and replaced	*Capacity of the government to effectively formulate and implement sound policies*	*Respect of citizens and the state for the institutions that govern economic and social interactions among them*
(1) Voice and accountability	(3) Government effectiveness	(5) Rule of law
Various aspects of the political process, especially civil liberties, political rights, and independence of the media	The quality of public service provision, the quality of the bureaucracy, the competence of civil servants, the independence of the civil service from political pressures, and the credibility of the government's commitment to its policies	The incidence of both violent and nonviolent crime, the effectiveness and predictability of the judiciary, and the enforceability of contracts
(2) Political stability	(4) Regulatory quality	(6) Control of corruption
The likelihood that the government in power will be destabilized or overthrown by possibly unconstitutional and/or violent means, including terrorism	The incidence of market-unfriendly policies such as price controls or inadequate bank supervision, as well as burdens imposed by excessive regulation in areas such as foreign trade and business development	Corruption, conventionally defined as the exercise of public power for private gain; this ranges from the frequency of "additional payments to get things done" to the effects of corruption on the business environment, to "grand corruption" in the political arena or in the tendency of elites to engage in "state capture"

Source: Adapted from Kaufmann, Kraay, and Zoido-Lobatón (1999).

The data rely upon the work of Daniel Kaufmann, Aart Kraay, and Pablo Zoido-Lobatón (1999) in identifying and defining six dimensions of governance, whose work has grown in aggregation in the past decade. This book uses the 2005 version. Hence, the definition of governance used in this book is also the definition Kaufmann et al. use: "governance [is] the traditions and institutions by which authority in a country is exercised" (see table 1.2). The first two dimensions speak to the processes of government selection, monitoring, and replacement: "Voice and accountability" describe the openness and responsiveness of a government to civil society and encompass the protection of civil liberties and political rights, as well as media independence. "Political stability" captures how likely a government is to be destabilized or overthrown by unconstitutional or violent means.[6] The second two dimensions indicate the extent to which a government is able to create and implement sound policies effectively: "government effectiveness" considers government commitment to its policies, the quality of a government's public services and its bureaucracy, and whether it has a competent and independent civil service; "regulatory quality" concerns the extent of market-unfriendly regulation, such as price controls or inadequate bank supervision, and the extent to which such regulations may have negative effects on foreign trade and economic development. The final two dimensions of governance involve citizens' attitudes toward the institutions of the state: "rule of law" measures the government's effectiveness in preventing crime, enforcing contracts, and maintaining an effective and predictable judiciary; "control of corruption" describes government success in curbing corruption, defined as "the exercise of public power for private gain" (Kaufmann et al. 2005:4), which ranges from demands for "additional payments to get things done" (66) to the distortion of the business environment to grand corruption in the political arena or in the tendency of elites to engage in state capture (5).

Since quality of governance is rooted in several determinants, among them income, population, and other invariant factors such as culture and history, no one would suggest that aid alone determines the quality of governance in developing countries. Instead, I examined four hypotheses:

1. Aid dependence worsens governance.
2. Different dimensions of governance respond to aid differently.
3. Disaggregating aid into technical cooperation and average grant element (both components of aid) results in different effects on governance.
4. Knack's findings overstate the negative impact of aid dependence on governance.

Regarding the first hypothesis, I found that aid dependence is statistically significant as an explanatory variable that negatively affects various dimensions of governance, whether instrumented or not, under cross-sectional analysis. When I applied a more sophisticated method of analysis to the second hypothesis, it was only partly proven; I found that the rule of law is the only dimension of governance hurt by aid dependence. Third, I found that two important components of aid, technical cooperation and average grant element, have statistically significant effects when considered with aid—both aid and technical cooperation hurt the rule of law. However, grants and aid help voice and accountability. Finally, regarding the fourth hypothesis, I concluded that Knack's findings do overstate the negative impact of aid dependence on governance. The findings were first reported and elaborated at length in Ear (2007a), an article that won the June Pallot Award for best article published that year in the *International Public Management Journal*, which, as of 2010, had an impact factor of 1.949 and ranks third out of thirty-nine public administration journals.

Knack may have been too pessimistic when he concluded that "higher aid levels erode the quality of governance, as measured by indexes of bureaucratic quality, corruption, and the rule of law" (2001:310), and later when with Jac Heckelman he wrote that "aid on balance significantly retards rather than encourages market-oriented policy reform" (2005:1). Under pooled TSCS, aid dependence explains very little of the variation observed in different dimensions of governance. It may be that the finding of a less prevalent negative effect than Knack reported is due to the attempts of the World Bank and other multilateral donors, beginning in the late 1990s, to use aid to positively affect governance, since Knack covered the period 1982–1995.

Nonetheless, one should indeed be concerned that many of the coefficients associated with aid are negative, even if they are not statistically significant. Aid or its components may have selective negative effects on governance; voice and accountability is the one dimension of governance that might enjoy positive returns. The ability to use aid to *positive* effect on governance—rather than just avoiding a negative effect—remains to be shown. The negative effects of aid dependence found by Knack and others might turn out to be diminished if greater attention is paid to the elements that make up aid itself.

Before this can happen, however, we must know more about how aid interacts with governance on the ground. Knack himself notes that "a case study approach should examine more closely the recent experience of high-aid countries with deteriorating institutional quality" (2001:326). Cambodia, while not cited by Knack as a potential case study, is highly aid-dependent and has experienced deteriorating institutional quality. The remainder of this chapter introduces an empirical examination of Cambodia's recent experiences with aid. I begin with an overview of the state's contemporary history and present governance and then move on to consider how aid dependence has affected Cambodian governance and to what extent donors have succeeded in exercising a positive influence.

Cambodia's Political Economy Context

Cambodia's Darkest Period

Cambodia gained independence from France on November 9, 1953, and for most of its modern history was led by His Majesty Norodom Sihanouk. Through the 1960s, Sihanouk's Popular Socialist Community movement formed agricultural cooperatives, emphasizing state-owned enterprises and launching numerous construction projects within the context of a market economy. From a long-term perspective, the Cambodian conflict can be said to have started on March 13, 1970, when a coup d'état against Sihanouk by his prime minister, Lon Nol, and deputy prime minister, Sirik Matak (a cousin of Sihanouk), led to the birth of the Khmer Republic. Under this new leadership, Cambodia abandoned its neutrality and sided fully with the United States against North Vietnam.

On April 17, 1975, Phnom Penh fell to the Khmer Rouge, a communist insurgent movement whose forces grew in strength when the deposed Sihanouk absorbed the movement into his government-in-exile. The Khmer Rouge then embarked upon the most far-reaching and disastrous social, political, and economic transformation in modern history. The new government, led by Pol Pot with nominal heads of state Sihanouk (in the first year) and Khieu Samphan, renamed the country Democratic Kampuchea. Currency and private property were banned.[7] Overnight, the country was transformed into a rural collective. Religion, class, and traditional family structures were abolished, intellectuals were executed, and money ceased to exist. Nearly all lawyers were killed. Indeed, wearing glasses was cause for elimination. The Khmer Rouge's motto—"To keep you is no benefit, to destroy is no loss"—made clear the position of the individual in society. Over the course of three years, eight months, and twenty days, nearly two million Cambodians (including my father) died of malnourishment, overexertion, and execution.

The massacre ended when the Socialist Republic of Vietnam, prompted by provocative border attacks by the Khmer Rouge, its former client, invaded in December 1978, capturing Phnom Penh on January 7, 1979. Thus, the darkest chapter in Cambodia's history ended with a quarter to a third of the population dead, and a new chapter began in which the country lost its sovereignty. The parties to the conflict were the Vietnamese proxy government of the People's Republic of Kampuchea (the country was renamed the State of Cambodia in 1989), which was backed by 140,000 Vietnamese troops stationed in the country; the Khmer Rouge, then situated on the Thai-Cambodian border; and a noncommunist resistance composed of the Khmer People's National Liberation Front and the royalist Funcinpec (a French acronym for "United National Front for an Independent, Peaceful, and Cooperative Cambodia," a political party formed by Sihanouk). The resistance groups formed the Coalition Government of Democratic Kampuchea and waged an insurgency against the Vietnamese proxy government, which was led by the Kampuchea People's Revolutionary Party. This party, which renamed itself the Cambodian People's Party (CPP) in 1991 before the transition to democracy and became the country's leading political force, was, by 1985, led by a troika that included thirty-three-year-old Hun Sen, who had defected from the Khmer Rouge to Vietnam and became prime minister that year, retaining the post for the next twenty-seven years and counting. The country's future political parties were very much born on the battlefield; they would naturally resort to violence and intimidation for political power.

From 1975 to 1989, Cambodia sank to its nadir. The major impacts of the conflict were overwhelming. There was a massive loss of human resources from death, disease, and displacement—hundreds of thousands of Cambodians (including my mother, four siblings, and me) became refugees, many of whom were forced to resettle in third-world countries. The UN estimated that most of the highly qualified Cambodians were living outside the country, among them Cambodia's best and brightest, systematically targeted by the Khmer Rouge as a threat to the regime (UN 1992:26). By 1993, the University of Phnom Penh, which had been among the best universities in Asia prior to the conflict, had "almost no books, few professors and only a handful of classrooms that were not shot to pieces" (Gibson 1993).

Peace Under the United Nations

On October 23, 1991, in Paris, the parties signed the Agreements on a Comprehensive Political Settlement of the Cambodia Conflict, a peace treaty to end the conflict and prepare the country for elections. The agreements assigned to the United Nations an unprecedented role: a $1.5 billion peacekeeping mission known as the United Nations Transitional Authority in Cambodia (UNTAC) would supervise the ceasefire, the end of foreign military assistance, and the withdrawal of foreign forces. UNTAC would regroup, canton, and disarm all armed forces of the Cambodian parties and ensure a 70 percent level of demobilization. Drawing delegated authority from a Supreme National Council composed of all parties to the conflict and chaired by Sihanouk, UNTAC would control and supervise the activities of the administrative structures, including the police; ensure respect of human rights; and organize and conduct free and fair elections. In effect, the country's sovereignty was entrusted to the UN, which was tasked with the imposing goal of constructing a democracy from the ashes of war and genocide.

These were lofty aims, and their implementation would have required a degree of control of the country that UNTAC never achieved. As I described in the Introduction to this book, when UNTAC's head attempted to enter a Khmer Rouge-held area and his car was stopped by a lowered bamboo pole, UNTAC was, bluntly speaking, neutered. Under the leadership of Yasushi Akashi, a Japanese international civil servant awarded the position as a result of Japan's financial largesse, the transitional authority lacked the resolve to enforce key elements of the agreement. This had long-term consequences for Cambodian democracy. Political parties remained heavily militarized, and the authoritarian state apparatus—handed down from the Vietnamese occupation and controlled by the CPP—was left intact.

In spite of these glaring failures, the international community had reason to pat itself on the back and declare the mission a success when Cambodians first entered the polling booths. From May 23 to 28, 1993, more than 4.2 million Cambodians, 90 percent of registered voters, voted in the country's first free and fair election. Funcinpec garnered 45 percent of the vote, while the CPP, led by Hun Sen, won only 38 percent. The remaining votes went to former noncommunist resistance allies that had been aligned with Funcinpec. The results were a surprise to observers, who had anticipated that the authoritarian CPP would emerge victorious. (I, for one, remember being convinced as a sixteen year old that the CPP would inevitably win because of its unfair advantage.)

The Politics of No Winners and No Losers

Although the election outcome looked good on paper, it soon became clear that democracy provided only thin cover for an essentially authoritarian political system. Unwilling to risk civil war after the elections, Sihanouk, who had by then become king once again—one who "shall reign but shall not govern," according to the Cambodian Constitution—brokered a compromise in which there would be neither winners nor losers. In a sign of politics to come, the wishes of voters were tossed out in favor of the demands of gun-wielding elites.

The CPP, which inherited the most formidable political and military machine in the country, forced its way into power. Following behind-the-scenes deal making, which consisted of intimidation and threats of social instability, the electoral spoils were divided privately as the CPP and Funcinpec entered into a coalition government. This forced marriage awkwardly established two prime ministers, one from each party. It was clear from the outset that the coalition government existed in name only, with Hun Sen occupying the center of power.

Further consolidation of CPP power occurred during the run-up to the second election, held in 1998. On July 5 and 6, 1997, First Prime Minister Norodom Ranariddh was ousted from power by Second Prime Minister Hun Sen. This resulted in more than seventy extrajudicial killings of mostly Funcinpec civilian loyalists. Although the precise details may never come to light, the general storyline is that a power struggle between Funcinpec and the CPP emerged as both attempted to recruit senior Khmer Rouge defectors. This led, for all intents and purposes, to a coup d'état. Forces loyal to the second prime minister launched violent and sustained attacks against forces loyal to the first prime minister (claiming that the former was ready to take sole power) in Phnom Penh and the surrounding area (Amnesty International 1997). In the aftermath of these events, there was no doubt who called the shots.

Politics in Cambodia today is predicated on power, prestige, and money, and the CPP, having effectively controlled the country for more than two decades, has all three in ample supply. Hun Sen is the longest-serving prime minister in Southeast Asia and among the longest-serving in the world. The CPP has consolidated control over the country from one election to the next. The party's political base is generally seen as coming from outside Phnom Penh. In 2003, the CPP came in second in the capital with 150,189 votes to the opposition Sam Rainsy Party's 217,663 and Funcinpec's 65,249. Its strength is at the village level, where it exerts greater influence on the people through its network of village, district, and commune chiefs. (The commune chiefs were, until 2002, entirely appointed by the CPP.)

Because the Cambodian electorate votes for parties, individuals are not elected per se. This results in considerable control over those elected (in contrast to some electoral systems where candidates themselves are elected—not the parties). As a result, party discipline is ironclad. Any deviations—and there have been very few—lead to an expulsion from the party and an automatic loss of position in the National Assembly or Senate. The way around this historically has been to mount an internal coup and take control of the party, as happened to the Buddhist Liberal Democratic Party in the first mandate government of 1993–1998. This also explains why some parties are eponymously named; the Sam Rainsy Party cannot be wrested from Sam Rainsy, for instance.

The July 27, 2008, national election results showed that the governing CPP had increased its National Assembly seats from seventy-three in 2003 to ninety and that the Sam Rainsy Party won twenty-six seats, whereas other parties, including the Norodom Ranariddh Party (created by Funcinpec's former head, Prince Norodom Ranariddh, after he was ousted from its leadership in 2006), the Human Rights Party, and Funcinpec itself, won two, three, and two seats, respectively. Despite the dismal showing of opposition parties at the polls, the CPP maintained a nominal coalition partnership in order to preserve stability. On January 18, 2009, Funcinpec and the Norodom Ranariddh Party signed an agreement with the CPP forming a Nationalist Alliance for the Commune Council elections in May 2012. The parties, while still separate, vote together.

The Character of Cambodian Governance Today

The trajectory of Cambodia's political and economic development following its triple transition from war to peace, from communism to electoral democracy, and from command economy to free market, as identified by Caroline Hughes (2003), has been mixed. On the political front, while democratic participation has expanded widely, democracy has failed to "consolidate" as a result of underdeveloped political institutions, rent-seeking in government, a lack of free and fair competition among political parties, and the underdevelopment of civil society to act as a check against government abuse. In spite of these shortcomings, the political environment in Cambodia remains highly stable; this stability is a result of one-party dominance by the CPP and the lack of a coherent opposition.

The regime has provided, above all else, the absence of war since 1998, when the last of the Khmer Rouge holdouts were demobilized. In that sense, it furnished Hobbes's Leviathan by exercising an increasing monopoly on the use of force, thus creating a state in Max Weber's definition of the term (without, unfortunately, the trappings of a modern rational bureaucracy). Cambodia had been on its way to becoming a failed state by the late 1980s, and this reversal could not have come at a more critical time. Balanced against this achievement, however, is the reality that there are virtually no checks on the power of the CPP. The judiciary is captured, and both the National Assembly and Senate are often powerless against the executive.

Cambodian governance is characterized by patronage. Indeed, the Heritage Foundation (2005) called a coalition deal brokered after the 2003 elections "patronage at its worst," with a single prime minister, 7 deputy prime ministers, 15 senior ministers, 28 ministers, 135 secretaries of state, and at least 146 undersecretaries of state. The patronage system runs both vertically and horizontally, across and within ministries. The solution from election to election had been to expand the number of positions—creating an entire Senate in 1999 to house the former chairman of the National Assembly and new cabinet positions, as evidenced by their growing multitudes in 2003—but this belies the true nature of political power in Cambodia. Only a few individuals hold it; the rest divide the spoils and are content to subsist on a modicum of influence. Key ministries for governance and growth include the Ministry of Economy and Finance, the Ministry of Commerce, the Ministry of Interior, the Office of the Council of Ministers, and—although a special case because of the guns it holds—the Ministry of National Defense. Although line ministries (Health, Education, Environment, etc.) are important in their own right, these ministries control far fewer fungible resources because donors have maintained significant audit controls.

Aid to Cambodia

Two major economic factors were at play by the time UNTAC arrived. First, the loss of aid from former Soviet Bloc countries[8] severely affected public sector finances and caused macroeconomic imbalance—an estimated budget deficit of nearly 4.6 percent of GDP in 1992 (World Bank 1994).[9] Aid dropped 35 percent from 1987 to 1988, while trade as a percentage of GDP stagnated between 1989 and 1990. Second, extremely high inflation and exchange rate instability subsequently emerged; for example, retail price inflation exceeded 100 percent for much of the early 1990s.

In 1989, when the Vietnamese army began to leave Cambodia, aid doubled, and in 1991 it tripled again (albeit from a very low base). In that year, UN secretary-general Javier Perez de Cuellar appealed to the international community to support Cambodia's rehabilitation efforts following the signing of the Paris Peace Accords in October 1991. This resulted in pledges and other commitments totaling $880 million when the first International Committee for the Reconstruction of Cambodia (ICORC) met in June 1992. New pledges of $119 million were added in September 1993 in Paris. In 1994, the total amount of aid committed to Cambodia at the second ICORC in Tokyo again reached more than $800 million through 1996.[10] From 2002 to 2010, the government received net aid of 94.3 percent of its spending (i.e., budget). Domestic revenues have not kept pace with expenditures, however, in reality cementing the RGC's dependence on foreign aid.[11]

The biggest bilateral donor to Cambodia has traditionally been Japan. (Technically, the European Union [EU] pledges more, but it is not an actual nation-state.) Pledges of foreign aid began to increase in 2008 (for the following year) to nearly $1 billion, a significant increase compared with all previous years (see table 1.3). Indeed, in 2008, Japan fell to third with about $113 million, and the EU came in second at $214 million (Xinhua 2008c). The lead-donor spot passed to China, which eclipsed all other donors, with a commitment of $257 million at that year's pledging session.

The Chinese–Cambodian aid relationship is mutually beneficial; through it, China solidifies its strategic interests in the region and gains access to Cambodian resources, whereas Cambodia gets economic development, unconditional funding for infrastructural projects, and the perception of being a strong ally to a country whose interests Cambodians have long understood to be tied to their own. "The People's Republic of China is our special development partner . . . very close friend and can be considered as siblings of Cambodia because . . . China help [sic] us timely [sic] responding to our requests and need [sic] without complicated conditions," said Prime Minister Hun Sen on November 2, 2011, but there are reasons to question the conclusion. There is no ethical dimension to Chinese aid money, and events such as the forcible repatriation to China of twenty members of the Uyghur minority in December 2009, just before the Chinese vice president visited the country to sign a $1.2-billion aid and soft loans accord, attracted howls of outrage from human rights groups and Western governments. When Cambodia falls under pressure from international bodies to reform its human rights abuses, corruption,

Table 1.3 Royal Government of Cambodia aid requests, donor pledges, and disbursements

Consultative Group Meeting	1996	1997	1998	1999	2000	2001	2002	2003	2004	2005	2006	2007	2008
(1) RGC requested next year	500*	449	N/A	450	500	500	480¹	N/A	500	N/A	513	N/A	N/A
(2) Donors pledged next year	500¹	450	N/A	470	548	556	635⁵	N/A	504	635	601	689	951.1
(3) Net ODA received (current $ million)	416.53	335.33	337.44	277.22	395.72	420.88	485.24	518.31	485.37	535.60	529.37	529.37	674.58
Location of meeting	Tokyo	Paris	N/A	Tokyo	Paris	Tokyo	Phnom Penh	N/A	Phnom Penh	Phnom Penh	Phnom Penh	Phnom Penh	Phnom Penh

Source: (1) Various news sources; (2) and (3) RGC (2004).

Note: * Upper range was $550 million, based on $1.6 billion for three years.

¹ DPA (2002) reported $485 million.

¹ UPI (1996) reported $518 million.

⁵ Revised to $514 million after redefinition of aid.

Does not include data for 1998, 2003, and 2005 when the CGM was not held and therefore no pledges were made. The 2006 CGM was rescheduled from December 2005. As reported in AP (2006c), the 2006 CGM saw $601 million pledged against $513 million requested by the RGC. Net ODA received from 1996 to 2008 from World Development Indicators (http://databank.worldbank.org).

oppression of its people, or misuse of power, it turns to China for financial support. In exchange, evidence suggests Cambodia finds itself serving nearly every Chinese whim—from enormous land concessions to dam building and other infrastructure projects—and suffering labor abuses, geopolitical backlash, social unrest, ecological degradations, and a deep and lasting threat to the country's democratic norms (Ear and Burgos 2010). In the case of the Uyghurs, the United States cancelled plans to donate 200 surplus military trucks to Cambodia. China responded by donating 257 military trucks and 50,000 uniforms. Then, when the United States announced it would not forgive more than $400 million owed from the pro-American Khmer Republic, China forgave Cambodia's Khmer Rouge era debt of a few million dollars.

Unlike the norm in other less-developed countries, which averages 20 percent of foreign aid taken up by technical cooperation (Land and Morgan 2008)—defined as "the transfer, adaptation or facilitation of ideas, knowledge, technologies or skills to foster development" (Ek and Sok 2008:11)—half of all aid to Cambodia goes to technical cooperation. Foreign aid used to transfer, adapt, or facilitate ideas, knowledge, technologies, or skills is less prone to corruption because the bulk of the funds go to international consultant salaries under the label of technical assistance or capacity building. The imbalance in the types of aid being offered to Cambodia has been a sore point since at least 2000, when Godfrey et al. published a path-breaking study on technical cooperation in Cambodia. Ek and Sok's analysis suggests that technical cooperation represented about 51 percent of the total foreign aid from 1998 through 2006, whereas country programmable aid (that is, aid for actual development activities) accounted for only 43 percent. The remainder was used for emergency relief and humanitarian and food aid (Ek and Sok 2008:11). Table 1.4, based on the activities of 31 donors, suggests the massive extent of their interventions relative to the RGC. This table refers only to official donors and does not include the hundreds of nongovernmental organizations (NGOs) operating in Cambodia.

In addition to aid flows from governments, NGOs numbering in the hundreds are heavily involved in Cambodian development. A 2002 count tallied 607 NGOs in Cambodia, of which 407 were local. NGO Forum, an umbrella organization, had ninety-four leading-member NGOs as of May 7, 2010, of which thirty-three were international NGOs. Two faith-based NGOs (World Vision and Catholic Relief Services) are members. Beyond these traditional NGOs are nonprofit and for-profit development consulting firms, such as Winrock International and Development Alternatives, Inc. (DAI), respectively. NGOs' goals and purposes are invariably noble in a country whose poverty rate remains appallingly high, encompassing more than one-third of the population. DAI's mission is to "make a lasting difference in the world by helping developing nations become more prosperous, fairer and more just, cleaner, safer, healthier, more stable, more efficient, and better governed."[12] World Vision International's vision is "for every child, life

Table 1.4   Selected indicators of aid dependence in Cambodia

Indicator	Year	Value
Number of donors	2003	31
Number of donor-supported activities	2003	410
ODA as percentage of GNI	2002	12.7%
ODA as percentage of imports	2002	16.7%
Reported external assistance flows	1996–2001	$2,672m
...compared to total treasury-executed expenditures	1996–2001	$2,122m
Percentage of total public spending accounted for by ODA in 2001	%	
Health	65.9	
Agriculture	67.4	
Transport	68.1	
Area/rural development	88.8	

Source: World Bank (2004b:111).

Note: GNI, gross national income; ODA, official development assistance.

in all its fullness; Our prayer for every heart, the will to make it so."[13] The financial contributions of NGOs to Cambodia's development have been substantial, total-ing about $96 million in 2002. International NGOs contributed some $78.9 million and local NGOs $17.3 million (NGO Forum on Cambodia 2002).

The activities of NGOs are diverse. According to Cooperation Committee for Cambodia, another umbrella NGO organization with more than 100 members, the major contribution of NGOs by sector is toward rural development (22 percent), fol-lowed by activities in education and training, health, and social development. NGOs are also involved in capacity building and institutional development; sharing infor-mation among NGOs, government, and donors; sectoral analysis; policy advocacy; and monitoring and evaluation of large-scale development activities (ADB 2005:3).

Costs of Aid Dependence in Cambodia

While aid was desperately needed for reconstruction by the turn of the millen-nium, several unintended and undesired consequences became apparent. Two are described by Godfrey et al. (2000):

> The scale of aid is such that it distorts the economy. In an aid-related version of "Dutch disease," a high proportion of Cambodia's scarcest resource, educated people,

is pulled toward employment in donor agencies and international non-governmental organizations or attached to projects as salary-supplemented counterparts. At the same time, donors and NGOs virtually take over the funding of education, health care, social welfare, rural development etc., while government spends most of its funds on defense and security.

(Godfrey et al. 2000:123)

The Dutch disease effect is particularly pernicious. Observed in the Netherlands in the 1960s, when large reserves of natural gas in the North Sea were first exploited, "Dutch disease" refers to the inflow of foreign exchange that deindustrialized the Dutch economy. In the case of Cambodia, aid crowds out other sectors, becoming a tradable sector financed by "revenues" in the form of aid. Donor-financed workshops and conferences abound, while civil servants are often abroad on "study tours" and even have their salaries supplemented. Meanwhile, civil servant salaries are marginally above the poverty line of about $0.45 per day per person, making their gravitation toward the aid sector almost a fait accompli. Yet civil service reform is not a high priority for the RGC for political economy and patronage reasons, enabling the abuse of public office for private gain. Salaries— still in the $20–$40 per month range—have increased, but they have not kept up with inflation. The Soviets used to joke, "They pretend to pay us and we pretend to work." The same can be said of civil servants in Cambodia. As a vice president of Cambodia's top private university told me in 2008 when I asked whether graduates might become civil servants, "If you look at government salary, unless you plan to be corrupted, you have no future in that."

The second problem described by Godfrey et al., in which aid allows government not to spend on basic services, is that of aid fungibility. According to the World Bank, "fungibility" is defined as the possibility for aid recipient countries to reduce investments of their own resources in the sector that receives aid and transfer them to other sectors of the budget (1998:130). A foreign expatriate manager with a dozen years' experience with a membership organization of local and international NGOs complained in 2005, "In some ways, donor projects have stifled government initiative, placing foreign agencies largely in charge of the government's service provision responsibilities" (1-1). Another foreign expatriate with five years' experience in international and local NGOs added: "In some ways NGOs can't avoid working with the government. In some ways they should" (1-2).

What the aid variant of the Dutch disease implies for Cambodia is the functional equivalent of brain drain into the aid sector from both the government and the private sector—widely acknowledged as the engine of growth in any country. This is what Knack calls the "siphoning of scarce talent from the bureaucracy"

(2001:310). State capacity is weakened when the best and brightest are neither entrepreneurs nor government policy wonks. Working for donors, they will naturally be donor-driven, and although the goal of aid may be development, with bilateral aid it is more often than not the donor country's foreign policy and national interest that take precedence. As the administrator of the United States Agency for International Development Brian Atwood testified to Congress, "Eighty-four cents of every dollar of aid goes back into the US economy in goods and services purchased," while "for every dollar the United States puts into the World Bank, an estimated $2 actually goes into the US economy in goods and services" (qtd. in Aristide 2000:13). In Cambodia, aid spent by donors on 700 international consultants in 2002 was estimated to total between $50 and $70 million, approximately equal to the wage bill for the country's 160,000 civil servants. Donor-financed consultants working in the RGC are paid upwards of 200 times what their Cambodian counterparts receive (ActionAid 2005:22).

Development Outcomes: Infant and Child Mortality, Poverty, and Inequality

A decade of Cambodian development has proven that technical solutions often fail in the face of political reality. Notwithstanding large annual infusions of aid and approximately 7 percent per year in per capita GDP growth from 2000 to 2010, human development indicators such as infant and child mortality rose after 1990 according to World Bank (2005a) data. For example, in 1990, 80 infants out of 1,000 died in their first year. By 2001, that number had increased to nearly 97 in 1,000. Although a jump over the course of a decade may be an anomaly, what gives confidence to this trend is the continuous rise across the years 1992, 1995, 1997, and 2000. Moreover, child mortality (under the age of five) also rose steadily from 115 per 1,000 in 1990 to 120 in 1995, 135 in 2000, and finally 140 in 2001. At the time, Cambodia's infant and child mortality rates were the highest in the region, higher than even those of Timor-Leste, which in 2003 had an infant mortality rate of 87 in 1,000 and a child mortality rate of 124 in 1,000 (the equivalent of 1995 Cambodia). But as happened with Cambodia's stubbornly high poverty rate (more on that later), a backward "projection" was done, and figures in the current world development indicators accessed online on February 24, 2012, show that infant and child mortality in 1990 has been adjusted upward to 87 (from 80) and 120 (from 115), respectively, whether rightly or wrongly, but certainly not fitting a trouble-free narrative of progress and development. (If only stock market returns could also be adjusted in this manner, we would all be winners!) Meanwhile, the maternal mortality ratio (national estimate, per 100,000 live births) increased from 440 deaths in 2000 to 472 in 2005 before dropping to 460.8 in 2008 (although notably still higher than in 2000). Moreover, inequality has increased dramatically, from a Gini coefficient of 0.38 in 1994, to 0.42 in 2004, and finally to 0.44 in 2007. (A Gini coefficient is an index that ranges between 1, the most inequitable possible outcome, and 0, the most equitable possible outcome.) Cambodia is on par with the Democratic Republic of the Congo and the Philippines in terms of inequality, and, in Asia, is only behind Malaysia, Bhutan, Nepal, and Papua New Guinea.

Illness can often be catastrophic. The high cost and low quality of medical care force families to borrow at usurious interest rates or sell their only assets— livestock and land. Yagura Kenjiro's village-level research found that illness spurs more land sales than crop failure. While floods destroy crops, for example, they also enable fishing, which produces income or provides protein. In contrast, "given the lack of health insurance and insufficient governmental support to the health-care sector, Cambodians have to bear all their own medical costs when they become sick," and microcredit, available in some areas, carries high interest rates and inflexible terms (Kenjiro 2005:780).

With respect to poverty reduction, indications as of early 2005 were that little to no progress had been made since 1994. This changed by late 2005 and early 2006, when the World Bank (2006a) announced a significant 12 percentage-point decrease in poverty over the previous decade based on household consumption data collected in 2004. The bank had recalculated the national poverty rate from 39 percent in 1993/1994 (Prescott and Pradhan 1997; World Bank 1999) to 47 percent using backward projection (World Bank 2006a). Thus, instead of announcing that poverty had decreased very modestly from 39 to 35 percent from 1993 to 2004, the bank announced that poverty had decreased from 47 to 35 percent. From 1993 to 1994, only 56 percent of Cambodian villages and 65 percent of rural areas were accessible to researchers; the remainder of the country was largely controlled by the Khmer Rouge (by then formally known as the Democratic Party of Kampuchea). The backward projection assumed that these areas were much poorer than the accessible portion of the country.[14]

However, sensitivity analysis reveals the lack of robustness in the 2006 World Bank findings. If the 2004 national poverty line (1,826 riels, or $0.45 per person per day) is increased by only 10 percent, or 183 riels ($0.045), the national poverty rate jumps to 41.6 percent from 35 percent. This 6.1 percentage-point difference represents a 17.4 percent increase in poverty. Caution should thus be exercised in interpreting the gains made in reducing poverty between 1994 and 2004. More worrisome, inequality was found to have increased significantly. In non-DPK parts of Cambodia that were surveyed from 1993 to 1994, the Gini coefficient for real per capita consumption was 0.35. As detailed earlier, this coefficient increased to 0.42 in 2004 and to 0.44 in 2007. While it is not unusual to see widening inequality during the transition from a command to a market economy, the World Bank noted that "inequality in Cambodia is somewhat unusual in that most countries in Southeast and East Asia saw levels of inequality start [to] widen only at later stages of development, when levels of average income and consumption were higher (and poverty headcounts lower)" (2006:vi). Rushdy notes more recently that "significantly inequality rose from 0.27 to 0.36 in rural areas, indicating that inequality has increased not only between rural and urban areas, but also within rural areas" (2009:5).

The Failure of Leadership and Political Will

Since it has been established that aid may distort the Cambodian economy by siphoning talent from government and the private sector, it is apparent that the country's tenuous balance between aid and governance needs to be recalibrated. There is an urgent need to focus aid on improving governance. To this end, the importance of domestic political will and political leadership cannot be overstated. This is a subject I explored in a 2005 essay in which I questioned precisely "how well words have turned into action when it comes to governance in the context of Cambodia's economy" (Ear 2005:17). After reviewing a decade of achievements and failures of governance in Cambodia, I found that political will exists to promote exchange rate stability, inflation control, a market economy, and World Trade Organization membership, as do corresponding policies. Support to combat corruption in a way that meets the standards of the UN Convention against Corruption is absent, however, as is a separation of power—particularly of the judiciary from the executive as required by the constitution. Citing the absence of credible signs of domestic leadership for reform, the World Bank abandoned its legal and judicial reform activities in Cambodia in 2004. Then, in August 2009, when the World Bank acknowledged that safeguards to a land titling project had been breached, allowing disenfranchisement and land-grabbing, the RGC terminated the project, citing the bank's "complicated conditions" (BIC 2010). Both of these outcomes strongly support the earlier global empirical finding that aid dependence hurts the rule of law.

If we accept that lack of political will and poor leadership are key factors responsible in the poor governance of Cambodia—factors that donors are unlikely to be able to shift and for which they do not bear responsibility—what can donors realistically hope to accomplish? To this end, I conducted an elite survey to gauge the impact of aid on governance.

Aid and Governance Elite Survey in Cambodia

Using the six dimensions of governance developed by Kaufmann et al. in their 1999 study of the relationship between governance and development—voice and accountability, political stability, government effectiveness, regulatory quality, rule of law, and control of corruption—I ask: What is the relationship between governance quality and the very large amounts of ODA Cambodia has been receiving?

To answer this and related questions, forty-three key informants in Cambodia volunteered to rate donor success across the six dimensions of governance (described in table 1.2), the findings for which I first detailed in Ear (2007b). These informants were selected from various sectors, but all were involved in an intense way with ODA flows and the performance of the Cambodian government. All of them had a minimum of three years' experience in Cambodia, and their mean level of in-country experience was eight years, with a median of seven years. These informants do not "represent" even the population from which they were derived, but they do represent a very deep set of experiences that can help explain the core dynamics of aid, development, and governance in Cambodia. They are deeply involved in Cambodian development (84 percent are employed in donor agencies or nongovernmental organizations) and have a great deal of professional expertise (89 percent functionally manage or advise).

The online portion of the survey was open to informants for a period of 10 days. Total usable responses totaled forty-three,[15] but the survey should be understood as representing only the views of those who responded.[16] These informants were drawn from a potential group (targeted individuals and large e-mail distribution lists on Cambodia) that probably is no larger than 200, given the number of individuals who received (or were forwarded[17]) the message and met the criterion of three years' professional experience working in development in Cambodia.

The survey instrument most likely reached a significant number of individuals in the donor and NGO community, as well as a few in the RGC who had the requisite credentials and Internet access. The response rate was approximately 21.5 percent of the relevant (informed) population of 200, although RGC respondents are underrepresented. Informants listed themselves as working for donor agencies (43 percent), international NGOs (25 percent), local NGOs (16 percent), and the RGC[18] (16 percent); many fell into more than one category.[19] Of these, 61 percent were foreign expatriates, 11 percent were Cambodian expatriates, and 27 percent were citizens of Cambodia only. More informants classified themselves as advisors (52 percent) rather than managers (37 percent), followed by those

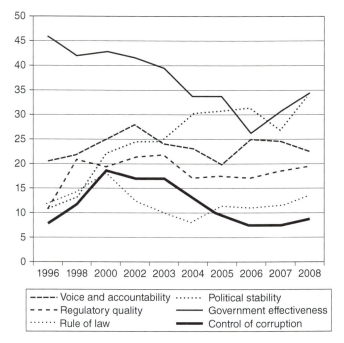

Figure 1.1 CAMBODIA'S PERCENTILE RANKINGS ON SIX DIMENSIONS OF GOVER-
NANCE (1996–2008). These numbers do not include 1997, 1999, and 2001, which
are not part of the dataset.

[*Source*: Based on data from Kaufmann, D., A. Kraay, and M. Mastruzzi (2009).]

working in an educational or research capacity (6 percent) and those classified
as "other" (5 percent).[20] Choices were not mutually exclusive, permitting informants to cross-list themselves.

Notably, the release of the Kaufmann et al. aggregated governance indicators,[21]
"Governance Matters VIII," launched on June 29, 2009, and covering the period
from 1996 to 2008, four years after the survey conducted for this book closed in
early May 2005 (days before "Governance Matters IV," which was released on May
9, 2005). Therefore, the rankings could not have been used by respondents and
could not have influenced them. "Governance Matters VIII" provides percentile
rankings for Cambodia for 1996, 1998, 2000, 2002, and 2003–2008 (missing in
this dataset, therefore, are three years: 1997, 1999, and 2001) across all six dimensions of governance. Cambodia's rankings for all dimensions suggest a turbulent
decade. However, some trends are evident (see figure 1.1). Cross-national rankings place Cambodia very low, at, or below the 34th percentile in 2008 across all

six dimensions and languishing since 2005 in the single digits for control of corruption. The only two areas in which Cambodia might be said to be moderately low (rather than very low) and improving are political stability and regulatory quality (both at the 34th percentile). The latter measure is not confirmed by local informants; however, it picks up a decline in formal regulation and its replacement by corruption (which is exceedingly high and worsening) rather than a real improvement in the business atmosphere.

Political stability in Cambodia is markedly higher than in 1996 (11.1 percentile), jumping to the 30th percentile beginning in 2004, dropping slightly in 2007 (due to an attack on freedom of expression, an incident that forms the basis of chapter 4). Regulatory quality has seen constant performance in the 40th percentiles, dropping to the 30th percentiles starting in 2003. It seems that Cambodia has actually gotten worse over time in terms of regulatory quality. In 2000, after the events of July 5 and 6, 1997, led to the suspension of aid from Germany and the United States in 1998 (UN 2000), most indicators saw some improvement, and those that did not improve remained constant.

The rule of law also saw little to no improvement. It languished in the mid-10th percentile and was at its worst in 2004, at the 8.1 percentile. Government effectiveness, in contrast, saw fluctuations in rankings throughout the period; much of the gains were made after 1996 (the worst year, in which Cambodia was at the 10.9 percentile). Finally, voice and accountability have seen mixed performance, peaking in 2002 at the 27.9 percentile but otherwise remaining in the low- to mid-20th percentiles in all other years. Cambodia embodies the French dictum: *plus ça change, plus c'est la même chose* (the more things change, the more they stay the same).

In contrast to the Kaufmann data, the survey explored the relationship between aid and governance as perceived by development experts. Although the Kaufmann data place Cambodia in the context of other countries in terms of governance performance, they say nothing about the success of donors in changing various dimensions of governance in Cambodia. The survey respondents were asked, for each of Kaufmann et al.'s six dimensions of governance, to "please indicate whether you believe that the donor community as a whole has succeeded in stimulating positive changes in Cambodia or if aid, in effect, is given despite government refusal to change (for example because of massive poverty or the country's tragic Khmer Rouge legacy)." The scores they assigned were to "reflect 'donor success' at effecting change in the government," as instructed by my survey.

Collectively, the survey results suggest that the donor community effected positive change in political stability (67 percent rated donor success in influencing political stability as medium to very high) and, to a lesser degree, voice and accountability (47 percent), but on balance the informants felt that donors had

Table 1.5   Informant ratings on donor success

	None	Poor	Medium	High	Very high	Total	None to poor	High to very high	Medium to very high	Rank
Voice and accountability	9%	44%	35%	12%	0%		53%	12%	47%	2
	4	19	15	5	0	43	23	5	20	
Political stability	10%	24%	31%	31%	5%		33%	36%	67%	1
	4	10	13	13	2	42	14	15	28	
Government effectiveness	16%	53%	28%	2%	0%		70%	2%	30%	4
	7	23	12	1	0	43	30	1	13	
Regulatory quality	20%	51%	22%	7%	0%		71%	7%	29%	3
	8	21	9	3	0	41	29	3	12	
Rule of law	33%	55%	10%	2%	0%		88%	2%	12%	5
	14	23	4	1	0	42	37	1	5	
Control of corruption	60%	33%	5%	2%	0%		93%	2%	7%	6
	26	14	2	1	0	43	40	1	3	

Source: Results of author's survey.

Note: The top percentage indicates total informant ratio; the bottom number represents actual number of informants selecting the rating. The question asked: "For each of the above six dimensions of governance, please indicate whether you believe that the donor community as a whole has succeeded in stimulating positive changes in Cambodia or if aid, in effect, is given despite government refusal to change (for example, because of massive poverty or the country's tragic Khmer Rouge legacy). The score below should therefore reflect 'donor success' at effecting change in the government."

failed to positively influence government effectiveness (only 30 percent rated donor effectiveness as medium to very high), regulatory quality (29 percent), rule of law (12 percent), or control of corruption (7 percent). Summary statistics for informant ratings concerning donor success across the six Kaufmann dimensions of governance are shown in table 1.5.

Political stability has the fewest "none" to "poor" ratings and the most "high" to "very high" ratings, making it the best-ranked dimension of governance in which donors are evaluated as having succeeded. A distant second, numerically, is voice and accountability, although informants qualified their rankings with a number of comments suggesting that, for a country without a history of democratic governance, Cambodia had come a long way. Rankings for all informants are consistent when examined under subgroups such as Cambodian only, Cambodian expatriate, foreign expatriate, or combinations thereof.[22]

That forty-three professionals working on development in Cambodia found that donors have been successful in effecting political stability (and to a lesser extent in voice and accountability) is an important outcome of the last decade of Cambodian reconstruction and development. The mixed success in government effectiveness and regulatory quality is troubling but not surprising given the lack of human capital in the country and the need for state-building in the early post-conflict period. Unfortunately, authorities' lack of political will to curb corruption and unwillingness to rein in impunity have not been checked by donors, who have also failed to control corruption or improve rule of law.

Indeed, as can be seen from the comments on ratings of "none" and "poor" for control of corruption, some informants suggest that donors have enabled corruption to increase. A foreign expatriate manager and advisor with six years' experience in donor and local NGOs who has researched and taught in Cambodia, and who concurred with the statement that high indebtedness and a high poverty rate put great pressure on donors to give even when the governance situation is disappointing, argued: "Donors have no real incentive to curb corruption, because they are not held accountable, nor are their activities very transparent. Donors are part of the problem of corruption in Cambodia" (1-3). Another foreign expatriate manager and advisor with a decade's experience with local and international NGOs who has worked on research and advocacy added that donors "don't control corruption in their own practices" (1-4). Referring to corruption, a foreign expatriate manager with eleven years' experience in an international NGO commented that donors "encourage it and support it at every opportunity" (1-5).

A foreign expatriate manager with over three years' experience with a donor agency wanted to rate donor success in control of corruption as –10 if possible (1-6). Those who rated donor success as "poor" did not mince their words either. A foreign expatriate manager and advisor with seven years' experience in an international NGO (1-7) and a Cambodian manager with four years' experience with a donor agency (1-8) agreed that there was an absence of prosecution for corruption, while a foreign expatriate manager with a dozen years' experience with a membership organization of local and international NGOs (1-9) specifically stressed two recent incidents involving the World Food Programme (WFP) (on Food-for-Work) and the World Bank (on demobilization). Indeed, six other informants named the World Bank as unsuccessful in controlling corruption, despite four mentions of the bank being successful by others. Meanwhile, two other informants cited the World Food Programme as unsuccessful in controlling corruption. Both cases are studied in greater detail in the following section.

Governance and Aid Effectiveness: Explaining the Major Results

Donors have played the role of doting parents and occasional disciplinarians to Cambodia. The embarrassment of inaction during the Khmer Rouge genocide has made them less willing to demand too much of Cambodia, making allowances for the burden of its history. They frequently qualify Cambodia's lack of progress with references to its terrible past and the absence of human capital following the Khmer Rouge period. McCargo argues: "Given Cambodia's recent history of bloodthirsty ideological dictatorship and civil war, the bar for what constitutes improvement is extremely low. Hun Sen and his cohorts 'get away with' authoritarianism because strongman rule is a lesser evil than mass murder" (2005:107).

Voice and Accountability Versus Political Stability

Elections are the culmination of a democratic process.[23] In Cambodia, elections seem to be *the* process (elections = democracy) in the eyes of the international community. This is an important lesson that the Cambodian People's Party learned after 1993 when it lost to Funcinpec. A brokered solution to the subsequent impasse called for no winners and no losers in the form of two prime ministers from each party. As McCargo has argued, "What happened under UNTAC in 1993 was the beginning of a pattern in which Hun Sen used the outward show of electioneering to legitimize the status quo rather than let power change hands," adding, "Elections in Hun Sen's Cambodia have become an exercise in political theater that the CPP uses to legitimize its power" (2005:99–100). Indeed, the threshold for free and fair elections is not particularly high, and it varies according to observers. Observers may visit only for the elections and thus remain unaware of the atmosphere of intimidation.

This may also help to explain why donor success in voice and accountability was perceived by informants as relatively good, with 47 percent rating its success level as medium to very high. In 1996, the leader of the EU delegation, Italian ambassador Leopoldo Ferri de Lazara, said, "If Cambodia is able to maintain [the] present political framework until the 1998 national elections, a democratic and normal life will have been achieved after years of war and instability." With respect to human rights and democracy, the ambassador declared that "E.U. policy [is] to allow sovereign countries to reach democratic status by their own means. This is a situation where the international community should help the Cambodians rather than condemn them.... Our approach on human rights is that we feel if we continue our development aid we will see results" (qtd. in REC 1997).

A retired diplomat described "crossing spades" subsequently with the counselor for the EU delegation based in Bangkok: "He challenged my assertion that Cambodia was not yet a democracy and dismissed the Cambodian opposition as 'trouble makers' for asking the [National Election Commission] to affect the recounting of votes at some places during the 1998 election" (retired diplomat 2003).

This view was reconfirmed in 2003 by then-UN resident coordinator and resident representative of the UN Development Programme Dominique McAdams: "Based on the criteria used to assess a country's degree of democratic participation, Cambodia is a free and steadily progressing country. This assessment is based on three main indicators: elections, a multiparty parliamentary system and free-media," adding, "When it comes to political parties, very frankly, I don't know any other Asian country that would tolerate the level of strong words used by the MP Sam Rainsy in his media papers or whatever." Conceding that expectations had not been met, she concluded "that the government may not have performed as well on judiciary reform or the issue of corruption may be the result of an over-ambitious reform agenda" (qtd. in Doyle 2003). Perhaps the secret to happiness, then, is to have low expectations.

There was a sense among the survey respondents that a Faustian pact had been made to promote stability at the expense of democracy. For example, a foreign expatriate manager, advisor, researcher, and teacher with six years' experience in donor and local NGOs commented that "donor funds have helped prop up an increasingly autocratic, despotic state" (1-3); a foreign expatriate donor official with six years' experience in Cambodia argued that "donors reinforce [the] status quo" (1-10); and a foreign expatriate manager, advisor, researcher, and advocate with a decade's experience with donor, local, and international NGOs noted that "the international community has and continues to happily underwrite authoritarianism (which in the long run isn't terribly stable, but donors don't object to the incremental expressions, such as the murder of MPs, etc.)" (1-4). A foreign expatriate manager with eleven years' experience in an international NGO added that "donors have succeeded at making the current government ministers into some of the richest, most secure officials of any 'democracy' in the world" (1-5).

Rule of Law: Capture of Justice Institutions

With respect to the survey's finding that donors have been unsuccessful in encouraging the rule of law (only 12 percent of respondents rated the success rate at medium to very high), the comments of a foreign expatriate manager and advisor with six years' experience in donor and local NGOs who has researched and taught in Cambodia are enlightening: "The state, including the army and the privileged elite are responsible for most of the crimes, both violent (e.g. land-grabbing) and non-violent (e.g. corruption, resource exploitation). Donor support has enhanced the state's impunity. The absolute inability of donor support to affect positive change in the justice system is a case in point" (1-3). In 2004, the World Bank stopped its traditional legal and judicial reform program in Cambodia due to an absence of political will and the likelihood that new justice institutions would be captured by the authorities. Today's judicial system in Cambodia is hopelessly corrupt. Several of Hun Sen's nephews, for example, have committed murder; one is known to have been sentenced to eighteen months in prison for a triple murder; in 2008, one ran over a motorcyclist and was comforted by military police rather than jailed afterward (regular police were allegedly too afraid to approach the nephew's vehicle for fear of getting into trouble). Much as happened during UNTAC, the Khmer Rouge Tribunal now taking place in Cambodia was supposed to be a shining example to Cambodian courts of how Western rule of law works, but it has instead been co-opted by the Cambodian judges working in its ranks. Kickbacks, corruption, and political interference by the Cambodian authorities have turned the court into a three-ring circus. It is doubtful the UN will ever allow itself to be taken down the Mekong in this manner again, but political expediency combined with weak institutional memory cannot rule out the possibility.

Efforts to reform Cambodia's justice system fall in the category of what Steve Golub critiques as "rule of law orthodoxy," which he identifies as "most prominently practiced by multilateral development banks" and defines as a "'top-down,' state-centered approach [that] concentrates on law reform and government institutions, particularly judiciaries, to build business-friendly legal systems that presumably spur poverty alleviation" (2003:3). Using Cambodia as an example, he explains: "A key assumption of ROL orthodoxy is that the judiciary is central to serving society's legal needs: Unless we fix the courts, many other legal reforms will fail" (Golub 2003:15). As examples, he quotes the World Bank's legal vice presidency: "The rule of law is built on the cornerstone of an efficient and effective judicial system" and the Asian Development Bank: "Although a daunting task, Cambodia has no alternative other than to overhaul the current judicial system if it is to lay a strong foundation for the nation's future development" (qtd. in Golub 2003:15). He concludes, however, that "these claims tie in with related assumptions that neither alternative roads to justice nor dysfunctional judiciaries are usable" and that "this package of assumptions ... is fatally flawed" (Golub 2003:15).

Golub's preference for "alternative roads" resonates with a singular exception to donors' failure in rule of law: the Arbitration Council, an independent tribunal established by law to decide on collective labor disputes that cannot be settled by conciliation. The council was established in 2003 according to the provisions of the 1997 Labour Law at the behest of the United States, which required Cambodian garment factories to meet Cambodian labor standards. (More than 70 percent of Cambodia's export dollars are from garments that go to the United States.) The council's founders were given the choice of being either independent without binding rulings or not independent with binding rulings. They chose to be independent, believing that the council's legitimacy would grow over time and that participants would voluntarily choose that rulings be binding. Without threatening political elites' hold on power, the council has succeeded where others have failed. As a result, the World Bank initiated a Justice for the Poor program in 2005 to explore possibilities of alternative dispute resolutions in land conflicts. While this is a positive sign, the inescapable conclusion remains that donors have not succeeded in improving the rule of law in Cambodia. Indeed, in 2009, the earlier mentioned World Bank land titling project saw safeguards breached and resulting abuse. The government pulled the plug on the project to avoid the embarrassment of having the project suspended or cancelled by the bank. But in March 2011, the bank's own inspection panel faulted the bank for having been deceived in the case of Boeung Kak Lake, located in the middle of Phnom Penh. The 133-hectare lake has been filled in by a Chinese-backed company headed by a Cambodian tycoon who is also a senator from the ruling Cambodian People's Party. The bank was duped into not allowing lake area residents to obtain land titles. In turn, the residents were offered $8,500 for their homes regardless of size or plot of land when the real estate market would have called for many times this amount. The bank atoned by suspending all lending to Cambodia in August 2011 until the matter of Boeung Kak Lake was sorted out. As of June 2012, the suspension of lending is still in effect despite a promise by the prime minister to require the company to set aside land for remaining residents.

Control of Corruption: Cambodia's and the Donors' Problem

In tandem with the donors' lack of influence in improving the rule of law has been a complete lack of control over corruption. Corruption consumes a significant portion of the economy—possibly as much as the entire aid budget each year. To combat it, Cambodia has been drafting an anticorruption law since 1994. A watered-down version, with asset declaration by public officials that is to remain inexplicably secret, passed the National Assembly in 2010. Lindsay MacLean notes that while "Many use [the lack of an anticorruption law] as an explanation for the widespread corruption in Cambodia and the culture of impunity that exists . . . a law is only the first stage of reform" (2006:9).

The results of a survey on governance and corruption in 2000 prepared by the World Bank in response to a request by the authorities for technical assistance for capacity building in enhancing governance and fighting corruption found that public corruption is perceived as a leading problem for citizens and enterprises of all types, with some functions of government—such as the judiciary, revenue collection bodies, and bodies managing public assets—rated particularly poorly (2000:iv). A more recent survey of corruption shows that unofficial payments (also known as a "bribe tax") amount to 5.2 percent of surveyed firms' gross revenues (World Bank 2004b), more than twice that measured in Bangladesh, Transparency International's bottom performer on the Corruption Perception Index (CPI) in 2004. Cambodia was ranked for the first time in the 2005 CPI at 130 out of 158 and fell further in the 2006 CPI to 151 out of 163 countries. From 2007 to 2011, Cambodia ranked in the range of 154 to 166 out of a possible 178 to 182 countries. Thus, it remained in the bottom 28. The cost of corruption has been estimated at $120 million per year by the World Bank (2004b) and at between $300 million and $500 million per year by Calavan et al. (2004). This latter figure suggests that up to 10 percent of Cambodia's then ~$5 billion gross domestic product is consumed by corruption.

A foreign expatriate manager and advisor with four years' experience in donor and international NGOs in Cambodia complained that matters had "deteriorated" since he began working in Cambodia in 1990 (1-11), while a Cambodian expatriate manager with a decade's experience in development quipped that "The anti-corruption bill is a joke," adding: "The whole government system, which is based on patronage mentality, has prospered out of control due to corruption that has benefited a select few. It would be too much to expect the top would do anything serious to cut their own throat and life line" (1-12). A Cambodian expatriate manager with seven years' experience in an international NGO and a national institution called for more "international pressure" (1-13), while a foreign expatriate manager and advisor with five years' experience with a donor agency went so far as to claim that donors "May have made corruption worse" (1-14). Clearly, something has gone terribly wrong with donors and the RGC when it comes to corruption.

Two cases of donor handling of corruption from 2003 to 2005 are particularly instructive. In 2004, the World Food Programme reported that more than $2 million worth of rice was diverted from its Food-for-Work scheme. The approach to dealing with this problem was at first very public: the subject was given a front-page article in the *Phnom Penh Post* (Woodd 2004a), which was followed by an interview with the then-WFP representative in Cambodia (Woodd 2004b). WFP's approach included prior consultation with Cambodia's largest bilateral donor and assurances of support by that donor as leverage on the RGC. At the time, the WFP representative put her foot down: "If [the government] did not accept anything [i.e., any responsibility] then we would have to seriously look at our future in Cambodia" (qtd. in McKenny 2005). The RGC quickly accepted the terms, taking responsibility and agreeing to repay the cost of the rice in principle following its own investigation.

Unfortunately, the $2 million figure was then disavowed by the WFP, which made it clear to the RGC that the amount in question was negotiable. On February 28, 2005, the RGC agreed to pay only $900,000. The WFP had suspended Food-for-Work for the duration, but it continued all its other activities in order not to hurt the "hungry poor" (qtd. in Cochrane 2005). The agreement came, coincidentally, after the WFP announced it would distribute 1,500 metric tons of rice to drought-affected populations. There was no apparent rallying around the agency by other donors, and no press releases concerning this matter were found either on the program's global Web site or its local one through mid-March 2005. The case was further complicated by the World Food Programme representative's coincidental and unrelated departure from Cambodia for another posting and allegations of local program staff's own complicity in the corruption (evidence of which was used as a foil for criticism of the RGC). Although some local staff did not have their contracts extended, no government official was ever punished.

In contrast, the case of the World Bank saw somewhat better results, even though the bank's initial approach was more muted.[24] At first, the bank took a very low-key approach to making any declaration of misprocurement in a demobilization project with the RGC. The Integrity Department of the World Bank investigated certain procurement irregularities concerning a bank-financed $6.9 million contract for the supply and maintenance of motorcycles. Misprocurement was declared on the contract on June 26, 2003, and the bank sought repayment of $2.8 million. The bank saw no progress. It was then reported in the media that a letter had been sent by the World Bank's vice president for East Asia and the Pacific that allegedly threatened that if reimbursement did not take place by February 15, 2005, the entire portfolio of more than a dozen bank-funded development projects would be suspended. This quickly produced results—the government immediately repaid the $2.8 million.

At an impromptu press conference on January 21, 2005, the prime minister suggested to reporters that the World Bank had brought into the tender process the private firms responsible for the corruption. Minister of Economy and Finance Keat Chhon had been more conciliatory when earlier interviewed by the Associated Press. He said, "It is regretful for me that such a problem has occurred. This was because there were loopholes in the implementation. . . . We must work to build good governance, so others stop suspecting that corruption was committed" (qtd. in AP 2005b).

Note the rather vague language and complete absence of responsibility in the minister's response.

To be sure, the World Bank's large size, its role as lender of last resort, and its stature as cochair of annual Consultative Group meetings gave it more leverage than WFP, but the case also suggests that the World Bank's threat to suspend its entire portfolio was credible, whereas the World Food Programme's threat to examine its future in Cambodia lacked credibility. Learning from past lessons elsewhere, the bank already knew by 2004 that "when abuses are discovered" due to corruption, donors needed to pursue "greater information disclosure, strengthened controls and supervision, engagement of communities and civil society organizations in project design and supervision as the norm, and better enforcement" in an effort to "significantly reduce the opportunities for misuse of ODA and, in doing so, contribute to clarifying the distinction between public and private resources" (World Bank 2004a:122). In the case of Cambodia, the bank failed to follow its own advice. It was generally mute about its actions, disclosing little information, in contrast to the World Food Programme. When it came to enforcement after abuses were discovered, however, the bank may have had the upper hand. After all, food is very different from money, and the bank's ability to penalize Cambodia through its annual performance-based allocation exercise known as the Country Policy and Institutional Assessment (CPIA) and, more immediately, by threatening to withhold millions of other project funds left the Cambodian authorities little choice. In refusing the bank's terms, they would have been penny wise but pound foolish.

Indeed, as MacLean points out, "A degree of political will for reform exists within the government, but the reality is that those in power have little reason to change a system that has secured them much power and personal wealth." He adds, "Stricter costs imposed by the donor community would serve to pressure the government and effect real change" (2006:10). These stricter costs materialized beginning in 2005, when the CPIA scores became public for the first time since they were introduced in 1980—something bank clients themselves had lobbied hard against—making the instrument more credible as a deterrent against poor governance performance. In February 2005, James Wolfensohn, then president of the World Bank, declared, "We have reduced our lending to Cambodia—as a response to the poor performance on governance indicators—but we have not reduced our commitment, nor our efforts to push for the kinds of reforms that are needed to bring about a better life for all Cambodians" (qtd. in World Bank 2005b). His announcement was based on the 2004 CPIA score for Cambodia, which had already been revealed to the authorities in a letter dated July 26, 2004. It is worth noting, however, that even in this "successful" case, those who committed the corrupt acts neither reimbursed their gains nor were prosecuted.

It was the RCG that provided the reimbursement, and its budget is de facto donor-supported with fungible aid.

The evidence in this chapter confirms what has become increasingly clear in the past fifteen years: that aid dependence is not, generally speaking, good for governance. Yet it has also shown that the effects of aid dependence on governance may not be, on the whole, as bad as Stephen Knack's research has suggested. The key task that remains is to isolate how to make aid work better by assessing how it functions in specific country contexts.

The dismal quality of Cambodia's governance is, of course, largely the result of the government's own lack of political will and poor leadership. Yet donors also bear responsibility for this outcome, given their deep commitments, financial and programmatic, to Cambodian institutions. Aside from bolstering political stability and, to a lesser extent, voice and accountability, donors cannot be said to have succeeded in improving governance in Cambodia. Political stability is the byproduct of a peace dividend sowed by Cambodian stakeholders and nurtured by the international community. Donors and the government were aligned on political stability—this much is apparent—and this was clearly the political bargain that was made in Paris in 1991 to move Cambodia from a state of war to one of peace.

Certainly, with respect to control of corruption and rule of law, Cambodia may be in worse shape now than it was a decade ago. It is also apparent that ODA has made it more feasible, through fungibility, to divert resources and engage in other corrupt practices. The failure to mitigate corruption shows how hard it is for donors to be tough on a country that is genuinely aid-dependent for the survival of much of the population.

Donors' failure to effect positive change in the rule of law is of another category; it shows insufficient donor attention to the issue or the application of dysfunctional models of institutional development—or both. Knack suggests that "a larger fraction of aid could be tied or dedicated to improvements in the quality of governance, for example, in the form of programs to establish meritocratic bureaucracies and strong, independent court systems" (2001:326). While judicial independence remains a serious problem in Cambodia and a meritocratic bureaucracy cannot function on salaries of $20–40 a month, donors such as the World Bank have already recognized that alternative justice mechanisms for the poor are needed. On the basis of what has been accomplished to date, however, ODA seems unlikely to be able to deliver large improvements in governance and in some ways may even contribute to its further deterioration.

All of this suggests that the relationship among aid, governance, and development is far from being as straightforward as politicians and captains of the aid industry once assumed. In fact, as the next chapter will show, aid may succeed in fostering economic growth, but for all the wrong reasons.

2

GROWTH WITHOUT DEVELOPMENT

The Garment, Rice, and Livestock
Sectors in Cambodia

BETWEEN 2004 AND 2007, Cambodia experienced double-digit per capita gross domestic
product (GDP) growth: 10 percent in 2007
and 2004, 11 percent in 2006, and 13 percent in 2005. Simultaneously, it ranked
among the worst countries worldwide in terms of governance indicators, coming
in at 130 out of 158 in the 2005 Corruption Perception Index (the year it was first
ranked), 151 out of 163 in 2006, and 162 out of 179 in 2007. If aid is bad for governance in Cambodia, and if bad governance is in turn bad for development, what
explains Cambodia's rapid economic growth?

In search of an answer, in this chapter I unpack the country's prevailing and prospective growth patterns and their associated governance patterns in three economic sectors. I analyze more than fifty detailed semistructured interviews with
government, nongovernment, and donor officials, as well as with businessmen, to
understand the dynamics of governance and growth in a successful sector, the garment industry; a nascent sector, rice; and a stunted sector, livestock.[1] My findings
suggest that Cambodia's recent growth is *not* a product of good governance and
that poor governance—as distorted by the effects of aid—is stifling the potential
for growth in the agricultural economy.

I begin the chapter with an examination of Cambodia's political economy context, paying particular attention to *oknhas*—Cambodia's political-economic oligarchs—and taxation. In the three sections that follow I present case studies of the garment, rice, and livestock sectors. In the chapter's conclusion I outline policy factors that might promote economic growth in Cambodia.

Governance and Growth in Cambodia

While the paradox of growth despite poor governance has been observed in a number of countries, it is particularly puzzling in the case of Cambodia. In Vietnam and China, growth has been strong despite governance that is lackluster by international comparison. But available governance indices suggest that both Vietnam and China are slightly better governed than their peer states (except with regard to political and civil liberties), which may explain their economic edge. This is not the case for Cambodia, whose government performs below its peer group average. Indeed, on two crucial dimensions—government effectiveness and control of corruption—the distance between governance in Cambodia and in Vietnam is substantial. Thus, it is particularly surprising that the accelerated growth seen in Cambodia has been sustained for a number of years.

Cambodia's recent economic growth is based in part on extraction in the forestry sector. Growth based on extraction is generally possible even in relatively poor governance environments. In fact, the extraction of gold, timber, precious stones, oil, and gas may even be facilitated by poor governance. Extraction-based growth can in turn fuel other sectors, such as real estate, construction, and trade. A member of the National Assembly noted that much of "the driving force of the growth" in Cambodia's economy has been "temporary" and lacking in strength; the member of parliament (MP) cited deforestation, gambling, and garment exports as three examples (2-1). The availability of old-growth forest has dwindled since the rapacious clear-cutting commanded by both the Khmer Rouge and the Cambodian authorities in the early to mid-1990s. As Stiglitz (2007) points out, globally, poverty and inequality follow extractive industries.

What growth requires of governance varies according to the (potential) source of growth and its desired effects. For instance, growth based on manufacturing, agro-processing, high technology, and services is likely to be more demanding of governance than growth based on extraction. Export-oriented manufacturing and agro-processing require a government that has sufficient capacity to enforce minimum standards, that can provide the requisite infrastructure, and that contains corruption sufficiently to allow such sectors to flourish. Unfortunately, the emergence of China as a major donor and investor bodes ill for Cambodia's governance. China's largess requires neither good governance nor human rights, only backroom deals and profitability. China has allegedly acquired the rights to some offshore Cambodian oil fields by purchasing a firm with preexisting claims. Recent geological work suggests that significant amounts of oil and gas may reside underground throughout Cambodian territory (Burgos and Ear 2010).

When governance harms growth, it may do so directly or indirectly. Directly, poor governance may become a binding constraint on growth if it fosters a business environment so bad that no or only very limited growth is possible. Indirectly, poor governance can contribute to other constraints on growth; for example, poor infrastructure frequently results from a combination of weak and patronage-based governance as much as from a lack of capital. Lack of access to or a high cost of capital may in part be caused by poor governance of the banking sector and by practices such as lending to political cronies or politically connected business groups at preferential rates.

Importantly, governance is more often an indirect constraint on aggregate growth than a direct one. Examples of direct constraints include highly oppressive administrations (e.g., Cambodia under the Khmer Rouge, North Korea, China during the Cultural Revolution, Zimbabwe) and situations of significant insecurity (e.g., during civil wars and insurgencies).

It is assumed, though yet to be satisfactorily researched, that growth is more likely to be equitable, inclusive, and environmentally sustainable as governance improves. Better governance is more likely to stimulate sources of growth that create significant and sustainable employment. Growth in poor-governance environments is more likely to rely on extraction, which entails environmental risks and fuels the informal economy, which itself has risks. Better governance is also more likely to enhance the social returns of growth by fostering better use of fiscal resources and policies for the public good.

Market failures such as poor infrastructure, financial instability, a less skilled workforce, poor urban planning, and environmental degradation are less likely to be addressed in countries with poor governance, with negative effects on both social and private returns.

What type of government is needed to stimulate growth? Mushtaq Khan has argued that good governance necessarily facilitates development. This is an important insight in the Cambodian context. What he characterizes as the "service delivery model" has failed to spur growth. This model, according to Khan, focuses on a range of services that states should deliver—in particular, public goods such as law and order, social security, and market regulation—and relies on competitive markets to deliver all other goods and services. It has not been particularly effective in developing states. Dani Rodrik describes what he calls the "institutional underpinnings of market economies" in five parts: "A clearly delineated system of property rights; a regulatory apparatus curbing the worst forms of fraud, anticompetitive behavior, and moral hazard; a moderately cohesive society exhibiting trust and social cooperation; social and political institutions that mitigate risk and manage social conflicts; [and] the rule of law and clean government" and concludes that economists "usually take [them] for granted, but which are conspicuous by their absence in poor countries" (2007:153).

Substituting a "social transformation model" for the service delivery model, Khan argues that it is necessary to consider the state's role in transforming precapitalist and preindustrial societies into dynamic capitalist and industrial ones. His examination of case studies suggests that governance reforms do not necessarily make market-driven growth more likely; indeed, no society is known to have developed by creating, first and foremost, institutions of good governance. The alternate approach that has emerged is a diagnostic one, which Rodrik describes as starting "with relative agnosticism about what works" and is based on the hypothesis "that there is a great deal of 'slack' in poor countries, so simple changes can make a big difference. As a result, it is explicitly diagnostic and focuses on the most significant economic bottlenecks and constraints" (Rodrik 2008:2). He concludes by saying that "[r]ather than comprehensive reform, it emphasizes policy experimentation and relatively narrowly targeted initiatives in order to discover local solutions, and it calls for monitoring and evaluation in order to learn which experiments work" (2008:2).

Another issue is that of stability and its relationship to other aspects of good governance, such as control of corruption or regulatory quality. Although stability is a necessary but not sufficient condition for growth to sustain itself, Khan and others believe that it is an absolutely crucial aspect of governance for growth. But too often the same people (elite groups) providing stability are the source of bad governance and impunity—a problem that plagues Cambodia. It is often unclear how events will unfold—will stability and the growth it triggers eventually lead to improved governance, or will bad governance and impunity eventually undermine growth and stability?

"The goals of good governance are desirable in themselves," Khan argues. He insists that "the starting point" for reform "must be good analysis of how patron-client networks in particular countries have allowed some types of value enhancing economic transformations and prevented other types" (2006:18). In this chapter I adopt Khan's approach to compare how these three sectors have experienced

Cambodia's recent development. Patron-client networks in Cambodia have allowed some types of value-enhancing economic transformations in garments—transformations that have found their way through rice (and agro-processing)—while inhibiting livestock exports. First, I consider two key distorting factors in Cambodia's business environment.

The *Oknha* Economy[2]

It is widely known in Cambodia that if one wants to do business, one needs to have *khnorng* (literally, "back" in Khmer). In recent years, businessmen have connected with those in the government as a way of obtaining *khnorng*; meanwhile, government officials enjoy gifts both personal and as party contributions, especially around the time of elections. And so a web of personal *kse* ("string") and *khnorng* is woven. The logic is simple—power, prestige, and money find a way to meet. The systems of *oknha* and *tipreuksa* ("advisor") are two good examples of how the three come together formally. To increase their personal gain, *oknhas* invest in those sectors that enjoy the highest returns with the shortest time horizons.

According to Duong (2008), *oknha* is a title of nobility, akin to peerage in the British system. *Oknha* is more prestigious and sounds more high-class than *ayadom* ("excellency"), as it implies not only a high position but also wealth. (Although I will not delve into it beyond a mention here, the proliferation of doctorates—earned, honorary, and, unfortunately, unearned—is an additional manifestation of the desire for prestige and validation: a preponderance of top Cambodian politicians claim PhDs from obscure universities.) On April 15, 1994, the government issued a subdecree to grant any citizen, Khmer or foreign, who contributes more than $100,000 to the state the status of an *oknha*. According to the office that grants the title, there are currently about 220 *oknhas* nationwide. Independent figures are unavailable, but according to an *oknha*'s personal assistant, the number increased by 200 in 2004–2008 (1-2).

Almost all the members of chambers of commerce are *oknhas*, and they are associated with the governing Cambodian People's Party (CPP). Some have joined politics. Three *oknhas* have become members of the National Assembly and six are in the Senate. *Oknhas* make contributions to the CPP and its elites, especially during elections. The same cannot be said of the opposition Sam Rainsy Party, whose secretary-general pointedly said: "*Oknhas* and other millionaires do not help us, and our party is not corrupt" (qtd. in Ros 2008). The deputy secretary-general of the Human Rights Party "indicated that the *oknhas* are not helping his party" (Ros 2008).

It is well known in Cambodia that some *oknhas* have engaged in illicit activities, including drug trafficking (particularly marijuana) and land grabbing. It is common to hear about *oknhas* accused of encroaching on valuable lands in Sihanoukville, Siem Reap, and Phnom Penh, among other choice locations. According to Oxfam GB, "The land holders who own larger plot [*sic*] of land (more than 500 hectares of land) are business people (30.77 percent), high ranking official bearing [the title] 'His Excellency' (23.03 percent), OKNHA (23.08 percent), arm[ed] forces [members] bearing [the title] 'General' (15.38 percent), and members of [the] National Assembly (7.69 percent)" (2007:2). The wealthy buying up large tracts of land for speculative reasons can be such a problem that it spawned a tax on nonproductive land. As the United Nations Office of the High Commissioner for Human Rights in Cambodia notes, "a large number of economic land concessions have been granted in favour of foreign business interests and prominent Cambodian political and business figures, including senators and oknhas," with no apparent benefit to "rural communities" or to "state revenues" (OHCHR 2007:2).

The relationship between politics and business runs deep in Cambodia. As mentioned previously, a total of nine *oknhas* are MPs and senators, and all of them belong to the CPP; more importantly, most ministers and many MPs have financial interests. Indeed, joint ventures in which politicians participate but do not invest are a well-recognized method of parlaying influence into assets. The idea of a conflict of interest is foreign in Cambodian culture and politics, in which the separation between public and private is seldom clear. A minister who receives a monthly consulting payment from a firm he "supervises" argues that he worked outside business hours. A minister's spouse owning a million dollars' worth of shares in a conglomerate registered by her husband's ministry raises few eyebrows. An incoming minister who owns a large business that he will supervise as minister argues that no conflict of interest exists if he hands the business over to his spouse. Often, inexplicable wealth is explained by exceptional business acumen on the part of the spouse. This situation, in turn, makes it difficult to enact an anticorruption law, much less implement one.

The prevalence of *oknhas* and advisors in Cambodia is a symptom of a bigger problem. Because of the way that power operates in the country, the government has created virtually no incentives for healthy economic development. Instead, development incentives are along the lines of short-term, get-rich-quick schemes, from extraction to land grabs. The "discount rate"[3] of authorities in conflict-affected countries can be higher than those of private citizens, since today's minister might be tomorrow's political prisoner. Thus, as Rose-Ackerman argues, "By accepting present gains, he gives up a future stream of revenue. This may be rational if the ruler has a higher discount rate than private investors because he fears being overthrown. The kleptocrat may value the up-front benefits of selling the public firm more highly than the private market" (1999:118). Overall, however, this represents a state failure. The market is "free," but it offers few opportunities for important sectors to develop.

Aid, Taxes, and Revenues

The regime has provided a business environment that is not unfriendly to the private sector. Cambodia is in fact quite open to business, with generous tax holidays in comparison to the investment regimes of other countries in the region, according to the cabinet deputy director of the Cambodian Investment Board (Hing 2002:5). For example, there is a complete exemption from the 20 percent corporate tax on profit. The exemption period begins from the first year in which the project becomes profitable (but before the offset of losses) according to the Embassy of Cambodia (n.d.). The duration of this tax holiday can be up to nine years. There is also a precedent for extensions of tax holidays. In June 2006, the Council of Ministers extended the corporate tax holiday on garment and textile factories by two years to companies registered before March 14, 2005 (Wasson and Kimsong 2006).

The influx of official development assistance (ODA) into Cambodia, which peaked at $48 per capita in 1995 for the 1990s, has now been nominally exceeded in 2007 ($49), 2008 ($54), and 2009 and 2010 (both $52). Meanwhile, revenue (excluding grants) did not improve from 2002 to 2010, peaking in 2008 when GDP growth began to slow and the bottom fell out of the world economy. Tax revenue averaged 8.9 percent from 2002 to 2010. Indeed, tax revenues never exceeded 10.6 percent of GDP during that period—an abysmal figure by world standards, on par with Niger, Tanzania, and Togo.[4] This is also reflected in anemic domestic revenue performance, which averaged 10.7 percent from 2002 to 2010.

Table 2.1 shows recent trends in aid, tax, and domestic revenues for Cambodia. The steady decline in net ODA received [as a percentage of gross national income (GNI)] from 2002 to 2010 is due to double-digit GDP growth rates, which in turn expanded GNI, the denominator. While only indicative, patterns suggest that for each year in which ODA and official aid (current $) increased, tax revenues (as a percentage of GDP) decreased, and vice versa. The same pattern repeats for revenues, excluding grants (as a percentage of GDP). The Country Policy and Institutional Assessment rating for revenue mobilization fell right in the middle of a Likert scale (1 = low to 6 = high) at 3 and was unchanged from 2005 to 2010.

Certainly, as anecdotal evidence suggests, authorities have prioritized contributions from *oknhas*, advisors, and their aspirants over facilitating the payment of

Table 2.1 Cambodia's aid, tax, and domestic revenues (2000–2010)

Indicators	2000	2001	2002	2003	2004	2005	2006	2007	2008	2009	2010	Average
Net official development assistance and official aid received (current $ million)	395.72	420.88	485.24	518.31	485.37	535.60	529.37	674.58	742.84	721.43	736.70	567.82
Net ODA received (% of central government expense)	N/A	N/A	120.7	119.8	111.2	112.1	84.7	95.2	83.8	62.8	58.1	94.3
Net ODA received (% of GNI)	11.2	11.0	11.8	11.6	9.5	8.9	7.6	8.2	7.5	7.3	6.9	9.2
Net ODA received per capita (current $)	31.8	33.3	37.8	39.8	36.8	40.1	39.2	49.3	53.7	51.6	52.1	42.3
Tax revenue (% of GDP)	N/A	N/A	8.2	7.5	8.1	7.9	8.2	9.7	10.6	9.7	10.1	8.7
Revenue, excluding grants (% of GDP)	N/A	N/A	10.3	9.4	9.8	9.7	9.8	11.2	12.5	11.1	12.2	10.5
CPIA efficiency of revenue mobilization rating (1 = low to 6 = high)	N/A	N/A	N/A	N/A	N/A	3	3	3	3	3	3	3

Source: World Development Indicators online (http://databank.worldbank.org).

taxes to the point that a niche industry has been created for the payment of taxes; the payments, which must be in local currency, are notoriously difficult to make, as tax officials cannot be bothered to count the cash and require taxpayers to wait in line for entire afternoons. One leading NGO with exceedingly close ties to the government had to appeal directly to the prime minister when it had difficulty paying its employees' payroll taxes. A money changer who processes hundreds of tax payments for businesses for a $35 fee per payment and trades between $2 million and $3 million per day from a rented storefront confided that it only paid $100 in taxes per month (2-3).

The tax collection system has led to weak state capacity in the postconflict period and has allowed a patronage system of informal revenue collection to blossom in which authorities do not need a "modern rational bureaucracy," just loyalty in the chain of hierarchy. Taking a cue from the findings of Tarhan Feyzioglu, Swaroop Vinaya, and Min Zhu (1998), who showed a negative empirical link between aid and tax revenues, Collier and Dollar write that "aid directly augments public resources and reduces the need for the government to fund its expenditures through taxation, thereby reducing domestic pressure for accountability" (2004:F263). Typically, this implies a change in the demand for accountability, since the latter is linked to taxation, which is reduced by aid's fungibility.

Similarly, so-called bribe taxes enable a regime of low tax revenue collection to become sustainable, since unofficial payments are off budget and serve the dual purpose of sustaining the system and serving the party. Prospects for reform are dim, as Hach Sok points out, "The fundamental and systemic cause of administrative dysfunction relates to the maintained patronage system that Cambodia does not seem to be able to relinquish. The patronage system is a form of hierarchical, social relationships in which no one is considered equal to anyone else," adding that it is "[r]einforced by a pyramidal structure, the patronage system is also total, and involves all levels of civil servants. In this way, all the administrative systems become strongly interdependent" (Sok 2005:3). He concludes that "[a]dministrative patronage is closely linked to the ruling political party organization. The deep rooted Cambodian political patronage system is strengthening. Each of those patronage units has its own group interest to protect, which is likely done at the expense of the nation and of the citizenry" (Sok 2005:3).

Given such gloomy realities, one must wonder how Cambodia has managed to grow at all, much less at double-digit rates. A closer look at three sectors will help elucidate what works, what doesn't, and why in the interaction between Cambodia's government and its economy.

Three Sectors, Three Outcomes

In the remainder of the chapter I discuss the garment, rice, and livestock sectors of the Cambodian economy. Each was identified in 2005 in *Cambodia and WTO: A Guide for Business*, published by the Ministry of Commerce and the Mekong Project Development Facility (MPDF) of the International Finance Corporation, as being a potential export sector, although the report carefully noted that "the selection of an industry does not mean that it, more than one not selected, is likely to be successful at exporting" (MoC and MPDF 2005:3). The success of the garment industry, the emergence of rice, and the challenges faced by the livestock sector provide valuable insights.

The Garment Sector: A Cambodian Success Story?

The garment sector stands out for its tremendous contribution to Cambodia's economic growth. According to the Economic Institute of Cambodia, the sector has added an estimated 2 percent annually to GDP since 1995, although this is tapering off (EIC 2007:12). It is undergoing a period of adjustment—one predicted at the end of 2005 with the expiration of the Multi-Fibre Arrangement that permitted Cambodia to export to the United States under a duty-free quota. A labor-intensive industry, garments have been monitored through Better Factories Cambodia, a unique program of the International Labour Organization (ILO) that "aims to improve working conditions in Cambodia's export garment factories," combining "independent monitoring with finding solutions, through suggestions to management, training, advice and information" (Better Factories 2008:1). Monitoring is done against a 480-point checklist twice a year; the checklist includes all codes that are relevant (Cambodian Labor Law, buyers' code of conduct, etc.). This obviates the need for buyers to conduct their own inspections.

According to Ministry of Commerce data, as of October 31, 2011, there were 300 "active factories" in Cambodia employing 326,751 workers (qtd. in Better Factories 2012:3). By Better Factories' own count, the 300 factories it monitors employed 345,364. According its data, three-quarters of the workforce is employed in factories with 1,000 or more workers (Better Factories 2012:4). Of these factories, approximately 175 are affiliated with a particular brand, such as Walmart, Gap, and H&M (2-4). Women make up 91 percent of the monitored workforce (Better Factories 2012:6), which has a very high turnover rate—nearly 50 percent even at one of the best and most renowned factories in Cambodia (2-5).

As such, the garment industry is unique. It is responsible for the country's minimum wage—respected primarily in the garment sector—of $55 per month. This minimum wage is both a blessing and a curse. It makes no distinction between better or worse factories, better or worse workers, as long as they work the allotted 9.5 hours per day, 47.5 hours per week. There is growing difficulty, moreover, in finding garment workers at this wage rate amid rising inflation, since such workers could make as much, if not more, in the countryside (2-6).

Background

In the 1990s, the Cambodian garment sector emerged in response to U.S. trade preferences.[5] In 1998–1999, the Clinton administration developed the U.S.-Cambodian Trade Agreement on Textiles and Apparel (1999–2004), which linked market access (increasing quota) to labor standards. Cambodia is the first country where a trade-labor arrangement was agreed to and implemented. This is not to say that labor has not figured into every bilateral and regional trade agreement the United States has entered into; since 1993, the United States has included these and other standards in almost every bilateral and regional agreement (Wells 2006). The difference is that such standards have not been enforced, while Cambodia's were enforced, with rewards in the form of increased quotas for compliance. In addition, the Cambodian garment industry benefited from garment buyers seeking to diversify their sources and from being located in a region that is strongly engaged in textiles and garments.

U.S. trade preferences were made conditional on the observation of labor standards. Cambodia became the first country in which ILO monitoring of labor standards was made mandatory.[6] Apart from benefiting workers, there appears to have been some economic payoff from this approach, as the Cambodian system appealed to buyers who increasingly based their brand on embracing ethical approaches to manufacturing.

To date, Cambodia captures only a relatively limited share of the value chain and the value added in garments. Cambodia is only involved at the "cut, make, and trim" phase (see figure 2.1). Almost all inputs for the sector are imported, and the country does not have a textile industry. More than 95 percent of garment factories are foreign owned, and a significant part of the profits are repatriated. Direct contributions to the government budget have been limited, since the sector enjoys import tax exemptions as well as tax holidays. In June 2006, 180 out of 270 firms then operating (specifically those firms that had applied for licenses before March 14, 2005) became eligible for an additional two years of tax holiday when the Council of Ministers acted to support the industry in light of increasing competition from Vietnam and China (AP 2006a). Nonetheless, the benefits to Cambodia have been substantial in terms of direct and indirect job creation and in terms of boosting overall GDP. Garments account for up to 80 percent of

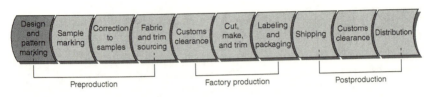

Figure 2.1 TEXTILES AND GARMENTS VALUE CHAIN.
[*Source*: Captured from USAID (2007:11).]

recorded exports, for nearly 350,000 direct jobs, and for approximately the same number of indirect jobs.

Garment manufacturing in Cambodia took off between 1997 and 2001 with high rates of job growth and a rapid increase in the number of factories. Since 2001, job creation in the sector has slowed down. Contrary to some expectations, the sector did not experience a rapid decline after the end of the Multi-Fibre Arrangement because China was restrained from exporting garments at will. Currently, however, the sector is coming under pressure. A significant slowdown of garment exports to the United States was recorded from the fourth quarter of 2007 through 2009. Overall, Cambodia's garment and apparel exports dropped 15.46 percent between 2008 and 2009 (May 2010). The first quarter of 2010 saw a modest increase of 7.24 percent from the first quarter of 2009, but the overall level remained below that of the first quarter of 2008. The first 10 months of 2011 saw garment exports rise to $3.47 billion—up 34 percent compared to the first 10 months of 2011.

The garment sector also lost nearly 30,000 jobs in 2009 but has since, as of October 2011, nearly recovered. A combination of factors weigh on Cambodian competitiveness in garments—productivity is lower than in key competitor countries, while some costs are higher (mainly informal payments/bribes, transportation, electricity, and costs related to labor disputes), and its key U.S. market was in a recession. (More than 70 percent of garment exports are destined for the United States.) The high cost and the unreliability of electricity are issues for factories using the national grid, as well as for those using their own diesel generators.

Garments likely has some *oknhas* involved, but because 93 percent of garment factories are foreign owned (GMAC 2010:10), there is little to no use in obtaining the title of *oknha* for foreigners, who cannot benefit from insertion into a patronage-based peerage system. One garment factory owner complained, "Oknhas have done nothing to help. They have no money, no knowledge" (2-7). The head of the industry's trade group, the Garment Manufacturers Association of Cambodia (GMAC), is Van Sou Ieng, a Sino-Khmer who was born in Cambodia, graduated from a French university in 1976, and has had a career in banking and finance as well as textiles (Ieng n.d.). While he lists his nationality as "Cambodia" (GMAC n.d.), he found himself hard pressed to deliver a speech or speak at all in Khmer in May 2005 at the launch of the Cambodian Economic Association. Such is the foreign character of the garment sector itself; this may have helped insulate the industry from capture. If nothing else, it offers greater potential for social capital formation through horizontal associational links when compared to domestically based sectors (2-7).

Reasons for Success
The Cambodian garment sector emerged in response to a big incentive provided by the United States and in the context of a strongly regulated regime at the international level, the Multi-Fibre Arrangement. From 1999 to 2004, Cambodia enjoyed preferential access to U.S. markets. There was a dual incentive for the government: looking good at the international level (and in particular in its relations with the United States) and gaining rents from the quota regime.

The garment sector could not have been so successful without Cambodia's transformation in the 1990s. In the 1980s, the People's Republic of Kampuchea would not have permitted freedom of assembly. One garment factory owner attributed the success of the sector to the fact that it is "strongly united." Speaking of GMAC, he noted: "Never before has Cambodia understood what is an association. Before, you were not allowed to get together. Now it has become very popular. [The i]dea has been accepted by government and private sector" (2-7). That owner's clear-cut recommendation was for donors like the World Bank to help fund secretariat functions for business associations. GMAC has all it needs because of its strong capacity and resources, but other associations are not so fortunate.

The garment sector has been able to generate some collective action by lobbying, enjoying better conditions for doing so than other business sectors in Cambodia. The sector is overwhelmingly foreign, so key actors have fewer preexisting ties that would facilitate individual deals. It is also relatively more uniform than other sectors: most players are of medium size, external, and face tough international quality standards and competition. GMAC's formation has been inextricably linked with that of the apparel industry in Cambodia and with the Ministry of Commerce. GMAC's own narrative of its formation is particularly telling: "In mid 1996, most of the garment investors, coming from such a diverse background as China, Hong Kong, Macau, Malaysia & Singapore, decided to form an ad hoc unit to represent them as a group" in dealings with the Ministry of Commerce, which oversees garment exports. The same year, the ministry, "working together with GMAC," succeeded in convincing the United States to extend Most Favored Nation status to Cambodia. "Thus began a journey of symbiotic cooperation between the garment manufacturers and the RGC that has stood the test of time until today," the narrative boasts.[7]

Created to represent disparate manufacturers as a group, GMAC has been led since its inception by Chairman Van Sou Ieng, with a secretary-general based in the secretariat of GMAC. This has provided stability for GMAC through strong leadership. In his role as chairman, Ieng also sits on a government committee that handles "all the consultation on labor law and regulation in Cambodia," according to his biography, and on another that resolves labor disputes through arbitration. He serves as head of a private-sector committee to facilitate export and business, as part of the Government–Private Sector Forum, and as vice-chairman of the National Training Board created by the Royal Government of Cambodia (RGC) in 1996 to coordinate long-term development plans for technical vocational education and training (Ieng n.d.). Ieng is not himself an *oknha* (or at least does not boast of being one, opting instead for the title "Mr."), but he has expanded beyond representing only garment manufacturers and is the president of the Cambodian Federation of Employers and Business Associations, founded in 2000, whose motto is "Turn to us for industrial harmony."[8] Currently, membership in GMAC is mandatory for all garment factories that wish to export. By virtue of its size, GMAC has some leverage in capping bribe taxes (unofficial payments) to authorities.

One of many examples of institutional capture in Cambodia is provided by the Cambodian Bar Association, which was founded in 1995 and captured in 2004 when senior government officials, including the prime minister, became lawyers by virtue of their positions in government. What explains GMAC's ability in *avoiding* capture by government interests? To begin with, GMAC represents more than three hundred members, making capture somewhat difficult. GMAC's twenty-seven-owner-strong Executive Council has three owners who hold Cambodian nationality. (In particular, two of the owners in fact represent the same company, Evergreen Apparel). As noted earlier, GMAC's own Web site boasts of the "symbiotic cooperation" between manufacturers and government that has characterized its activities;[9] given that the government requires GMAC membership for exporters, it is unclear who captured whom. Is GMAC an agent of the RGC and the RGC its principal, or vice versa? What is crystal clear, however, is that the sector has succeeded despite numerous challenges and is a leading contributor to Cambodia's growth. A turning point came on March 13, 2005, when commerce minister Cham Prasidh spoke to GMAC's general meeting in Phnom Penh in support of plans to reform the garment sector in order to keep it competitive. The minister emphasized the ties of dependence between his ministry and the garment sector: "If you do not see the reform at the end of this year, you will not see Cham Prasidh as the Minister of Commerce again. . . . In order to help the garment sector to survive, we must cut all the under-the-table costs." He added, "How can I still be a commerce minister if the garment industry dissolves?" (qtd. in Prak 2005).

Since garment quotas no longer exist to generate economic rents per se, it is Cambodia's World Trade Organization (WTO) membership, to which it acceded on October 13, 2004, that now allows access to developed country markets. At that time, China had joined the WTO in 2001, albeit with strings attached, and Vietnam would join in 2007. Thus, whatever economic rents Cambodia enjoyed are slowly being eroded by increased competition. Moreover, rent-seeking by the economic police (Ministry of Interior) on the way to and from Sihanoukville port, by customs officials (Ministry of Economy and Finance), and by CamControl (the Cambodia Import-Export Inspection and Fraud Repression Directorate-General, an arm of the Ministry of Commerce), among other agencies of government (although reduced from several years ago), must be carefully negotiated and vigilantly monitored by GMAC.

Collective action via GMAC and the Government-Private Sector Forum (GPSF) has resulted in some improvements to the sector's governance environment. In mid-November 2008, at the fourteenth GPSF, following a request by Van Sou Ieng for a 30 percent cut on Cambodian export fees to assist exporters, the prime minister announced a 10 percent cut. Several years ago, GMAC agreed with the government that it could negotiate informal fees with all government departments for the benefits of its members.

According to an NGO representative, the garment sector is paying 10 percent in informal payments (2-4); given its more than $3 billion in exports, this is at least $300 million under the table, but only people with a position in the supply chain can touch the money. The garment industry has also been able to achieve some improvements in the operation of the transport and export-import processes. According to industry representatives, however, all these arrangements require constant monitoring and enforcement in order to avoid slippage. Often, what has been agreed at the ministerial level and with customs in Phnom Penh does not get telegraphed to the ground level, where provincial authorities operate fiefdoms. Collective action by a single sector has nonetheless been sufficient to solve some major issues.

Constraints on the garment sector may be classed into three categories. Purely technical constraints include a reduction in demand due to the worldwide economic recession. This is entirely outside the Cambodian authorities' control. The second category, of indirectly governance-related constraints, includes the following:

1. High labor turnover: Turnover reached 48 percent at one factory I visited. While high labor turnover is due to a variety of factors, improved public service provision (health, education, and infrastructure) through better governance could alleviate this constraint.

2. High number of strikes: Labor-management relations remain poor and are often due to miscommunication. Even lower-level management is foreign, particularly Chinese, a source of language and cultural problems.

3. High electricity costs and unreliability: This is due to high tariffs on electricity and poor governance of public infrastructure.

4. High cost of transport: This is due to high fuel costs, poor roads, and informal payments.

5. Low productivity: Though this is partly a technical constraint, it is also a consequence of low government investment in health, education, and infrastructure, all of which lag behind Vietnam's ability to provision these services.

Of constraints that are directly related to governance, the only example is the high cost of export.

Labor Relations

Perhaps somewhat surprisingly, the sector faces labor disputes, which are more frequent in Cambodia than in competitor countries. Three reasons appear to account for this: The international regime that was put in place in Cambodia has had unintended consequences, labor unions are highly fragmented, and garment factory management is weak. There are some signs that the three parties concerned—garment factories, labor, and government—are seeking to improve the situation.

Adherence to ILO labor standards is monitored in Better Factories-supervised garment factories. While one might expect this to result in good labor relations, this has not in fact been the case. The number of labor unions has proliferated. Currently, more than 1,000 unions are registered. Although only around 440 are estimated to be active, this is still a large number considering that formal sector employment is limited and few informal workers are unionized. Eighty percent of factories have active unions, averaging about 1.4 per factory (2-4).

Unions are dominated by male workers, even though the garment-sector workforce is predominantly female. Union organizers have used the threat of strikes to extract bribes from factory managers; initially, managers may also have found it easier and cheaper to buy off union leaders than to address issues of concern. As would be expected, this has generated incentives for the creation of more unions. Although it is in contravention to the law, individual workers often belong to multiple unions, as dues are modest ($0.25–$0.75 per month). Their position is not unlike those civil servants who must carry multiple political party ID cards for the sake of political survival.

There is some indication now that entirely self-serving unions are diminishing and more comprehensive federations of unions are emerging. The National Union Alliance Chamber of Cambodia, founded in May 2007, claims to represent more than 200,000 workers (of which 75 percent are from the garment sector, with the remainder being teachers and informal sector workers). It brings together eleven smaller federations and two individual unions. The chamber claims to be politically unaffiliated, while its members have a range of political affiliations. Another major union in the garment sector is the Free Trade Union of Cambodia (claiming around 80,000 members). The government has not been very supportive of labor union consolidation, possibly out of concern that such consolidation could create alternative power centers. Such concerns are also evidenced by the fact that three leaders of the Free Trade Union have been killed in recent years.[10]

Frequent strikes can also be attributed to poor management. Reportedly, many factory managers have been unable to establish a communication regime that would resolve issues before they spill over into strikes. Issues may be of a petty nature, such as failure to repair broken toilets or to provide a shelter for bicycles and scooters (what Cambodians call "motos") with which workers commute to work (2-7). In most factories, even lower-level management is foreign rather than Cambodian, which is perceived to contribute to poor communications.

In combination with poor infrastructure and costly utilities, strikes also constrain investment in the sector. There are ongoing efforts to change the regulatory framework with a view to smoothing labor relations. The main proposition is to establish a rule of "most representative union" (defined as the status of possessing the highest level of representativeness) so that collective bargaining at each factory would become possible. There is no discussion yet of sectorwide collective bargaining.

Tripartite negotiations over labor rules take place through the Labor Advisory Committee, which can decide on government laws and regulations. Furthermore, under the International Labour Organization scheme, an Arbitration Council was established as an independent body whose function is to resolve collective labor disputes that could not be resolved by conciliation. The council was born in 2003 according to the provisions of the 1997 Labor Law. It sits at the apex of labor dispute resolution. However, as detailed in chapter 1, the Arbitration Council's decisions are nonbinding and it does not have enforcement power, so that even if it formally settles a dispute, the dispute may reappear due to lack of implementation. Parties can and have sought binding arbitration, however, because of the council's excellent reputation as an independent organization.

Outlook and Implications for Governance and Growth

The garment sector is an example of how "good enough" governance may facilitate growth in Cambodia. The sector has generated demand for improvements in governance that have had some impact, with positive spillover in other sectors. However, there is as yet little evidence that the sector has the potential to be a catalyst for other forms of light manufacturing. An entrepreneur and former secretary of state acknowledged, "We know very well that [the] garment industry is not durable." He expected the United States and other clients of the industry to "move on to another favorable quota country" (2-8). A staff member of a conglomerate agreed: "[The] garment sector is good, but it's not long term" (2-2). Other Cambodians noted that the garment sector had received special protections that would not last and that the sector would "have to diversify" beyond its dependence on the United States and the European Union if it hoped to survive (2-9, 2-2, 2-10, 2-1). A member of parliament summarized this view: "As this economic activity is totally dependent on the preferential rate agreement from Europe and US. . . . It will disappear as soon as these consumer countries stop their preferential trade policy" (2-1). Current government ambitions are focused on footwear and on agro-processing. Moreover, once the preserve of only one or two ministers, Special Economic Zones abound. Twenty-one have been approved, but only seven have occupants.

The intense involvement of external stakeholders—from the U.S. administration's design of trade preferences to the role of the International Labour Organization to the overwhelmingly foreign origin of investors to various donor projects that seek to improve the sector's productivity—has been important in bringing about this success of employment-intensive growth. The special regime allowed the sector the space to develop its relative competitiveness. Now the sector faces new challenges as costs rise in a declining market. Thus far, the governance improvements achieved have been largely incremental. It is unclear whether a continued gradual approach to solving some bigger and "lumpy" governance-related issues, including labor relations problems, will succeed. Solving these issues would not only help the garment sector survive and flourish but would also remove significant barriers for other sectors, improving Cambodia's overall competitiveness. Given the performance of the government to date, however, it is not clear whether this is feasible.

The Rice Sector: A Unfinished Story?

In 2000, agriculture's value added as a percentage of Cambodia's GDP was 37.8 percent. Though this share has been declining due to continued growth in garments

Table 2.2   Agriculture in Cambodia (2000–2010)

Indicators	2000	2001	2002	2003	2004	2005	2006	2007	2008	2009	2010
Agriculture, value added (% of GDP)	37.8	36.2	32.9	33.6	31.2	32.4	31.7	31.9	34.9	35.7	36.0
Agriculture, value added (annual % growth)	−0.4	3.6	−2.5	10.5	−0.9	15.7	5.5	5.0	5.7	5.4	4.0
Agricultural land (% of land area)	27.0	27.7	28.3	28.9	29.6	30.3	30.9	30.9	31.5	31.5	N/A
Employment in agriculture (% of total employment)	73.7	70.2	N/A	N/A	N/A	N/A	N/A	N/A	N/A	N/A	N/A
Rural population (% of total population)	83.1	82.5	82.0	81.4	80.9	80.3	79.7	79.1	78.4	77.8	77.2

Source: World Development Indicators (http://databank.worldbank.org).

and tourism, nearly 80 percent of Cambodians continue to live in rural areas and depend on agriculture. It has picked up since 2008 (34.9 percent) and reached 36 percent in 2010. There is a consensus that the development of agriculture and agro-processing are key for Cambodia's survival in the global economy following the end of the preferential quotas for the export of garments to the United States and the European Union (Godfrey 2003; World Bank 2004a; IMF 2004; RGC 2004a; Sciaroni 2004; NGO Forum 2002). Table 2.2 summarizes the importance of agriculture in Cambodia since 2000; 2003 and 2005 were double-digit years for growth of value added in agriculture.

While the total cultivation acreage of rice has shrunk marginally and agriculture itself has been shrinking, it still exceeds both tourism and garments combined. Rice accounts for nearly a quarter of GDP in agriculture; more than three-quarters of rural households grow rice. As Jehan Arulpragasam et al. point out, in Cambodia and Vietnam, "most of the poor earn a living by growing rice, and the rice culture permeates the farming traditions of the region" (2004:199). According to a Ministry of Commerce study, "the cultivation area for rice production accounts for approximately 90 percent of total cultivation acreage in Cambodia," making rice "the most significant industry for the prospective development of Cambodian society and economy including its food security" (MoC and JICA 2001). Rice is indeed the most important staple for Cambodians and essential for food security reasons. Today more than 9 million out of 14 million people are involved in rice farming or make their living from rice farming.

Background

The story of rice is in many ways the story of agro-processing, an area of well-recognized value addition that Cambodia has yet to tap effectively. The reasons for this are numerous. First, Cambodia lacks an extensive irrigation system. As one member of parliament explained, "Our rice culture is completely dependent on rainfall; as a result, we can have too much rain or not enough rain. These jointly contribute to damage the rice plants" (2-1). Growing rice is not a highly capital-intensive activity per se when irrigation is available, but milling rice requires energy, capital, know-how, and transport. Unfortunately, investment in the agro-processing sector is weak as a consequence of high energy, credit, and transportation costs (2-11). In addition, the time horizon required to recoup investment capital is too long to be attractive to in-country investors. According to an advisor from the Ministry of Commerce, "During the last three or four years, people who have money bought land. They don't want to get something that is low return" (2-9). This is an important difference between the rice and garment sectors that clearly relates to uncertainties created by governance problems and the rents required to overcome them.

The rice sector was for many years domestically oriented, but it has increasingly become export driven because of rising world prices and surplus production in recent years. During the 1960s, Cambodia was one of the key rice-exporting nations in the world, exporting far more than Vietnam and falling third behind Thailand and the United States in terms of net exports of milled rice.[11] Today, Cambodia is a small official exporter, with Vietnam its primary customer; unprocessed rice is sold to Thailand and Vietnam, which then process it and export it overseas (2-11).

Yang Saing Koma, a champion of the System of Rice Intensification, which enables higher yields with less water by spacing seedlings farther apart, and head of the Centre d'Etude et de Développement Agricole Cambodgien, a local agricultural NGO, has noted the "steady increase in rice production," which rose by 50 percent from 1997–1998 and 2007–2008, and the "new opportunity" (Koma 2008) for Cambodian farmers that surplus rice production and rising world prices present. The Cambodian government, he explains, has correspondingly announced plans to dramatically increase rice exports. In fact, the RGC announced that it would export 120,000 tons of rice to Guinea at a "friendship" price of $600 per ton (AKP 2008). Although this is a major discount compared to international prices, it does not take into account that Cambodian rice is 35 percent broken and is therefore considered low grade compared to long-grain Thai or Vietnamese rice, which is less than 5 percent broken. As one rice miller explained, "For now we can still follow the old system and we can export to Africa. They don't demand much quality" (2-11). Regardless, intervening events saw the failure of the agreement for technical reasons, including the fact that the two nations could reach no agreement as to how the rice would be paid for, and Cambodia refused to send rice before payment was received. The same failure reportedly happened with a rice deal involving Senegal that was announced in April 2008 (Xinhua 2008a). Notably, a joint venture announced in 2009 between the Ministry of Commerce-owned Green Trade Company (GTC) and Indonesian rice miller Racharvali that was said to have the potential to pump from $300 million to $500 million into Cambodia to set up rice-processing plants has also evaporated (Ros and Vireze 2008).

Asian and Middle Eastern investors could become a driving force in the development of Cambodia's rice sector. Both Kuwait's and Qatar's prime ministers visited Cambodia in 2008, and Prime Minister Hun Sen visited Kuwait in January 2009. During this visit, according to foreign minister Hor Namhong, the Kuwaiti government signed a Memorandum of Understanding with Cambodia to construct a $350 million hydropower dam and irrigation system in Kompong Thom Province. The dam will produce 40 megawatts of power for the surrounding area and provide irrigation for 130,000 hectares of rice land (Leopard Cambodia Fund 2009), all of which could come into service for rice cultivation to Kuwait (Walsh 2009). Minder (2008) revealed that Cambodia is also in talks with several Asian governments (including South Korea and the Philippines), as well as Middle Eastern governments (such as aforementioned Kuwait and Qatar) to receive as much as $3 billion in agricultural investment in return for millions of hectares in land concessions to be leased for between 70 and 90 years, according to Suos Yara, the undersecretary of state responsible for economic cooperation at the Council of Ministers.

In 2005, the Ministry of Commerce and the World Bank-managed Mekong Project Development Facility did not pin much hope on "Cambodia's chances of returning to its status as a major rice exporter" (MoC and MPDF 2005:3). A Ministry of Commerce business guide remarked that "Only one Cambodian rice mill can operate to export standards"; this mill is believed to be owned by Angkor Kasekam Roongroeung Co., Ltd. (AKR), which has exported to France and Belgium (2-12). Not unlike what happened with garment exports to the United States, however, an arbitrage opportunity is unfolding in rice. Cambodian rice millers and buyers have become increasingly aware of the opportunity presented by the European Union's Everything But Arms trade initiative, which reduced duties on rice for least-developed countries like Cambodia to zero as of September 1, 2009.

Cambodian agents are teaming up with international partners to exploit the opportunity (2-13, 2-12). One producer, based in Battambang Province, has created a joint venture with an international rice buyer to export rice to Europe in relatively modest quantities. Its exports are expected to quadruple under the Everything But Arms initiative. A completely new rice mill capable of producing at least ten tons per hour, and possibly up to four times this much, has also been established in Oudong, Kandal Province, with what is said to be Southeast Asia's most advanced paddy rice dryer, capable of drying twenty tons per hour. With multimillion-dollar funding from French investors who have rice milling expertise and who will direct initial exports to France's La Réunion Island, this new entrant appears poised to shake up the industry.

The sector's prospects are limited, however, by its poor potential for collective action. The battle for supremacy among the rice milling trade associations began with the clash of the Federation of Cambodian Rice Millers Association (FCRMA) and the government-recognized National Cambodian Rice Millers Association (NCRMA). The main national rice producers' group is the NCRMA, which was set up in 2003 with help from an NGO funded by the U.S. Agency for International Development (USAID). Its board comprises the Ministry of Agriculture, Forestry and Fisheries officials, rice millers, and rice traders. According to Development Alternatives, Inc., "Although the NCRMA is an established body, capacity is low, and additional support is needed to build capacity for effective representation of industry interests" (DAI 2008:122). The FCRMA was set up as an alternative to the NCRMA due to claims of vested interest among the NCRMA board in 2000. It is made up of nine associations of provincial rice millers (122).

Neither group covers the entire country nor any obvious majority of rice millers. One rice miller told me: "No, I'm not part of either one of them. I know I won't benefit from that. Nowadays, only one-third of rice millers are part of the associations" (2-14). Indeed, only nine provinces claim members, covering less than half the country (2-13, 2-14). Provincial rice millers' associations themselves are slowly becoming more influential, with the Battambang Rice Millers Association said to be among the most developed (2-16). (Battambang is Cambodia's perennial rice bowl, famous for the best-quality rice and highest outputs.) Organization of the sector has also been assisted by efforts to improve public-private sector dialogue at various levels. At the local level, rice millers' associations are linked to local chambers of commerce.

Collective organization in the rice sector compares unfavorably to the creation of GMAC in 1999. In 2008, following a global surge in rice prices, GTC and its ally NCRMA were initially named as the only two entities authorized to export shipments of more than one hundred tons of rice (the equivalent of only two days' worth of production for Cambodia's largest rice mills) without a license. AKR, which has on its board Chan Sarun, Minister of Agriculture, Forestry and Fisheries, was soon granted a license to export in excess of one hundred tons, though this could have been for a single shipment or a single year, subject to renewal and more fees being paid. In choosing to allow only a few firms to export rice without a license—under the pretext of the need to maintain food security—the Ministry of Commerce has taken an approach quite different from the one it used for garments. It tried to capture, if not corner, the market. By April 2010, the government relented and scrapped the licensing requirement. U.S. quotas were tied to the Cambodian garment sector's improvements in complying with conventions of the International Labour Organization.[12] No such incentives exist in the case of rice production or milling. One niche that could emerge is in organic rice production, but market demand is still very limited, and dedicated production would be problematic (2-9, 2-16, 2-12).

How Is the Sector Establishing Itself in a Challenging Governance Environment?
More than 65 percent of Cambodians engage in rice production, making collective action difficult, if not impossible. The challenge is even greater due to the legacy of the Khmer Rouge; extreme agro-communism under the Khmer Rouge was an unmitigated disaster, and the experience made vigorous pursuit of collective action unpalatable to the Cambodian people (Frings 1993).

There are several big rice millers and many small ones, but the small ones have increasingly gone out of business and trade paddy rice to Vietnam for milling. Of the remaining 200 to 300 rice mills said to exist (2-17), there is little evidence that their owners are themselves *oknhas*, at least not at any higher rate than entrepreneurs of similar small and medium enterprises. As a rice miller lamented, "*Oknha* . . . do not invest in any long-term business, they only invest in business that [will] give them profit tomorrow" (2-11). Indeed, if immediate profitability is any indicator, only a handful of *oknhas* are known to operate in the sector. The structure of the industry is described as "small potatoes" and "little guys"; "the ones who grow are foreigner or well-connected domestics" (2-17). Rice is estimated to enjoy a nearly 20 percent internal rate of return, which would be respectable almost anywhere else, but in Cambodia, land speculation is far more profitable (2-17). One informant reported one big rice mill with both government and *oknha* involvement, while another big mill processes 50,000 tons of aromatic rice per year (2-15). A bank employee stated that although currently there is not much lending for agro-processing, his bank is preparing to move in this direction by lending for a rice mill with a 50 percent government guarantee (2-18).

Cambodia's low yields relative to neighboring countries and its inability to export to developed countries due to lax hygiene standards and logistical difficulties are partly due to technical problems, but the government also bears some responsibility. While the authorities could do much to improve irrigation and water management, as well as extension and research services, they have no control over Cambodian seeds and soils, which are poor compared to those of neighboring Vietnam and Thailand. Other indirectly governance-related constraints include the following:

1. Poor access to credit: Better governance, through the creation of locked paddy rice warehouses as collateral (as opposed to the prevailing use of immovable property with a 50 percent leverage to value), would make credit more available.
2. High cost of transport and storage: As in garments, this links to high fuel costs, but high transport and storage costs are also the result of corruption on the road to the port of Sihanoukville.
3. Expensive and unreliable energy supply: This is due to high tariffs on electricity and poor governance of public infrastructure.

Finally, there is a direct governance-related constraint, in that any attempt to mill or trade rice above the local level must contend with the high level of "informal payments."

As high energy costs were discussed with respect to garments, an appreciation of how they affect rice milling provides a parallel. In 2004, the president of the FCRMA complained: "The rising cost of fuel has increased production costs and the price of our rice. The sudden increase in the price of fuel from around Riels 2,000 [$0.50] to almost Riels 3,000 [$0.75] has reduced our profit margin by US$2.50 per ton," adding, "There are around 300 rice mills in our federation and, on average, we mill around 500 tons per year [per mill]. Hence the forgone profits for our members, resulting from higher fuels costs, is an estimated US$375,000" (qtd. in MPDF 2004:3).

Although Cambodian rice millers cannot compete with their counterparts in Vietnam or Thailand—just across the border—because of these constraints, the export of paddy (unmilled rice) is not seen as a key blockage; that is, there are no known entrenched interests seeking to stop it. Although exporting robs Cambodia of the ability to add value to an unprocessed commodity, paddy rice, it does provide invaluable income to Cambodian rice farmers (2-19, 2-10). An agricultural advisor argued, moreover, that there are no large inefficiencies in the rice marketing chain; that is, the middlemen that are part of it are there for a reason and are needed (2-15).

As in garments, economic rents must invariably be shared with the economic police during the transport of rice within Cambodia; customs officials control the

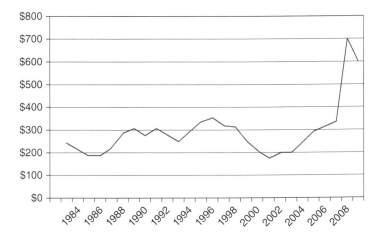

Figure 2.2 THE SPIKE IN THE PRICE OF RICE IN 2008 ($/TON FREIGHT ON BOARD). White rice, 100% second grade; f.o.b. Bangkok, indicative traded prices. (*Source*: International Rice Research Institute.)

borders, so any official or unofficial export must also go through them; and line ministries such as Agriculture, Forestry and Fisheries no doubt play another important role in rent-seeking. Having learned from its experience with garments, the Ministry of Commerce is acting not just as a gatekeeper of rice exports but also as a seller for rice between Cambodia and the international system. The decision to remove rice export licensing requirements from the Ministry of Commerce was finally endorsed by the prime minister on April 27, 2010. At the launch of the Government-Private Sector Forum in Phnom Penh, he said, "We have to nullify applications for licenses to export rice from Cambodia through the Green Trade Company now. . . . It is barrier for all rice traders at the moment" (qtd. in Chun and May 2010).

Farmers have reacted to economic opportunity by increasing output. When Cambodia banned the export of rice out of fears for food security, farmers were hurt financially, as their output could no longer be sold to neighboring Thailand and Vietnam. Rice millers were also doing a brisk business during this period, able to buy low and sell high in-country, driven in large part by international prices.

Export Regime: Cambodian Rice and the Opportunity of Everything But Arms
International rice prices have increased significantly in the past two years. The very strong increase is from 2005, peaking in 2008 and causing a world rice crisis, only to then drop in 2009 but remain well above pre-2008 levels, as can be seen in figure 2.2.[13]

The very strong increase has been a surprise, but it is also a problem, as it has led to speculation, hoarding, and a ban on exports for India, Vietnam, and Cambodia (since lifted). Expectations are that prices will remain relatively high, although lower than their peak in the spring of 2008.

Ultimately, whether Cambodians seize the day with rice exports will depend largely on the rice millers of the country being able to exploit opportunities. The prospects are not particularly encouraging at this stage. Collective action in rice has thus far not produced the results evident in garments. Not only does rice have millers' associations that are still fighting for legitimacy, it also lacks a certifying entity that could facilitate exports. Awareness of Everything But Arms is not enough to make the leap from domestic to export-quality production. One rice miller, who had not in fact even heard of Everything But Arms, expressed doubt that Cambodian rice would meet the necessary standard to be exported to the EU. He argued that to make rice an exportable commodity required "a very big company with lots of money," but no Cambodian rice miller had the required funds. He opined that if the government were to give $10 million to a collective of rice millers that would in turn use it solely to fund a major export initiative, "we can make it." Instead, the weak collectives in the rice sector would "split that money for their own business," while the government would focus its efforts on stockpiling rice for sale to keep prices down. He noted that for the cost of 100,000 tons of rice, the government could pay to process 2 million tons of rice for export. "What we are doing is like leaving money in the bank, while we should better invest it," he said (2-13).

Outlook and Implications for Governance and Growth

The government and donor programs are now shifting focus from food security to a more market-focused approach. Minister of Commerce Cham Prasidh has initiated a Trade Sector-Wide Approach Program (SWAP) to consolidate ongoing trade and trade-related reforms. The program aims to contribute more significantly to job creation, investment promotion, supply capacity enhancement, and thus economic growth by adopting an integrated approach to policy development, capacity building, institutional reform, and implementation through improved governance and accountability, and government is said to be taking serious measures. The SWAP also involves the Ministry of Mines, Energy and Industry and the Ministry of Agriculture, Forestry and Fisheries. It provides a framework under which the government will then develop various concrete projects with specific donors. There is a second SWAP/Program Based Approach being prepared on agriculture and water that involves ten development partners. Donors and government are also seeking to link trade and agriculture efforts. These projects are operational.

The Ministry of Agriculture, Forestry and Fisheries is keen to increase its role in promoting sanitary and phytosanitary (SPS) measures, and it has sent some representatives to China for study. Currently, Cambodian exporters who wish to meet SPS measures for the export of rice can hire the services of a laboratory such as Intertek Testing Services of Cambodia. The difference between Intertek and Better Factories is simple: Better Factories was externally imposed and provides a kind of public good subsidized by donors. Moreover, membership in GMAC is required for export, and membership requires compliance with Better Factories. Intertek is merely one of a handful of inspection, testing, and evaluation services firms in Cambodia that will test compliance with SPS measures for exporting Cambodian agricultural firms. Its work is not subsidized by any donors and is certainly not free.

Currently, the regime for ensuring that sanitary standards are met is fragmented, and competition around it between the Ministry of Agriculture, Forestry and Fisheries and the Ministry of Commerce's CamControl is a repeat of what is known to have happened with livestock (covered in the following section): CamControl is the quality arm of the Ministry of Commerce, launched for the purpose of ensuring WTO compliance, which the ministry championed and for which Commerce is the focal ministry; other line ministries, including the agriculture ministry, do not feel that Commerce has the right to venture into their technical "turf," since it has no technical expertise. More control over the sanitary standards regime invariably means more rent-seeking opportunities for one ministry at the expense of another.

While the two licensed big rice exporters from 2008 to 2010 are connected to the government (with one supervised by the Ministry of Commerce), it is also known that outside this duopoly some independent rice millers have better relationships with Agriculture than with Commerce. Even the leadership of the National Bank of Cambodia is said to have owned shares of a rice mill that successfully exports to Europe. The allegiances are therefore fractured across government, though all officials involved belong to the Cambodian People's Party.

What is apparent is that Cambodia will need to find buyers in order to clear markets. These could be in China, the Philippines, Africa, and India, or they could be in Europe, an option made more attractive by Everything But Arms. Much like garment buyers, rice buyers will play an important role in stimulating investment as well as signaling what level of certification buyers want, whether it be broken rice (which can be used to make rice flour), organic rice, paddy rice, husked rice, semi-milled rice, etc. This offers interesting parallels to garments, minus a certifying/audit mechanism like Better Factories, a dispute resolution mechanism like the Arbitration Council, or the strong leadership of GMAC.

The Livestock Sector: A Dream Deferred?

At the time of the 1993 United Nations Transitional Authority in Cambodia elections, if anyone had asked what Cambodia's main growth sectors would be, the answer likely would have been agriculture and tourism (Sciaroni 2004). While tourism has become Cambodia's second most important source of foreign exchange, agriculture has failed to deliver on its promise, declining steadily from nearly half of GDP in 1995 to 34 percent from 2008 to 2010. Livestock (cattle, pigs, and poultry) accounts for about a third of that agricultural GDP. The population of cattle and buffaloes is approximately 2.5 million, as is the number of farming families in the country (FAO 2007b:30), and Cambodia is one of the few countries in the region with an excess supply of livestock.

The demand for meat is growing rapidly in Southeast Asia, and because the majority of large ruminant livestock in Cambodia is held by small village producers and a quarter or less of cattle are currently exported, an opportunity to increase production and address rural poverty exists. Yet much of the story of the livestock sector in Cambodia is of potential deferred and opportunities unrealized. The story begins with a lack of government extension services and murky regulations. Smuggling is a significant problem in domestic production of swine, while Cambodian cattle are frequently smuggled across the border for sale in Vietnam due to the high cost of certifying and transporting them for official export.

Background

Livestock's importance in the lives of poor smallholders is recognized by the numerous NGOs that work on livestock and the (relatively few) donors that have projects or project components that include livestock. Livestock is "the most important source of cash income" for rural Cambodians, bringing the poorest 40 percent of households as much as 19 percent of their income. Surveys indicate that cattle are held by 62 percent of households, pigs by 46–54 percent, and poultry by 74–75 percent (Ifft 2005:2). And although livestock represents almost 7 percent of the economy, the government allocated less than 0.03 percent of total expenditures to activities in the sector, according to a livestock official (2-21).

The livestock sector, like other sectors of the Cambodian economy, continues to suffer from the legacy of the Khmer Rouge period. Cambodia remains one of the countries most affected by landmines and unexploded ordnance in the world. The consequences to livestock have been severe, though no statistics are available. In addition, veterinarians were among the "bourgeois intellectuals" targeted by the Khmer Rouge. Such professionals, like my father who was a small-time pharmacist in Phnom Penh and died of dysentery and malnutrition, or my wife's murdered father, whose only crime was to know how to use a syringe to inject medicine and to make a living out of it prior to the Khmer Rouge's rise, were considered enemies of the people. One of the few veterinarians who survived the period and returned to Cambodia estimates that competent veterinarians who have received training of an international caliber number fewer than ten nationwide (2-22). Morbidity and mortality of livestock are severe. Livestock professionals have estimated overall poultry mortality rates of 30 percent, with a rate of 30 to 40 percent among pigs (2-23, 2-21). With such high figures, the returns to preventive veterinary care are significant.

In addition, the sector is heavily taxed, both officially and unofficially. According to a private sector manager, when a Cambodian villager sells a cow to a buyer, the buyer must pay 10,000 riels ($2.50) to the chief of the commune, 15,000 riels ($3.75) to the veterinarian (a government official who clears the cow for export), 10,000 riels to the governor of the province, 3,000 riels ($0.75) to the police, and 3,000 riels to the military police. This amounts to 5.8 percent of the cost of a 200-kilogram animal, or 11.6 percent of the cost of a 100-kilogram animal (2-24). Sellers of cattle require a letter from the authorities proving the provenance of the animal; its age, owner's name, and other details; and permission for transport, sale, or both.

Transporting cattle requires another set of payments. One informant explained that on a 330-kilometer stretch of road, he had to give his truck drivers $100 in cash (5 to 10 percent of the load value) to pass through mostly illegal checkpoints manned by military and police authorities (2-24). When payments are not made as demanded, authorities can cause a delay of a few hours in the searing sun, which guarantees the cattle's expiration. Cattle rustlers combat such demands for payment by firing on officials who attempt to stop them or, if stopped, by insisting that they are military officers (Hunt 2004).

Donors have produced a large number of plans for the livestock sector but have failed to achieve tangible results. Nearly half of all aid has gone to technical assistance, leading to a situation in which capacity development is sacrificed to a "mountain of reports" and "cut-and-paste" consultants who offer nothing new in terms of high-level policy advice but whose English is "beautiful" according to the secretary of state in the Ministry of Commerce (qtd. in Kate 2004). What the agriculture sector requires, according to a 2004 IMF report, is "sharper focus on building simple infrastructure rather than . . . more studies and reviews" (IMF 2004). At the same time, to use the language of Scott (1976), the moral economy of the peasant has been replaced by the exchange economy in Cambodia. According to AusAID, relief-type assistance has, in some instances, established a handout mentality: "One district leader warned the team against supporting any form of credit that was not solidly entrenched within a bank. If locals thought there was government involvement, this official noted, they would refuse to repay any loans" (2004:4).

*Why Has the Sector Failed to Establish Itself in a Challenging
Governance Environment?*

Like rice, livestock is not known to enjoy a large number of *oknhas* per se. This could
be a revealed preference by *oknhas* or ostensibly a quality/quantity trade-off (few
oknhas, but particularly well-connected ones such as Mong Reththy). Among the
oknhas known to operate in livestock, one specializes in egg production for the city
of Phnom Penh, supplying hundreds of thousands of eggs. His facility is not up to
international standards, however, and a partner complained that biosecurity measures are needed whenever thousands of poultry cohabitate to prevent the spread
of diseases like avian influenza (2-25). Another *oknha* successfully exported cattle
to Malaysia but shut down the venture in 2005 after complaining of excessive corruption (see the next section). Since then, no new official exporters of cattle have
emerged, a fact that speaks volumes about the sector's insurmountable problems
both internally (with respect to corruption) and externally (with respect to SPS
measures).

A major difference between this sector and the rice and garment sectors is the
absence of livestock trade associations—no federation of livestock producers or
exporters is known to exist. Collective action in the context of low social capital
(much of it destroyed during the Khmer Rouge period) is difficult, leaving the
more vertically prevalent patron-client relations of producer and middleman, economic police, customs, and so forth, all the more powerful in determining the fates
of producers and exporters. The easier way out is always the informal way, since it
takes a lot of money to become formal.

Constraints on the livestock sector are in some ways similar to those on the
rice sector. Technical and indirectly governance-related constraints operate in the
implementation of SPS measures, in the lack of abattoirs that meet international
standards, and in poor veterinary care, which results in high mortality rates among
livestock. Each of these technical constraints would benefit from greater government involvement to establish standards and improve resource allocation. Livestock producers also struggle, like rice millers, with insufficient access to credit;
better governance could make credit more widely available. Directly governance-
related constraints on the sector include rampant corruption and rent-seeking—
one consignment of cattle was stopped nineteen times by the police and military
for a total fee collection of $250 (MoC and MPDF 2005:61)—as well as extensive
smuggling of pigs into Cambodia from Vietnam.

High costs to exit the country are one problem; unofficial payments for transport within the country are another. This is important insofar as domestic abattoirs
are concerned. Currently, there is no known abattoir of international standard
supplying meats to Phnom Penh. Animals are slaughtered and sold the same day,
without benefit of refrigeration. Domestic demand is met in this manner. Only

Cambodia's supermarkets and DANMEATS, a butcher, are known to have supplies of refrigerated meats for the expatriate market.

With the notable exception of Development Alternatives Inc., a grantee of USAID that helped pig farmers describe their plight on paper and transmit it to the authorities, donors are not sufficiently engaged in realizing the potential of the livestock sector, as it is currently grouped among products with potential for trade promotion that have limited or no technical assistance (2-16). State capacity in the sector is also weak (and maybe the role of the public sector is little defined in relation to the sector). On balance, the state has been a hindrance rather than an enabler, primarily because no single producer of livestock can yet be a market-maker. As mentioned previously, authorities have made the transport and official export of cattle so onerous that Cambodia's only exporter of livestock was forced to shutter its doors. In 2004, quite ironically, a costly biogas facility built and donated by Japan's New Energy and Industrial Technology Development Organization opened next door, relying on the ample manure of that exporter's cattle to generate electricity. When the manure stopped "flowing" in 2005, so did the electricity. Interaction between external factors—the international regime and the competitive power of neighboring countries—and domestic factors have conspired to stunt the sector.

Cambodian Livestock and Its Discontents
Livestock has been shown to hold significant, mostly untapped potential for the economy—80,000–150,000 head were exported *unofficially* circa 2004—that could be critical to Cambodia's overall prosperity through exports. More recent impressions from NGO representatives who work on livestock could not confirm the quantity but did confirm that there were a "lot of unofficial cattle exports, not many official" (2-26, 2-20). The development of the official export sector, which would require the imposition of SPS measures, could be a major boon in poverty reduction.

Indeed, a July 30, 2008, story in the *Viet Nam News* complained that "Hundreds of cattle are brought into Vietnam from Cambodia every day, at the risk of exposing the population to possible diseases as most are believed to be not thoroughly quarantined," adding, "More and more people are lured by the high profit margins of VND200,000–250,000 [$12.50–16.30] from smuggling an animal." "Cattle rustling," as the practice is better known, is nothing new and has been used since time immemorial to move cattle unofficially across borders and states. The DPA (2008) noted that border police in both countries were powerless to stop the illegal trade because "most of the dealers are backed by high ranking officials." It is apparent that certain groups have much vested in the continued trade of cattle from Cambodia to Vietnam. Titthara May, a customs officer at the border in Kampong Rou district, said there was little he could do to stop the smuggling, that he was in a "simple position" and had no real ability to make arrests. "We know everything but we need to keep quiet," he said. Another border police officer said that when local authorities did attempt to prevent a cattle truck from crossing, the truck's passenger fired at them. "Since then," he explained, "they have waved every truck through" (May 2008).

According to one NGO worker familiar with the livestock sector, Cambodia had to allow smuggling of pigs from Vietnam because it was unable "to compete with neighboring countries in terms of production cost" (2-27). An economics researcher noted that ministers would only regulate smuggling if they had a financial incentive to do so: "Being a minister is a business. They grant project [sic] if they have interest. If current project give money, smuggling is fine" (2-17). This laissez-faire attitude rankles for individuals like the manager of an international conglomerate, who told me that smuggling and corruption were "severe" problems for his company and noted that they paid taxes to the government and paid the price of corruption "while others only pay for corruption," yet the government does not use its tax revenue to "pay officials to do a good job" (2-25). Nestlé-Cambodia had to close its canned milk producing facility due to "an estimated $500,000 per month in potential sales" lost to "competition with smuggled Nestlé products" (MPDF 2004:3) from neighboring countries.

As one informant noted, summing up a common complaint, there is "too much corruption in livestock." He continued: "When we got everything officially from the government, we still had to pay. We cannot compare with Vietnam. We have to pay for license, so last minute we had to close," adding, "We lost around $1.5 million with Malaysia joint venture. License or no license, you still have to pay money." Indeed, NGO representatives have advocated getting rid of trading licenses, but they warned, "It's very hard to get people to work against the power at large" (2-26, 2-20).

The case of the failed joint venture in livestock export between Cambodia and Malaysia suggests the extent to which corruption and smuggling, combined with a dysfunctional business culture, conspire against success in livestock exporting. An agricultural and livestock expert argued that the venture failed because the Cambodian tycoon involved was "a kind of quick-in quick-out businessman" who was "only pushing for short-term benefit." "They do business but they don't think about the quality of their business," the informant explained. The venture exported old and chewy beef to Malaysia, he claimed, rather than investing in good breeding and good feed for its cattle (2-28). A government official blamed the Malaysian market: "Malaysians are so fussy about the quality of cows," he said, that the venture had to be "very selective when buying cows from people." Another company that exported cattle to Vietnam "didn't mind about the quality," however, and that company "bought all the cows," making it impossible for the new company to compete (2-29).

An agricultural advisor involved in the Malaysian joint venture for the government noted a number of problems, particularly rising beef prices and a consequent rise in smuggling. "We do not have any policy to control speculation yet," he noted (2-30). On the bright side, there is talk that a new joint venture with the same Cambodian partner will engage a UK-based firm to reenter the cattle export business.

Money is certainly being made all across the livestock sector, but the rents are shared not by the domestic producers of livestock but by the gatekeepers—those empowered to allow the entry of pigs into Cambodia from Vietnam and the export of Cambodian cattle to Thailand and Vietnam. Thus, rents are likely shared among CamControl, the economic police, and customs. A number of informants spoke to the difficulties faced in the movement of livestock and the commune-based origins of taxing authority on livestock. One official report noted the extent to which bribes were required by "different authorities" on the national roads, remarking: "In each province transporting costs and administrative charges are paid to the Governor's office, veterinarian, economic police (the economic police have many different levels: ministerial, provincial, and district), the Livestock office (i.e. in two provinces in Kampong Thom and Rathanankiri), [and] other police (e.g. military police)." All such fees are "unofficial," and "[t]here is no receipt given" (GPSF-ABAP 2004). In rural areas, commune councils have the power to tax local products, including livestock. Thus, the payment of transport fees begins at the commune and works its way up the chain. A veterinarian and livestock advisor told me: "The development of commune livestock markets with a direct link to the market chain as a means of creating volume and clout [is essential]; otherwise producers remain price takers" (2-31).

Government has had little political will or interest to engage in developing the sector because the costs of doing so outweigh the benefits. Achieving SPS measures for livestock would require long-term vision, capital, and technical knowhow, none of which *oknhas*, advisors, or donors are yet willing to invest in. Local cattle, moreover, are considered inferior and of poor quality (2-25). In the area of livestock, there are said to be protected networks in the trade of cattle across the border to Vietnam and Thailand (2-2), to the detriment of those wishing to export through official means, via a port. The export cost for a container sent to Vietnam or Thailand is reportedly less than half the cost via the Autonomous Port of Sihanoukville (2-17).

Outlook and Implications for Governance and Growth
The livestock sector continues to suffer from a governance-disabling environment, whether by acts of commission (unofficial payments, banning and then lifting a ban arbitrarily) or acts of omission (no concerted SPS efforts or abattoirs of

international standard or even on an experimental basis). Informants suggest that in the absence of an *oknha* to fight the corruption, small and medium enterprises would be hard pressed to face off against myriad provincial and national authorities (2-2, 2-5). Ultimately, the trade-off to consider is the value of domestic production and export versus smuggling.

Growth has failed to transform this sector primarily because smallholders are involved and cannot collectively engage with authorities (2-32). Without what the management of a domestic conglomerate called "Mafia roads" controlled by smugglers who facilitate transport, avoidance of unofficial payments is impossible (2-2). Moreover, the enforcement of SPS measures is required as of January 1, 2008, per Cambodia's WTO terms of accession, if the country is to export "officially" to other WTO member countries. The onerous cost of meeting these standards virtually guarantees that the issue will fail to gain traction, whether because of lack of government intervention or private sector clout, leaving much of Cambodia's livestock official export potential unrealized in the near to medium term. Sanitary and phytosanitary measures are simply too costly at this stage in Cambodia's development.

Because the sector is not dominated by any large players and is provisioned by smallholders, contestation with the state has also failed to materialize. This represents an opportunity for the creation and active engagement of a business association to represent the interests of businesses exporting cattle legally.

Cross-Sectoral Comparison

Garments, rice, and livestock are three sectors that could be promising in Cambodia. Yet only one is vibrant (garments), while another is emerging (rice), and the third is stunted (livestock). Comparing these three sectors has underscored the importance of governance for growth and how governance can improve and support growth in some sectors and not others. It has also confirmed that Cambodia's economic growth in recent years has occurred not *because of* government action but *in spite of* it.

Evidence suggests that two factors may help explain the success of the garment sector. The first is the presence of a private-sector organization, the Garment Manufacturers Association of Cambodia, that produced collective action to lobby authorities for negotiated industrywide rent-seeking rates and international drivers/incentives, such as an overwhelmingly foreign presence in garments, along with quota exports to the United States linked to minimum labor standards that produced enough rents for all parties involved. The second is the exceptional relationship that evolved between GMAC and the Ministry of Commerce, which qualifies as what Nicolas Miesel and Jacques Ould Aoudia call a "governance focal monopoly": "certain public governance institutions" acquire "the capacity for co-ordinating private interests by positioning themselves as the unavoidable focal point of governance relations" (Miesel and Ould Aoudia 2008:38). Institutions in this position "foster dialogue and coordination among public and private elites in which confidence is inextricably created on a basis that is *simultaneously* interpersonal, process-based and institutionalised" (38). Establishing a garment sector in Cambodia proved a win-win proposition both for foreign investors and local stakeholders inside and outside the government.

The rice and livestock sectors compare unfavorably by contrast. No credible private sector organization for collective action exists in either sector, though rice has competing milling associations whose membership is diffuse both geographically and politically. Livestock does not enjoy even that modicum of organization, in part because of a lack of social capital, which was destroyed during the Khmer Rouge period. Moreover, in both rice and livestock, foreign involvement is minimal compared to garments. Livestock had foreign involvement in the export of cattle through a joint venture with a Malaysian partner, but that ended in 2005, allegedly because of onerous unofficial payments. Rice may have an opening in exports to the European Union; however, this will require stringent compliance with sanitary standards, and the overall demand for Cambodian rice is unlikely to be significant given Thailand and Vietnam's dominance in the sector. In summary, what is clearly different among garments, rice, and livestock is the involvement of international players, the creation of new opportunities (as opposed to the dividing or displacement of preexisting rents), and the generation of social capital to fight long-ingrained patron-client networks.

Across all three sectors, only a handful of constraints persist. Certainly both rice and livestock suffer from related problems with certification and access to credit, problems that were resolved in garments or that never existed in that sector. The constraints that cross all three sectors may be summarized as energy and informal payments.

Collective action through entities like GMAC that require membership to export may be a solution; however, rice millers will have to build the needed social capital to win trust for a leadership fraught with suspicion. There is a credibility problem in the assignment of the right to export at the low threshold of one hundred tons exclusively to only a handful of entities. Scrapping this licensing requirement was a recognition that the authorities could not have their cake and eat it too.

Certification also requires attention. In garments, certification was imposed externally by the U.S. government and executed by the ILO's Better Factories program. There is currently no equivalent authority in Cambodia for rice or livestock.

For rice, organic certification and SPS measures compliance loom large, while Everything But Arms represents the creation of only modest economic rent opportunities at this stage. For livestock, SPS measures compliance remains terribly elusive.

The problem with energy costs, as mentioned in the garment sector case study and reiterated for rice, illustrates the political economy choice authorities must make. Reducing reliance on unofficial payments and increased domestic revenue collection through a broader range of taxes than those imposed on fuel (with a pass-through to electricity) will require political will to change a system that has worked for decades and proven itself reliable in bringing the governing CPP revenues for the gifts needed to incentivize and possibly intimidate voting in rural areas (Hughes 2006). The same can be said about moving away from estimated tax regimes and the gray area of unofficial payments toward wider collection of value-added tax by enlarging the formal economy. Ultimately, the question is one of national ownership for development—the essence of this book.

The three sectors tell us that political stability is a necessary but not sufficient condition for success—that quality of governance was good enough for garments, may be good enough for rice, and has certainly not been good enough for livestock. The country's ability to maintain growth will depend largely on keeping the gains made in political stability while moving to improve quality of governance—and not just for the acts of commission but also for the acts of omission, which are too often forgotten. The role of aid and donors has been limited in explaining the success or failures observed. Too often the work is at a high policy level, while the reality on the ground differs markedly. When donors got involved on the ground—as in the case of the pig breeders—they managed to eke out a victory for a few months. Oftentimes, policy decisions are linked to a greater political narrative involving *oknhas* like Mong Reththy. As the cochair of the Private Sector Task Force on Agricultural and Agro-Industry, he has the ear of the prime minister and asked at the meeting for a "review of export procedures" because he believed that taking a look at these procedures and eliminating the license requirement would "help bring about transparency and suitable costs for the export of agricultural products" (qtd. in May 2010). In the most recent case of the lifting of the requirement for export licenses on rice, he was right in the thick of the action.

How Aid Does or Doesn't Matter

Aid dependence has exacerbated problems in the Cambodian economy. Leaders who depend on foreign aid become less accountable to their people—outcomes

that deviate from what Paul Collier described as "the spread of fiscal accountability" as a "consequence of warfare" in the nineteenth-century European context
(2009:175). One of the obstacles to fiscal accountability today is foreign aid. As
Collier describes the European transition, "Step by step, the predatory ruler of the
mini-state had evolved into the desperate-to-please, service-promising, modern
vote-seeking politician" (176). Today's predatory ruler is instead buffeted by availability of foreign aid—in Cambodia's context, Western aid in the 1990s and early
2000s and now Chinese, Vietnamese, and South Korean foreign aid and investment. Indeed, Collier's lesson learned is summarized as follows: "The governments of the [poorest] bottom billion [people] have not engaged in international
wars to anything like the same extent as did the European states of the nineteenth
century," adding, "The resulting reduced need to tax has been reinforced by aid: in
the typical country of the bottom billion the government gets around a third of its
expenditure met by aid. The combination of modest military spending and high aid
has left the tax burden quite light: often around 12 percent of GDP." He concludes
that "[t]his level of taxation has been too low to provoke citizens into demanding
accountability" (Collier 2009:179).

The international community's failure to prevent Cambodia from drifting
more and more toward a one-party state when it was reliant on Western aid is a
major one.[14] This only goes to show that elections do not a democracy make. Overall, it appears that aid from the West has become increasingly irrelevant in light
of ever looser conditionality and noncredible threats (in the perennial exercise
of admonishing the authorities for failing to meet benchmarks but pledging more
foreign aid than requested). Cambodia now relies increasingly on aid from countries that do not care about democracy, the rule of law, or poverty reduction. As
has often been said, success has many fathers, but failure is an orphan. Western
donors will surely take pride in their support for health, education, and social sector improvement generally that would otherwise have been largely ignored by the
authorities (or even actively undermined by ongoing corruption). They will claim
they have helped reduce poverty dramatically, that they were essential to achieving double-digit growth, that Cambodia is a democracy thanks to them, and that
there are fewer political murders. They will take credit for stability. The real failure
of Western aid to Cambodia can be seen, however, in the continuing improbability
of a state that collects about as much from its citizens as it receives in foreign aid,
and sometimes considerably less. This speaks directly to Collier's point on fiscal
accountability—not in the age of warfare but in the age of foreign aid.

The definition of ODA, which is calculated annually by the Organization for
Economic Cooperation and Development, is as follows: "Flows of official financing administered with the promotion of the economic development and welfare
of developing countries as the main objective, and which are concessional in

character with a grant element of at least 25 percent (using a fixed 10 percent rate of discount). By convention, ODA flows comprise contributions of donor government agencies, at all levels, to developing countries ("bilateral ODA") and to multilateral institutions. ODA receipts comprise disbursements by bilateral donors and multilateral institutions."[15] Thus, the assumption that foreign aid is for "the promotion of the economic development and welfare of developing countries as the main objective" is in fact definitional. However, the devil is in the details. Foreign aid can be terribly self-serving—not least when it is tied aid, that is, aid that requires the recipient country to buy or hire from the donor country. This is true of Fly America rules[16] as well as of Chinese and South Korean aid, which are notorious for their requirements that the recipient country import workers and buy equipment from the donor country. Every carrot has a string attached.

How much credit should donors get for establishing the conditions that led to what Guimbert called an "episode of rapid growth" in Cambodia? From 1998 through 2008, Cambodia grew at nearly 10 percent per year, but there is little evidence to suggest that donors were actually the driving force behind this growth. Indeed, Guimbert's analysis suggests that the growth was "driven by the coincidence of a set of historical and geographic factors (including opportunistic policy responses), together with the use of natural assets (although in a nonsustainable way) and the elaboration of productive sector-specific governance arrangements" (Guimbert 2010:back cover). The reference to historical and geographic factors, natural assets, and governance arrangements are economist-speak for special conditions that were one-offs and unlikely to be repeated. This chapter describes just those conditions in its discussion of the garment sector. As Guimbert notes, "Several of these factors are unfortunately not self-sustaining, and the global economic crisis of 2008–09 is exposing these vulnerabilities."[17]

As the next chapter on avian influenza suggests, when donors continue to throw money at Cambodia's problems without taking significant steps to address quality of governance, the results are discouraging.

3

AN INTERNATIONAL PROBLEM

The Cambodian Response to Highly Pathogenic Avian Influenza

I N JANUARY 2005, Cambodia's first confirmed victim of highly pathogenic avian influenza (HPAI) was discovered—in Vietnam. This led to the publication of news accounts critical of Cambodia's notoriously weak health infrastructure. A March 5 *Wall Street Journal* article by James Hookway entitled "In Rural Cambodia, Dreaded Avian Influenza Finds a Weak Spot" related the valiant efforts of Cambodia's "chief flu-hunter at the cash-strapped Ministry of Health," whose "emergency budget for educating [Cambodia's] 13 million people about bird-flu dangers" was a mere $2,500 (Hookway 2005). I argue that such coverage confirmed an extant image of Cambodia as a hapless nation-state, so fragile and incapable that it had failed to protect—indeed had murdered—its own citizens in the mid-1970s. Now, after more than a decade of donor intervention to "develop" the country, Cambodia risked being ground zero for the next global pandemic.

Playing its part as an "infected" country, Cambodia received a pledge of $32.5 million from donors at the January 17–18, 2006, International Pledging Conference on Avian and Human Influenza in Beijing (World Bank 2006c). In 2008–2009, at least 15 implementing partners were slated to spend $22 million to combat HPAI and promote pandemic preparedness in Cambodia in the areas of animal health;

human health; information, education, and communication; and pandemic preparedness itself. So severe was the concern that the United States, which, following the events of July 5–6, 1997, had barred direct government-to-government support of Cambodia while giving hundreds of millions of dollars to nongovernmental organizations (NGOs), allowed an exception for the U.S. Centers for Disease Control and Prevention (CDC) to work directly with the government of Cambodia. The CDC has funded HPAI activities in Cambodia since 2005 to strengthen animal and human surveillance systems, train animal and human health frontline workers to detect and respond to disease outbreaks, and run a communications program to foster a national change in relevant behaviors.[1]

Given the critical risk posed by HPAI and the huge infusion of aid that Cambodia received to control the risk of an HPAI epidemic, it is a case that I believe offers a contemporary and critical opportunity to assess the effectiveness of aid in shaping Cambodia's public policy, as well as the ways aid dependence influences the Cambodian response. Cambodia's experience since the disease was discovered on a farm outside Phnom Penh in January 2004 reveals important aspects of how this developing country with limited resources and capabilities has responded to a crisis that has global public health implications and, in turn, how the global response to the crisis has affected Cambodia. Cambodia's response to HPAI demonstrates the pervasive weakness in the nation's policy process. The state's response revealed evidence of poor governance, lack of political will as manifested in an unwillingness to commit state funds, and a failure to protect the livelihoods of the poor. Meanwhile, the case of HPAI has also revealed donors' failure to coordinate plans or to take appropriate steps to protect and educate the poor. Instead, donor responses have tended to focus on preventing the spread of HPAI to the developed world. Taken together, these shortcomings suggest the persistent weaknesses of the Cambodian state and the failure of the international community to address the problem effectively in the context of a major health crisis.[2]

The Emergence of HPAI in Cambodia

The severe acute respiratory syndrome (SARS) coronavirus caused a near pandemic between November 2002 and July 2003, with 8,273 known infected cases and 775 deaths worldwide, a case-fatality rate of 9.6 percent (WHO 2004). Twenty-eight countries and territories were affected within 10 months. These included most of Southeast Asia—with the notable exceptions of Cambodia, Brunei, Myanmar, Laos, and Timor-Leste, which had by then become independent—but the virus went well beyond Asia, involving the United States, Canada, Germany, the United Kingdom, Italy, and Sweden in the developed world. The emergence of SARS was a precursor to the global policy response to HPAI. The SARS virus made travelers fearful that travel by plane would carry a risk of contagion. In this way, SARS framed the downside of globalization and worldwide travel and cast the developing world's relationship to the developed world in a new light. SARS became a rallying call for what to do about places like Cambodia, where the health infrastructure, destroyed by decades of war and plagued by corruption, could barely function. But SARS was only a test of Cambodia's emergency response system. HPAI was the real emergency.

By December 2003, HPAI had already infected both Thailand and Vietnam. It was only a matter of time before the disease would reach Cambodia through cross-border trade, much of which remains unofficial. Anticipating as much, the Cambodian government temporarily banned the import of birds and poultry eggs from Thailand and Vietnam on January 13, 2004 (Xinhua 2004). Nonetheless, within ten days, Cambodia had detected its first outbreak of avian influenza on a farm outside Phnom Penh. At least 3,000 chickens were reported to have died on at least three farms near Phnom Penh; two days later, as part of a policy of destroying poultry in an area surrounding HPAI outbreaks, 10,000 chickens were culled (AFP 2004; JEN 2004b).

Another year passed before Cambodia's first confirmed human victim succumbed to HPAI. A twenty-five-year-old woman from Kampot Province infected with the virus died at a hospital in Vietnam in January 2005. The woman's brother had died of similar respiratory problems weeks before but had not been tested for HPAI. The government responded by once again banning the import of live birds and eggs from Vietnam and Thailand (JEN 2005a). The second identified human victim, a twenty-eight-year-old man, also in Kampot Province, died in March; he had become ill following contact with a sick chicken (AP 2005a). This cycle of outbreaks, victims, and bans would continue for another two years but mysteriously stopped approximately one year before the July 2008 national election and then, like clockwork, resumed in December 2008. In total, twenty-two animal outbreaks were confirmed between January 2004 and June 2012, and there have been nineteen human cases, only three of whom survived.

In March 2005, modest resources began to trickle into Cambodia to combat HPAI; the Japanese government donated 30 motorbikes and about $50,000 in cash to assist Cambodia's emergency HPAI projects (JEN 2005b). The third and fourth Cambodian victims succumbed in April. In October, U.S. Health and Human Services secretary Michael Leavitt signed an agreement with Cambodia pledging $1.85 million in assistance for HPAI surveillance and capacity building (U.S. Department

Figure 3.1 SUPER MOAN. From left to right, next to Super Moan (Super Chicken): Meas Kimsuwaro [Under Secretary of State, Ministry of Agriculture, Forestry and Fisheries (MAFF)]; Dr. Chan Sarun (Minister, MAFF); Dr. Kimiko Uno (Food and Agricultural Organization representative); and Joseph Mussomeli (U.S. ambassador to Cambodia) pose for a photo with Super Chicken and a decontamination suit model during the USAID donation of personal protective equipment handover ceremony in Phnom Penh, May 17, 2007. USAID donated 4,500 sets of bird flu protection equipment to MAFF.

(*Source*: Courtesy of the U.S. Embassy, Phnom Penh.)

of State 2005). Three months later, at the January 2006 donor conference in Beijing organized by China, the European Commission, and the World Bank, more than 100 countries pledged $1.9 billion to combat HPAI, half of which would go to Asia (Japan Times 2006; World Bank 2006b).

At the November 4–6, 2006, Water Festival in Cambodia, the Academy for Educational Development, an American NGO funded by the U.S. Agency for International Development (USAID), introduced a "superhero" character to increase public awareness of how to prevent HPAI from appearing and spreading. Developed during an academy workshop with Cambodian government officials, "Super Moan" (*moan* means "chicken" in Khmer) is a "broad-breasted rooster with a familiar red cape and strong opinions about healthy behaviours" (AED 2007). Super Moan (see figure 3.1) was used to convey the importance of fencing in poultry and quarantining new poultry to prevent transmission. Appearing in public service announcements, on posters, and in booklets, he later showed up in costume at community theater performances throughout the country as well as in cartoon form in television commercials. Strongly associated with the United States because of USAID funding, Super Moan was simultaneously exported to Laos as "Super Kai," becoming part of the global HPAI landscape.

The response of the Cambodian government to this point had been far from systematic. In late January 2004, when it was dealing with the nation's first outbreak of HPAI among chicks near Phnom Penh, a coalition of Asian governments, the United States, the European Union, and international organizations agreed to create an Asia-wide HPAI veterinary surveillance network (JEN 2004a). Nearly simultaneously, the prime minister of Cambodia issued a *prakas* (ministerial declaration) on the creation of a national interministerial committee on HPAI.[3] This committee would deliberate on important issues, such as compensation and vaccination. The Ministry of Agriculture, Forestry and Fisheries established multisectoral committees in every province for the control of HPAI, but these committees failed to detect any HPAI outbreak until after a human victim had been identified— a failure that led to conflict between the agriculture and health ministries.

While the line ministries fought over who should have discovered what first, the issue of pandemic preparedness built momentum. Up until this point, Cambodia did not have a coordinated plan for avian and human influenza, although it had separate plans for animal health and human health. In July 2007, the National Comprehensive Avian and Human Influenza Plan was released. In a foreword, the prime minister wrote, rather alarmingly, that "a human influenza pandemic is inevitable." He ended, "Strong leadership, organisation and co-ordination, and clear lines of accountability and communication will be key in pandemic preparedness and response," adding, "The Royal Government of Cambodia [RGC] respectfully calls upon all relevant national and international partners to play their part in together overcoming the threats of the influenza pandemic" (RGC 2007:1). Reading between the lines, one cannot help but feel that "play[ing] their part" could also be read as "paying their part" when it comes to international partners. At this time, three task forces were created by the authorities to handle information, investigation, culling, and disposal. The first of these, known as the Information, Education, and Communication Committee, had met twice as of May 2008, and it nominally controlled the message on HPAI that was being transmitted to the Cambodian people.

In fact, the World Health Organization (WHO), the Food and Agriculture Organization of the United Nations (FAO), and the United Nations Children's Fund (UNICEF) had held an ad hoc meeting on March 14–16, 2006, 16 months prior to the release of the government's plan, to identify priority behaviors to control HPAI. As this move suggests, international actors would be the prime movers. In July 2007, the FAO held a series of three training courses in Phnom Penh to teach village health animal workers from 24 provinces in Cambodia how to conduct surveillance for bird flu and respond to outbreaks (Xinhua 2007b). A total of 4,703 health animal workers were trained by the end of that month; the total had reached 5,405 workers and 578 village chiefs by February 2008 (Cereno 2008:11–12). Before the end of 2007, Australia had pledged to provide up to $6 million to combat HPAI in Southeast Asia (Bernama 2007); MEDiCAM, with Food and Agriculture Organization support, organized the first of a series of community forums to educate isolated rural communities with little or no access to television and radio about HPAI (Xinhua 2007a); Cambodia and the United States signed a bilateral agreement whereby USAID would provide the Cambodian government with $5 million to fight HPAI over the following year; and an additional $1.9 million in U.S. funds were earmarked for Cambodia as part of a USAID grant to the Food and Agriculture Organization (FAO 2007a). In March 2008, the World Bank approved another $6 million to support Cambodia's national avian and human influenza plan. In addition, Japan and the AHI facility, a multidonor organization consisting of the European Commission and eight other nations, provided $3 million and $5 million, respectively, for the same purpose (World Bank 2008a). All of these funds aimed to help the Cambodian government address the risk of HPAI both within and beyond Cambodia. The extent to which they failed to do so reveals some of the ways aid has distorted important aspects of Cambodia's governance.

Failure of Governance

Experts identified several aspects of the Cambodian government's response to HPAI as problematic or otherwise noteworthy. Perhaps the greatest failure of the government in reacting to HPAI was its unwillingness to compensate poor poultry keepers whose chickens had to be destroyed, or culled, by agents of the state. Though the policy process that led to this decision is opaque, it seems clear that government officials relied on personal interests, misinformation, and a reluctance to spend state or even donor funds out of concern that this would set a bad precedent for accountability—namely, that the authorities could later be expected to compensate people when causing harm to them (i.e., when it expropriates or destroys their property, as in the case of real estate, or when it culls their poultry). Bureaucratic squabbling, particularly between the health and agriculture ministries, highlighted turf wars that had as much to do with rent-seeking and patronage struggles as they did with differing levels of competence between the ministries. Finally, the threat that HPAI posed to tourism, on which a number of high government officials depend for rents, seems to have significantly influenced the authorities' handling of the disease, which included allegations of positive results suppression—at least on the animal side of testing. Notably, there were no animal outbreaks reported from May 20, 2007, to the July 27, 2008, national elections, whereas neighboring Laos, Vietnam, and Thailand all had outbreaks. Each of these failures of governance is linked to the relationship between the government and international donors.

Culling Without Compensation

Following the onset of the first HPAI outbreak in poultry on January 23, 2004, a 2005 report by Vétérinaires Sans Frontières for the Food and Agriculture Organization noted that "financial compensation to producers" whose fowl were "officially HPAI-infected" was urgently needed in order "to compensate for their losses and to encourage disease reporting by producers in the future" (VSF 2005:2). By mid-July of that year, however, a decision had in fact quietly been made by the Cambodian authorities not to adopt a compensation policy. A short paragraph in the tenth weekly "Bulletin on Avian Influenza in Cambodia" published by the FAO and WHO representatives indicates as much: "H.E. Chan Sarun, Minister of Agriculture, Forestry and Fisheries, sent a letter on Monday 4 July [2005] to H.E. Lu Lay Sreng, Deputy Prime Minister and Minister of Rural Development, in response to his request in exploring the possibility of funding compensation for poultry culling in Kampot Province. H.E. Chan Sarun clearly explained that MAFF/RGC's policy does not allow to pay compensation to the farmers" (FAO and WHO 2005:1). The appearance of this paragraph in the bulletin confirmed that discussion regarding compensation had reached the highest levels of government and come to nothing. No published record exists of this decision or how it came about, but one government official claimed that it came from the prime minister (3-1). By this point, three confirmed deaths had taken place in Cambodia.

International pressure on Cambodia to adopt a compensation policy extended well beyond Vétérinaires Sans Frontières. David Nabarro, the senior UN system coordinator for avian and human influenza at UN headquarters in New York; Douglas Gardner, the UN resident coordinator and UN Development Programme resident representative to Cambodia; and Michael O'Leary, the World Health Organization representative to Cambodia, among others, all raised the issue. The minutes of the second Partnership Meeting on Avian and Pandemic Influenza on February 20, 2006, hosted by Gardner, suggest that donors had evolved from merely reporting the RGC's internal deliberations about compensation to demanding that the authorities present at the meeting clarify the government's policy. In response, Kao Phal, the director of MAFF's Department of Animal Health and Production at the agriculture ministry, reported that "the Ministry has no compensation policy but is providing incentives to farmers with support from FAO." He listed these incentive efforts as including "technical support to farmers to improve bio-security in the farm, provision of protective gear and equipment for culling, disposal of affected poultry and disinfection of poultry premises" and noted that "[t]o strengthen surveillance and early response, MAFF buys ducks from farmers to be studied" (UNRC 2006:3). Of course, all these activities are donor-financed, which the director conveniently fails to mention when he adds that "[c]ommunication materials have been distributed to farmers so they understand more about the disease. Training for village animal health workers is continuing, providing some 1,900 with protective equipment, pump spray, disinfectant, gloves, masks, posters and small calendars with hotline numbers" (UNRC 2006:3).

Why did the RGC choose not to compensate for culled birds (or to vaccinate live ones)? Based on interviews with experts, it appears that the RGC did not wish to spend its own resources—resources it did not in fact have. One donor staff member remarked, "The government doesn't have any budget for that" (3-2). Nor did the RGC wish to borrow or use donor resources for this purpose; the abuse of a guns-for-cash program had taught government officials that paying handouts to citizens, even to incentivize responsible behavior, was a poor policy choice in Cambodia (3-3). One government official made the point—a point I heard from several different sources—that "to get compensation," poultry owners would cheat, putting sick chickens among healthy ones: "They make all the chicken sick and they will get the money." "This is what happened in Thailand," he noted, and he argued that compensation programs in Japan, Vietnam, Thailand, and Indonesia had also failed (3-1). His view suggests that RGC leaders had concluded, whether credibly or not, that compensation policies were ineffective elsewhere and therefore would not work in Cambodia. Moreover, there were the logistical difficulties of implementation to consider. David Nabarro said that for Cambodia, "It's a question of ensuring that the government is comfortable about some of the challenges of administering a cash compensation scheme." Such schemes "are not easy to administer, and governments need to feel confident they've got the right mechanisms to do so" (AP 2006b).

The decision not to compensate was an unpopular one, and the government official quoted previously rushed to explain that some forms of compensation were being offered:

For example, in Kampong Trach, Kampot, a farmer borrowed money from ACLEDA Bank—2,000,000 Riel to raise ducks. When those ducks got sick, we asked him to kill them. He claimed 500,000 Riel for compensation. We had money and we didn't want to risk losing it. An anonymous organization gave me money to buy the ducks. But I didn't do so. At that time, if we gave money to the farmer, there were many other farmers nearby who would have asked for compensation when their ducks died. No, we can't [buy as a way to compensate]. If it happens when we investigate, we can do that. But when the case is disclosed, we can't. Our staff felt pity for that farmer, but we could not give him money. I took his picture crying. When I returned, I met the minister. When he saw the picture, he said he would work it out. I heard that he asked the chief of department of agriculture in Kampot to visit the farmer and give him money quietly. This is how we compensate.

(3-1; edited by the author for clarity)

HPAI experts in Cambodia tended to scoff at such stories of ad hoc compensation. One remarked, "I read a document, I'm not sure who said that, but they said 'At some points, some people are compensated.' There is no compensation scheme at all" (3-4). Another noted "All they want is honesty from the government that there will be no compensation for culling. Government was not clear and not official. No vaccination has been done in Cambodia nor any compensation" (3-5).

Indeed, an FAO evaluation of activities in Cambodia from 2002 to 2007 recommended "restocking of culled farms" (FAO 2007b:31) in addition to compensation, as did a government official (3-6). Ek (2006) suggests that authorities were in fact practicing some restocking, although this clearly was not systematically instituted. He quotes MAFF Department of Animal Health and Production director Kao Phal, who said: "Compensation is not there, but we are trying to replace their sick chickens with healthy ones for new breeding. If we keep paying out compensation, what will we do if big farms have all their poultry die?"

Bureaucratic Politics and Patronage

Quarrels, rivalries, and competition among political parties, ministries, and departments are commonplace in any country, and Cambodia is no exception. The Ministry of Agriculture, Forestry and Fisheries dealt with the livestock implications of HPAI, whereas the Ministry of Health was responsible for its human implications. Because animal surveillance was intended to warn of risks to humans, the discovery of the seventh human victim—at a time when no animal outbreaks had been detected—created immediate tension between the ministries (3-5, 3-1).

Subsequently, the eighth and ninth victims were discovered accidentally when an unrelated hospital-based study by the U.S. Naval Area Research Unit 2 found the virus in their blood. Once again, the agriculture ministry had not discovered the ill birds before the Ministry of Health found the human victim. Sick poultry would serve as canaries in a coal mine do, warning of impending disaster. Agriculture officials noted, however, that the Ministry of Health had similarly failed to identify the human victim.

The rancor between the two ministries extended to a competition for HPAI funding. The more experienced Ministry of Health was seen by informants as a seasoned implementer of donor funds, whereas the agriculture ministry was perceived as having less capacity in managing large donor resources. When the focus shifted to pandemic preparedness, the National Committee for Disaster Management (NCDM) entered the picture as a relatively new institution founded in 1994 that could bridge various national and international players and coordinate the Cambodian HPAI response. The competition for funds among these three governmental units grew out of underlying patronage struggles linked to donor resources. The turf wars between ministries are as much about the ability to extract profit from discretionary power (taxation, licensing fees, etc.) as they are about obtaining vehicles and salary supplements.

A project director—in government—bemoaned having to leave one donor for another because he would not be permitted to receive pay from both. He weighed the pros and cons of each carefully. Of course, at the end of the day, this would not be his only revenue stream. Staff in the ministry must pay up the pyramid, a normal feature of working the "system." Per diems for trips within the country or abroad are "taxed." Decisions to extend contracts are "taxed." But the story is all too common in aid-dependent countries: without its own resources (because of an unwillingness to raise official revenues), the state and its functionaries rely on aid. In turn, the functionaries reflect particular interests both inside and outside the state; thus, in the parlance of van de Walle, a "ventriloquism" (2005:67) occurs, with benefits accruing to both sides (money flows and promotions happen).

The competition for resources first between the agriculture and health ministries, and then among these ministries and the NCDM, is apparent only if one considers how money flowed prior to HPAI. Because the Ministry of Agriculture, Forestry and Fisheries oversees good governance of the forests (among other natural resources), long a contested area between donors and the RGC, it has not had a particularly good image in the eyes of donors (3-7). Animal health, moreover, had not been a high priority for donors; given that human health was already so weak, the health ministry had a long-established record of receiving and processing

Receipts	2008	2009	2010
Net ODA (USD million)	743	721	737
Bilateral share (gross ODA)	61%	65%	68%
Net ODA/GNI	7.6%	7.2%	6.8%
Net private flows (USD million)	450	244	253

For reference	2008	2009	2010
Population (million)	13.8	14.0	14.1
GNI per capita (Atlas USD)	660	690	760

Top ten donors of gross ODA (2009–2010 average)	USD million
1 Japan	139
2 Asian Development Bank special funds	79
3 United States	78
4 Global Fund	54
5 Australia	51
6 International Development Association	43
7 Germany	40
8 EU institutions	35
9 United Kingdom	29
10 France	29

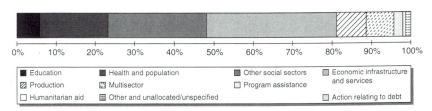

- ■ Education
- ■ Health and population
- ■ Other social sectors
- ☐ Economic infrastructure and services
- ▨ Production
- ▨ Multisector
- ☐ Program assistance
- ☐ Humanitarian aid
- ▦ Other and unallocated/unspecified
- ☐ Action relating to debt

Figure 3.2 AID AT A GLANCE CHART—CAMBODIA.
[*Source*: Based on OECD (2011.)]

significant donor resources. In fact, according to the Organisation for Economic Co-operation and Development, the Global Fund to Fight AIDS, Tuberculosis and Malaria ranked fourth among Cambodia's top donors from 2009 to 2010 and the health and population sector accounted for nearly a quarter of bilateral resources from 2009 to 2010 (see figure 3.2).

At the same time, greater funding for animal health has become available: the World Bank's HPAI project, which stewed for several years until it was finally disbursed in 2009, notably allocated $5.8 million to animal health, $3.5 million to human health, and $1.7 million to pandemic preparedness (3-8). As with any pendulum, there will be swings back and forth as different interests coalesce and divide the funding pie. Figure 3.3 shows the current breakdown of committed funds.

The Ministry of Health's track record in managing funds gave it an edge over other entities in the initial years (precise data for which is unfortunately not available), while the Ministry of Agriculture, Forestry and Fisheries' large share, thanks to the World Bank project, has already been cited as a pretext to refocus attention

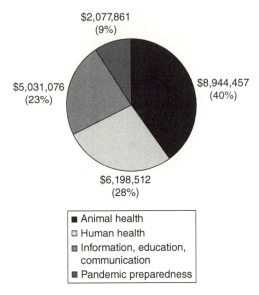

Figure 3.3 CAMBODIA'S AVIAN INFLUENZA AND PANDEMIC PREPAREDNESS PIE (2008–2009).

[*Source:* Calculated from UNRC (2008).]

on human health once again. One HPAI expert pointed out that the World Bank viewed the Ministry of Health as having "capacity in managing finance," whereas the agriculture ministry lacked that capacity; the health ministry was also perceived as being "way ahead" of the agriculture ministry in its HPAI preparedness, while the latter ministry "doesn't even have any budget on that" (3-8). The historical strength of the health sector as a recipient of donor funds gave "health people" a feeling of "ownership" of HPAI, while agriculture professionals saw the situation quite differently (3-9).

A health expert noted that the Ministry of Health has done a better job of setting up an effective reporting structure at the provincial level "with help from NGOs," whereas the "sub-national level structure" of the agriculture ministry was "limited and not smooth," with poor delegation, "making it less responsive to any events reported on the hotline." Thus, even though "the animals die first before the disease gets transmitted to people," workers in animal health occasionally learned of outbreaks "from human doctors" (3-10). The tension between the two ministries was strong enough that, according to one donor staff member, they could "barely collaborate," although HPAI forced them to work together (3-11).

The tension between government units has made it difficult for cooperative projects to succeed and has hampered the policy-making process. A series of workshops that took place in May 2008 on pandemic preparedness offers a case in point (UN System 2008:2). The organizers did not invite the agriculture ministry at the national level but instead involved provincial-level participation. One official posed the question why a preparedness plan had been developed without the agriculture ministry's participation, and he promised to call a meeting "to clarify this." One of the organizers reported that the national-level agriculture ministry had not been invited to participate because only eight of twenty-four sectors involved in this "multi-sectoral response project" had been invited. He noted that the agriculture ministry would be invited "after we draft operational goals and objectives for the project," and he added, "If we invited the ministry to participate all the times, we will not able to get information from the field."[4] The agriculture ministry had developed a reputation for being difficult to work with on HPAI. A donor staff member remarked: "MAFF agued that animal health is the most important issue, and MAFF is the only institution which has authority in this sector. MAFF definitely refuses to cooperate with other institutions if the next outbreak cases occur" (3-2). As another donor staff member and doctor argued, "MAFF has to understand too, in the 'pandemic' stage, animal health doesn't matter anymore, but [rather] food security, human health, prevention, behaviour modification" (3-11).

The World Bank's $11 million Avian and Human Influenza Control and Preparedness Emergency Project (of which the bank funded $6 million and other donors funded the remainder), involving the agriculture and health ministries as well as the NCDM and, formulated in 2006, took two years to eventually be signed. In a June 2006 draft of the project document, the responsibility for implementation was put on the government, but this shifted to the Food and Agriculture Organization, WHO, and UN Development Programme in an April 20, 2007, draft before the project ground to a halt because of a disagreement between the World Bank and the United Nations over who would have the final say over audits. Finally, a February 14, 2008, version of the project reverted to government implementation.

The struggles of the project following passage by the bank's board underscore the human resources constraints and bureaucratic politics of project control and implementation. Two respondents, a donor staff member and a government official, emphasized the difficulty faced by NCDM in its effort to coordinate the health and agriculture ministries and the various international stakeholders in the project (3-12, 3-1). The government official said that NCDM "would like to take control over this project," when its assigned job was simply coordination. He complained that it was very difficult to identify "who is responsible for the project" (3-1).

The Threat to Tourism

One important factor distorting the government's response to HPAI was the threat that the virus posed to the tourism sector. Tourism accounts for around 14 percent of Cambodia's gross domestic product (GDP) and has clearly stood out in the past decade for its tremendous contribution to growth. Tourism has been the main contributor to growth in the services sector, which held the largest sectoral share of GDP (41 percent) in 2007 and is increasingly important given concerns that garments will continue to decline due to the Great Recession. Cambodia's Angkor Wat, located in the tourist Mecca town of Siem Reap, was one of 13 finalists for the New Seven Wonders of the World list, taking in more than 100 million votes.

The fear of tourists being scared off affected the policy process surrounding HPAI response by disincentivizing the need for active surveillance. Many of Cambodia's senior leadership have huge financial stakes in luxury hotels and the tourism industry through joint ventures in which they have invested little or nothing. Lower revenues hit their pocketbooks directly. Concerns over HPAI and a possible pandemic could be expected to scare tourists away, given Cambodia's limited medical facilities. (Aside from SOS International, which specializes in medical evacuations, there are no hospitals of an international standard in Cambodia.) This made the country's tourism sector particularly vulnerable to HPAI.

While it is not clear who specifically suppressed the HPAI response in Cambodia, it is known that one of Cambodia's most powerful politicians did not believe that the threat of HPAI was severe but instead saw it as a donor-driven concern (3-13). This official would have been deeply engaged in any decision concerning compensation, surveillance, and funding. Luckily for Cambodia, HPAI did not jump from animals to humans en masse, and there was no discernible drop in visitor arrivals.

Donors' Failures but Government's Responsibility

The role of donors and NGOs in Cambodia cannot be overstated, as shown in the case of Super Moan—even if donors are careful to note that it was created in a workshop with government officials. Although donors are a diffuse group with as many interests as organizations, their numbers are simply staggering. As Scoones and Forster quote one informant: "In Cambodia there are 22 donors active in the health sector. There are over 200 NGOs also and 109 projects. You can imagine how useful it would be if everyone could work in a co-ordinated way" (2008:55). Indeed, while funding for Cambodia's national HPAI plan stood at $22 million for 2008–2009, an informant mentioned in passing that a current health project funded by the World

Bank and other donors will total $100 million. Cambodia now ranks as one of the top ten recipients worldwide of avian influenza funding commitments in absolute and relative terms (i.e., per case and per outbreak) according to the most recent available funding data, despite its relatively small number of human cases. Cambodia's funding far outweighs that of other countries. Egypt, with 151 human cases, saw commitments of only $238,411 per human case. Vietnam and Indonesia, which had 119 and 178 human cases, respectively, saw pledges of approximately $1 million per case. Thailand has suffered twenty-five cases (of which seventeen resulted in deaths) but is not among the top recipients of animal and human influenza funding (Ear 2011a).

As the World Bank's influenza project—on hold for two years as it swung back and forth between UN and government implementation—shows, the question of what happens to large amounts of uncoordinated donor aid remains open. How does donor intervention work when the absorptive capacity of the state is low (or high in the wrong ways)? The bank declared misprocurement in 2003 on the demobilization project, and by June 2006 it had uncovered financial malfeasance affecting seven additional bank projects. Indeed, there was even talk from then-World Bank president Paul Wolfowitz of cutting off Cambodia completely. In August 2011, World Bank president Robert Zoellick suspended new lending to Cambodia over evictions of Boeung Kak lake residents and the bank's failure to title residents' land. As of this writing (June 2012), the suspension was still in effect but was rumored to be soon lifted.

A number of those familiar with the HPAI picture in Cambodia were critical of donors for using scare tactics without making effective contributions to the HPAI prevention effort. A veterinarian complained of donors, "They work on people's fears." Arriving "with money dripping out of their ears" did not make these actors effective; on the contrary, he argued, "We couldn't get anything done" (3-13). One manager who worked for a donor noted: "It was not so much about the country." "As a result," he said, "most of the time we saw the government staff went busy with trainings supported by donors and didn't have time to implement their actual work" (3-14).

Indeed, donors' failure to target their interventions appropriately is a common cause for complaint. An HPAI expert noted that if the goal was to assist poor countries while developing effective HPAI control measures, the policies that would best achieve this would focus not on creating "systems of control in countries where, to the majority of owners, the disease is only of minor importance but its associated movement controls are a major hindrance to their effective pursuit of economic livelihoods" but instead on "developing cheap effective vaccines with which farmers . . . could dependably protect their stock" (3-15). Another expert argued that "money only is not enough." More important is "rural development," which "cannot be done in a few years." He argued: "Some partners don't want to admit this aspect, because they have limited funds and time" (3-16).

Less than five years after Cambodia's first confirmed HPAI outbreak in poultry in January 2004, the global HPAI funding picture looked less certain. With no predicted human pandemic, there was concern that "flu fatigue" may be the "biggest threat that we have now," according to Dr. Julie Hall, deputy regional adviser on communicable disease surveillance and response with the World Health Organization's Western Pacific region (qtd. in Bennett and Gale 2008). Indeed, flu fatigue could spell disaster in more ways than one to the constellation of interests built around the $2.7 billion pledged worldwide to the animal and human influenza industrial complex (of which $2 billion has been committed and $1.5 billion disbursed; Jonas 2008:6). Several of those I interviewed argued that such fatigue is already apparent in Cambodia. An HPAI expert noted that with the "immediate emergency . . . gone," it had become more difficult to obtain funding (3-3). The government has used the media to amplify HPAI prevention messages (3-2), with both positive and negative consequences. A veterinarian and consultant (3-13) reported watching a January 2008 satellite broadcast in Cambodia and saw an exchange that Bernard Vallat, head of the World Organisation for Animal Health (known by its French acronym as OIE), had with reporters in which he noted: "The risk was overestimated. . . . We have never seen such a stable strain. . . . It was just nonscientific supposition" (qtd. in MSNBC 2008). This message was quickly clarified with a press release from the World Organisation for Animal Health emphasizing the ongoing need for preparedness (OIE 2008).

The Cambodian case reveals two significant lessons to be drawn from the donor response to HPAI. First, protecting livelihoods cannot be assumed; it must be made explicit in the form of "pro-poor" HPAI risk reduction. Donors overlooked livelihood issues owing to their own self-interest in containing a potential global threat. Because 90 percent of poultry is raised in backyard villages, almost any positive impact on poultry (or livestock) can be considered pro-poor. The high cost of targeting the poor (to prevent leaks to the nonpoor) is often raised as an issue in the developing world and elsewhere. Focusing assistance and development programs on livestock owners (including poultry) in Cambodia is a win-win proposition for poverty reduction and the protection of livelihoods.

Second, greater government-donor coordination and oversight is needed to align national and international interests. Ultimate responsibility for the success or failure of policies in Cambodia must rest with the Royal Government of Cambodia, however, since ownership of national development plans cannot be in the hands of donors. Poor governance and pervasive institutional failures have hindered disease control in Cambodia. Effective responses and effective governance must go hand in hand. A rushed, emergency-oriented response to HPAI may indeed have undermined already weak governance capacity in Cambodia, fuelling patronage networks and encouraging rent-seeking behaviors.

Perceptions of Effectiveness

Government

A remarkable number of external actors became involved in Cambodia's HPAI response. Most obviously, the international community provided millions in development aid. In addition, more than 160 NGOs developed HPAI-related activities in Cambodia.[5] The U.S. government took on a very active role in funding HPAI activities through USAID and the CDC. The political economy of HPAI in Cambodia also encompassed informal arrangements and private sector actors. Conducting interviews across this vast array of actors was impossible, but to increase the likelihood that a larger number of knowledgeable individuals could be reached, a confidential elite survey was launched on May 27, 2008, and sent to 308 e-mail addresses[6] of individuals known to be involved in HPAI work in Cambodia.[7] The results offer a glimpse of how government and donors intervened against HPAI across animal, human, livelihoods, pandemic preparation, or some other dimension of the respondent's choosing.[8]

Respondents were then asked to rate a series of statements and to add written comments to their ratings. A majority of respondents agreed or strongly agreed that, given resource allocations, the RGC had intervened effectively and appropriately among humans, among animals, and in pandemic preparedness (56, 54, and 60 percent, respectively). Regarding work with humans, one respondent noted Cambodia's "strong surveillance team at national and provincial levels," characterizing it as "very active" (3-15). Another noted the government collaboration with UN agencies (3-4). Regarding animals, one person remarked, "the interventions seem appropriate" (3-13).

However, only 33 percent of respondents agreed or mostly agreed that the government had intervened effectively and appropriately in protecting livelihoods. Clearly, this effort was understood to have been shaky at best. While one respondent felt the damage to livelihoods was limited because of the short duration of outbreaks (3-13), others were left totally unimpressed: "Nothing is done to take care of the livelihoods of the smallholders," one person remarked, adding, "In fact, there is no record of any discussions on compensation for loss of poultry in the event of outbreak" (3-8). This was not the only criticism. Regarding efforts to protect humans from HPAI, one informant claimed that "instances of suspected [cases were] not being investigated" (3-20). Indeed, comments in the area of protecting livelihoods were among the harshest.

Respondents were also asked about which organizations, both in government and among donors, were "successful" and which were "unsuccessful." Among successful entities, the Ministry of Health and its Communicable Disease Control (CDC) Department received two mentions each for a total of four mentions out of sixteen successful entities named, twice as many as the next highest (USAID and the agriculture ministry). Respondents mentioned the "very strong commitment from leaders of CDC" (3-21, 3-13).

Finally, respondents were asked about Cambodia's preparedness and surveillance (both active and passive) for an influenza-like disease today. Respondents were in agreement that Cambodia's preparedness and surveillance (both active and passive) had improved over time.

Donors

Donors received better marks than the Cambodian government in terms of effectiveness in HPAI interventions among humans and animals: 77 percent agreed or strongly agreed with donor success among humans, and 67 percent agreed or strongly agreed with donor success among animals. One respondent wrote that donors had "strongly support[ed]" and responded "quickly" to human outbreaks (3-17). Another noted that donor funding of human and animal initiatives had been good (3-18).

Like the government, however, donors were dismally rated on protecting livelihoods, with only 38 percent of respondents agreeing, and none strongly agreeing, that donors had effectively and appropriately intervened, given resource allocations. More surprisingly, only 43 percent of respondents agreed or strongly agreed that donors were effective in pandemic preparedness interventions. Highlighting donor constraints, one respondent wrote that "Donors wish to help the RGC to control AI, but can't put any pres[s]ure on the RGC" (3-19). Ownership is a serious problem not just in Cambodia but in the developing world, and a donor-driven agenda can sometimes result in wag-the-dog effects where the government nominally leads by nominally "chairing" a committee or thematic working group, but donors are in fact calling the shots.

Ultimately, HPAI interventions are only a small part of a much bigger aid system that has not served Cambodia particularly well in terms of building local capacity for ownership and fiscal independence. Have HPAI interventions been more or less successful than other activities in Cambodia? In some ways, functioning in emergency mode, expectations will be lower than those of longer-term development activities, not unlike what Cambodia saw in the early postconflict period when reconstruction and rehabilitation were job one. In other ways, an entire aid system has been built in Cambodia and local capacity has improved considerably since 1993. It is unlikely, however, that the performance of emergency aid to control HPAI would be superior to that of normal development aid.

Ultimately, the emergency response proved too focused on donors' naked self-interest in preventing the spread of a potentially global disease at the expense of rural Cambodians. With authorities more than happy to oblige in exchange for additional aid, the losers were poor poultry producers. Traditional development aid, while deeply flawed when tied to donor countries, still aims to reduce poverty and improve livelihoods. The reality, however, is that far too few resources end up doing so because so much money is used for technical cooperation, which is spent on international consultant salaries.

Government, Donors, and Risk

In order to understand the trade-offs policymakers face in weighing the risks of HPAI and how these impact poor people, it is important to examine their interplay. Developed in an online exchange among experts and codified by Otte and Roland-Holst (2008), a typology of the risks of HPAI for government and donors is described as follows:

1. "the risk HPAI poses to poor people's poultry,"
2. "the risk HPAI in poor people's poultry poses to the poor themselves,"
3. "the risk HPAI in poor people's poultry poses to not-so-poor people's poultry and related business interests," and
4. "the risk HPAI-affected poor people represent to humanity as initiators of a global pandemic."

(Otte and Roland-Holst 2008)

This final risk, Otte and Roland-Holst argue, "is driving the international response," while the third risk drives national responses. Turning to the first two risks, they note that neither can be expected to be of much concern to poor people. The risk of HPAI to poultry is lower than the risk of the poultry "dying from a plethora of other causes," and the risk to the poor from HPAI is likewise small compared to "other disease risks."

This analysis holds true for Cambodia, where international donors have proven to be concerned primarily with the risk that HPAI will spread from Cambodia to the rest of the world. Donors' inattention to other fatal viruses afflicting Cambodia that do not threaten the developed world helps to make this case. Swiss pediatrician Beat Richner, the founder of several hospitals in Cambodia, became furious at the disparity between the reaction to HPAI and the lack of attention to a dengue fever outbreak. Dengue claimed 407 lives (Khoun 2008) out of some 4,000 dengue fever cases in 2008, a death rate of 10 percent (Xinhua 2008b), in comparison to HPAI's single-digit mortality. According to Richner, the additional cost for his Kantha Bopha Hospitals Foundation caused by the dengue epidemic in 2006 was $7 million, yet "Neither a member of the International Community, nor the WHO responsible on the Dengue Program, nor the Cambodian Government have made any gesture of financial contributions" (2007:15). Richner argues that HPAI attracts more attention because it "is a threat to the Western world." Dengue, on the other hand, poses "no threat to the United States or Europe, so nobody's interested."

It is also the case that Cambodia's rural poor have not responded to the risk of HPAI with the level of concern that the international community thinks it merits. While awareness of HPAI and personal protection measures is high, according to Ly et al., "most rural Cambodians still often practice at-risk poultry handling," and "family members of H5N1-infected patients, who knew about HPAI risks, still prepared dead or sick poultry for household consumption during massive die-offs, because they observed that neighbours with the same behaviour did not become sick" (2007:131). This gives a new spin to the concept of "neighborhood effects," defined by Dietz as "community influences on individual social or economic outcomes" (2002:539).

As the Centre d'Etude et de Développement Agricole Cambodgien (CEDAC) notes, "Particularly with the experiences of partial culling and involvement of children in the campaign, it is doubted whether HPAI is really serious or not. Thus, not many rural people and poultry producers believe about the seriousness of HPAI," adding, "It seems that they are not willing to collaborate with the technical departments and authorities to prevent HPAI outbreaks" (CEDAC 2007, para. 10). Not surprisingly, what Ly et al. conclude is that "Behaviour change involves comprehensive and multidisciplinary intervention, which combines risk perception communication and feasible and practical recommendations, including economic considerations," adding, "We speculate that it is hardly feasible to sustain good poultry-handling practices if access to personal protective equipment is cost prohibitive, particularly when disease occurrence poultry die-offs are common" (2007:131).

Subsequent research by anthropologist Ben Hickler revealed that the indigenous taxonomy of poultry disease in Cambodia needs further consideration. Cambodians have long been aware of *dan kor kach*, or Newcastle disease, "a seasonal sickness with heavy mortality, generally regarded as natural and harmless to humans (though harmful to livelihood)" (Dy 2008). *Dan kor kach* "is seen as impossible to prevent and difficult to treat," and the term *pdash sai back sey* ("avian influenza") is "new and frequently confused with *dan kor kach*" (Dy 2008). One informant recalled raising poultry that would perennially suffer from *dan kor kach* and was resigned to heavy losses but never thought much of it (3-6). He attributes current difficulties in convincing farmers of the risk of HPAI as inextricably linked to Newcastle disease. Hickler's report concludes that in order to be effective in terms of behavior change, HPAI communication strategies must monitor and manage both terms, even if these "may not be concordant with bio-scientific categories" (2007:30).

Otte and Roland-Holst observe that "the problem of non-aligned interests between important 'parties'" affects efforts to manage the risks from HPAI to more affluent poultry producers and to international health. This misalignment has consequences for the effectiveness of strategies to combat HPAI. Early attempts by Cambodian national authorities to cull infected birds—and even all birds within ten miles of infected birds—struck the poor as "overzealous," with the result that the cure seemed worse than the disease. This gave rise to a fifth risk, "namely, that keeping and marketing poultry is constrained and thereby, at least partially, removed as an activity from the livelihoods and (more ominously) subsistence food portfolios of poor people" (2008).

Indeed, Otte's and Roland-Holst's typology of risks at the national and international levels serves to highlight the difficulties found in Cambodia. The risk that HPAI in poor people's poultry poses to not-so-poor people's poultry and related business interests is relatively small given the nature of Cambodia's poultry industry, which is overwhelmingly backyard-based. But who is making the case for poor people? In the Cambodian context, this would typically be the donors (when they are not making their own case), but with respect to HPAI, donors had dual motives—not simply to combat poverty but also, and more importantly, to protect their own countries.

Conclusion

My analysis of Cambodia's political economy of avian influenza reveals key challenges, obstacles, and opportunities for responding to both HPAI and other global epidemics. HPAI showed that donors, not surprisingly, are motivated by self-interest—at the expense of the poor. HPAI activities have been overtly focused on detecting and preventing a pandemic that threatens the donor countries themselves.

Indeed, complacency and lack of foresight by both donors and the authorities are evidenced by their failure to focus on zoonotic diseases such as Newcastle, fowl pox, and cholera that occur more frequently than HPAI. However, I argue that ultimate responsibility for the success or failure of policies in Cambodia must rest with those in charge—the authorities themselves—and the lack of good governance and political will speak for themselves in the pervasive institutional failures that have plagued Cambodia's political economy. These failures are by no means limited to HPAI alone. Actions speak louder than words, and authorities have been unable or unwilling to commit state resources, although they eagerly welcome donors' funds to keep HPAI and pandemic preparedness programs going into the near future. Of greater concern is the precipitous increase in cases in 2011. Prior to 2011, Cambodia had only ten confirmed cases of HPAI from 2005 to 2010, of whom two survived. In 2011 alone, there were eight confirmed cases, none of whom survived. In January 2012, there was one confirmed case of a two-year-old boy. After being treated without success by private doctors, he was admitted in critical condition at the nonprofit and completely free Angkor Hospital for Children (not affiliated with Beat Richner) in Siem Reap province. The boy survived.

Finally, whether rightly or wrongly, I believe that Cambodians and their government perceive the risks posed by HPAI to be low. Cambodia's epidemic waves were mild, and the numbers of human cases were few compared to neighboring countries, although 2011 clearly should serve as a wakeup call with a near doubling of human cases and no survivors. In contrast, based on data through 2008 donors have committed $35 million to Cambodia, placing it seventh among the top ten recipients of HPAI funding, fourth in terms of per case and per death and second in terms of per capita and per outbreak funding (Ear 2011b:71). As of June 2012, Cambodia remains in the top ten recipients of animal and human influenza funding.

On the whole, the gaps between intentions and implementation in the response to HPAI in Cambodia suggest the persistent weakness of the Cambodian state and the failure of the international community to address this problem in a positive way. The next chapter considers the problem from another angle, investigating the status of civil society in Cambodia through a case study of 2005–2006 human rights activism.

4
SHALLOW DEMOCRACY

Human Rights Activism and the International Community

DEMOCRATIZATION IS GENERALLY seen as necessary for the advancement of human rights and freedom of expression. This is particularly true in Cambodia, where the effects of years of civil war continue to permeate every level of society. Nation-building efforts, driven by outside actors over the past few decades, have concentrated on a political approach to democracy assistance (Carothers 2009), in which international aid is directed toward core political processes and institutions, such as elections and politically oriented civil society groups.

Meanwhile, nonviolent popular protest, opposition unity, youth movements, and election monitoring observed in some countries have served as warning signs; government officials afraid of democracy are able to analyze such movements and step up concentrated repression tactics in their own countries (Way 2008). For example, the Arab Spring that swept Tunisia, Egypt, and Libya remains unfinished in Syria and Yemen. Such tactics came to light in Cambodia during election campaigns in 2003. Even as international agencies began to promote public discussion and debate on television and radio programs, there existed an "ongoing climate of intimidation, vote-buying and incivility of rhetoric in the villages and on politically-aligned radio stations and newspapers" (Hughes 2005:3) that served to undermine the open dialogue that is a necessary precursor for democratization.

Although the United Nations Transitional Authority in Cambodia intervened in 1993 to establish democracy and hold elections, no real transfer of power resulted from the election process. Instead, as discussed in the introduction, Hun Sen—the election's loser—manipulated the situation to the extent that he became prime minister, though he shared the title with Prince Norodom Ranariddh. Elections do not make democracies. Hun Sen maintains control of the media, the government purse strings, and wealthy campaign donors, while his dominant Cambodian People's Party continues to employ voter-intimidation tactics to this day (McCargo 2005). The combination of money, prestige, and power is nearly impossible to beat. While interventions by international agencies and domestic democratic institutions have prevented Cambodia from slipping back into cycles of civil war, they have not enabled the country to establish enduring peace (Mukherjee 2006). A hollow democracy has evolved: democratic processes exist but have not translated into functioning democratic institutions, such as independent courts and legislatures.

International assistance has failed to bring about meaningful reform because it too often has been directed toward short-term stability efforts, such as successful election processes, rather than long-term changes, like as power sharing and the development of a loyal opposition (Zeeuw 2005; St. John 2005). In fact, the dominant political party has been able to utilize mechanisms obtained through democratic procedures to cultivate and strengthen its patronage relationships with voters, government officials, and business tycoons (Un 2005). The organization of political parties within Cambodia's democratically elected government has complicated rather than facilitated democratic consolidation (Albritton 2004; Hughes 2001). Although sociopolitical changes have brought democratic decentralization to rural areas (Ojendal and Sedara 2006), benefits from the growth of the garment industry have not trickled down to the majority-rural population—evidence of the lack of democratic consolidation in the country (Beresford 2004).

Nonetheless, the case for democratic consolidation and for the development of a framework for human rights and freedom of expression is not lost. Since patronage networks are too deeply entrenched within the political culture for politicians to overcome, many look to civil society as the necessary reforming body in Cambodia (Un 2006). Both international and internal approaches to the development of civil society would benefit by changing their focus from short-term stabilization efforts to long-term transformative goals that embed sustainable democratic processes in society (Lambourne 2009). Emphasis needs to be placed upon individual rights and security, which are crucial to any civil society actor's ability to partake in the democratic process (Lizée 2002).

Much of the existing literature on human rights struggles, civil society, and democratic consolidation efforts in developing countries emphasizes political abuses and human rights violations, proposing theoretical approaches to address these issues. Studies of human rights violations in the garment industry in Cambodia (Hall 2000), repression tactics following criticism of election campaigns (U.S. Department of State 2006), and the disregard of democratic procedures during power struggles (Pongsudhirak 2008) examine the failure of democratic processes and freedom of expression to take root in Cambodia without suggesting concrete tactical responses. In this chapter, as I analyze the activities surrounding the arrest and subsequent release of Cambodian human rights activists from 2005 to 2006, I dissect the strengths and weaknesses of coalition activities and recommend future efforts to promote freedom of expression and human rights as democratic processes in Cambodia.[1] After providing an overview of the events, I consider the national, international, and regional responses, in turn, and then consider their implications for activists in Cambodia.

Activism and Arrest

As noted in the Introduction to this book, the anti-Thai riots of January 29, 2003, were instigated by unsubstantiated rumors spread on the Internet, radio, and by the Cambodian prime minister that a Thai actress had disparaged Cambodia's internationally acclaimed Angkor Wat temple and that the Cambodian Embassy in Thailand had been ransacked, resulting in casualties. After the riots, Cambodian authorities constrained freedom of assembly, with a few exceptions. Among these, a May Day (Labor Day) rally attended by 4,000 people on May 1, 2005, was permitted; this inspired human rights activists to join with their labor colleagues in organizing another large rally for International Human Rights Day (IHRD) on December 10, 2005. At that rally, attended by more than 10,000 participants, a banner was displayed containing handwritten comments that, according to the Ministry of Foreign Affairs and International Cooperation, accused the Hun Sen regime of treachery for selling land to the Vietnamese, characterized its leaders as having "bloody-stained hands," and remarked, "This is the second Pol Pot regime" (MoFAIC 2006). The banner referred to a border treaty with Vietnam that the government had signed in October; many Cambodians felt that the treaty gave away land to Vietnam to which Cambodians had long staked a claim. News accounts, verified by informant interviews (4-1, 4-2), indicate that the banner adorned the Cambodian Center for Human Rights (CCHR) booth during International Human Rights Day.

International Human Rights Day had been authorized by the government and organized by 63 human rights and development organizations, labor unions, federations, and youth associations. It successfully brought more than 10,000 people together at Olympic Stadium. The Royal Government of Cambodia (RGC) permitted the event with stipulations as to what could be discussed (4-3, 4-4, 4-5). The organizers established a committee that reviewed all speeches and made a number of changes to tone down criticism of the government. The rally was described as innocuous and festive by informants (4-6, 4-7, 4-8, 4-9, 4-10, 4-11) and as a "nonstory" by a journalist in attendance (4-12). The fact that human rights abuses would stem from a day celebrating human rights would later be perceived as bitterly ironic by a senior diplomat (4-13).

At around 11:00 A.M., CCHR staff members were informed by the IHRD organizing committee that the authorities had complained about the banners used in the CCHR stall.[2] The banners were removed without incident. After the celebration, at around 4:30 P.M., a CCHR truck returning to the CCHR office was stopped by the authorities, who demanded to search the vehicle. CCHR staff refused to permit this because the authorities did not have a court order to search. After the intervention of the UN Office of the High Commissioner for Human Rights in Cambodia, the vehicle was allowed to proceed. That evening, local television broadcast images of scrawled remarks on the banner in question and announced that there had been a "breach of trust," according to a nongovernmental organization (NGO) advisor (4-9).

The regime had already targeted several individuals for criticizing the border treaty, including Mom Sonando and Rong Chhun. Sonando, a well-known independent journalist and the owner of Beehive Radio, was arrested on October 11, 2005, for broadcasting an interview with a Cambodian border activist in France who criticized the supplemental border treaty. Though Sonando, who conducted the interview, challenged the views of the interviewee repeatedly, he was charged under Articles 62 and 63 of the UNTAC Law of September 10, 1992, with defamation (which carries a maximum one-year prison sentence) and later with disinformation (up to three years in prison), as well as "incitement of others to commit a criminal offense without the offense being committed" (one to five years' imprisonment; Licadho 2006a). The charges resulted from complaints filed against him by the government and the National Assembly.

Rong Chhun, president of the Cambodian Independent Teachers Association, was arrested on October 15, 2005, in Banteay Meanchey Province while trying to cross the border into Thailand. He was apprehended in connection with an October 11, 2005, Cambodia Watchdog Council press statement criticizing the border agreement with Vietnam. Chhun had signed the statement along with other members of the Cambodia Watchdog Council, a lobby group of trade unions and associations that Amnesty International described as being affiliated with the opposition Sam Rainsy Party. Chhun was charged with defamation and incitement of others to commit a crime without that crime being committed (Licadho 2006a). Three other individuals associated with the statement—Ear Channa, Men Nath, and Chea Mony—were already abroad when authorities sought to arrest them.

In the context of these October arrests and the official response to the IHRD banner, CCHR staffers began making extensive preparations for a meeting with municipal authorities on December 13, 2005. During the meeting, Yeng Virak, executive director of the Cambodian Legal Education Center and head of the IHRD organizing committee (because no one else had volunteered to take on the responsibility), reportedly explained that following the complaint by the authorities, the banner in question had been removed and that he himself had never even seen the banner, having requested its removal by telephone. On December 31, Virak and Kem Sokha, president of the CCHR, were arrested. Both Virak and Sokha had made the conscious decision to remain in Cambodia when they suspected authorities would attempt to arrest them. This principled stand served as an example to other activists (4-2).

The arrests had a chilling effect on human rights activism in Cambodia. On that day, a meeting of IHRD organizers disbanded when it was rumored that four or five more individuals who had signed documents with the municipal authorities concerning IHRD and worked on security matters for the event would be targeted for arrest (4-14). A statement that had been in the works until then was left uncompleted (4-14). Authorities questioned by the *Cambodia Daily* at the time claimed that no further arrest warrants had been issued. On January 4, 2006, however, Pa Nguon Teang, deputy director of the CCHR and in charge of the organization's Voice of Democracy broadcasts, which are transmitted by Beehive Radio, was also arrested in Stung Treng on the Cambodia-Lao PDR border. A national meeting of provincial activists, planned to take place in Phnom Penh in January 2006, was cancelled. Provincial representatives reported that they were required by local authorities to obtain permission to leave their provinces (4-15, 4-7). Even in Phnom Penh, it was alleged that municipal authorities sought organizers of large NGO events to *teutool khoh treuv* (literally, "to accept right and wrong") for any and all actions resulting from their event (4-16). If unknown persons were to hand out libelous pamphlets during the event, organizers would be held accountable.

After the initial October 2005 arrests, some human rights leaders left the country; they admitted that their departure was a direct result of the arrests (4-17). These leaders subsequently returned to Cambodia. Following the December 31, 2005, arrests, a number of individuals involved in IHRD went underground (4-4). Certain human rights leaders left the country to lobby the international community or to avoid the possibility of imprisonment (4-18, 4-11). Their exodus had a dampening effect on freedom of expression. It also had an unanticipated positive consequence—the absence of leaders presented an opportunity for everyday citizens at the grassroots and for junior managers who normally rely on human rights and union leadership to step up and gain visibility (4-19 and 4-20).

National Response

In October 2005, authorities characterized the first wave of arrests as preventive measures designed to protect national security and foster stability harmed by criticism of the supplemental border treaty. Advocates in civil society reframed the issue as one of freedom of expression. A conference on freedom of expression in Cambodia was organized by the CCHR and held at the Phnom Penh Hotel on October 24, 2005, during which representatives of thirty-one organizations signed a "Statement on the Exercise of Freedom of Expression in Cambodia." Several people I interviewed suggested that this was a turning point, marking the beginning of a coordinated response to the restriction of freedom of expression (4-21, 4-2, 4-22, 4-23, 4-24). On November 28, more than twenty organizations formed the Alliance for Freedom of Expression in Cambodia.

Many of the activities that took place following the December 31, 2005, arrests were organized by an ad hoc "post-December 31 core group" of individuals, who did not participate as representatives of their organizations. The group's size is unclear; people I asked estimated it to be between four and twelve members.[3] Although the membership was fluid, participants were able to organize many events in a short period of time, and informants felt these activities had an important impact. The organizers met secretly on a daily basis, sometimes twice per day, to strategize. The committee is believed to have planned most of the events described in the following discussion.

A yellow ribbon symbol was created by a staff member of the CCHR and adopted by the Alliance for Freedom of Expression. The campaign's purpose was "to push the National Assembly to reform laws on expression, participation, legislation and criminal defamation and press freedom" (MC&D 2005). By the end of

November 2005, the Alliance for Freedom of Expression began to distribute 60,000 yellow ribbons. A full-page advertisement in the *Cambodia Daily* on December 1, 2005, announced the distribution and explained, "I wear the Yellow Ribbon because I demand Freedom of Expression in Cambodia."

In total, 100,000 yellow ribbons are said to have been distributed, though the effort was not without difficulties. Initial distribution at local area markets was stopped by market authorities. The impact of the campaign was mixed. One labor informant asked, "Things like yellow ribbons may be meaningful to Phnom Penh, but what about the rest of the country?" (4-7). A youth association head noted that people would wear yellow ribbons when these were distributed at public forums of the CCHR but would later take them off because they were afraid of the police (4-25).

On January 7, 2006, a delegation of supporters brought law books to the notorious Prey Sar prison for Yeng Virak, along with food for the other detained activists.[4] The delegation was told that the books and food could not be delivered, and at least one of the detainees reported not having been informed of the visit. At this demonstration, as a symbolic gesture, one hundred caged birds were freed outside the prison by participants, including Alex Sutton, the country representative for the International Republican Institute, which funds the CCHR.

The following Saturday, January 14, 2006, 75 to 150 members of human rights organizations, unions, and other groups again gathered in front of Prey Sar prison to show support for the imprisoned activists. On January 11, Yeng Virak had been released from pretrial detention, and he attended the January 14 event. The wives of Mom Sonando, Kem Sokha, and Pa Nguong Teang, the sister of Rong Chhun, and the brother of Kem Sokha attended (Licadho 2006b)—part of a conscious strategy by organizers to focus on the victims' families rather than the organizations (4-11). The gathered protesters held yellow balloons representing the color of the Alliance for Freedom of Expression and wore yellow ribbons to demand freedom of expression in Cambodia. Families of the detainees spoke to the crowd, which released balloons and birds, chanting, "We demand freedom of expression!" One of the detained activists reported seeing the birds, which gave him hope. People then walked to a nearby pagoda to pray for the release of the four detainees.

By mid-February 2006, more than 180,000 thumbprint petitions had been collected demanding freedom of expression—in particular, they called for the release of the detainees (even though this had already happened), the dropping of the charges against them, and the end of prosecutions for criminal defamation. According to the CCHR, the organization collected 164,367 petitions, while the Youth Council of Cambodia (a new umbrella youth organization) was credited with gathering 14,756. Other petitions were collected by unions and labor associations,

such as the Informal Development Economic Association, Cambodia's Independent Civil Servants Association, and the Coalition of Cambodia Apparel Workers
Democratic Unions, among others.

The Cambodian Center for Human Rights had been holding public forums at
the rate of three per month on average, but following the arrests there was a desire
to increase the frequency to three per week (4-8, 4-26). In January 2006, a total of
eight CCHR Public Forums took place. They were used to highlight the absence
of the detainees, to collect thumbprints, and to publicize the Yellow Ribbon Campaign. A forum attended by 200 villagers was held in Siem Reap on January 4, at
which the mission director of the United States Agency for International Development (USAID) spoke (Berthiaume and Prak 2006). He referred to comments by
the German ambassador to the *Cambodia Daily* on January 3 alluding to the possible economic impact of the arrests. Those comments were remarkably frank,
according to a senior diplomat, and showed an increasing (if temporary) diplomatic response (4-27).

A forum in Kandal Province on January 6, 2006, was attended by the U.S. ambassador. Another forum in Takeo on January 10 drew 800 people. It was in Takeo that
the umbrella Youth Council of Cambodia began to assist the effort. Subsequent
forums took place in Kampong Cham on January 12 and in Phnom Penh on January
15; at the latter, the vice-president of a union spoke, as did the U.S. deputy chief
of mission. A sizeable number of union members were present.[5] Following this
came forums in Prey Veng on January 19, Kompong Speu on January 24 (attended
by about 500 people), and finally Battambang on January 27. The minimum attendance starting on January 10 was 350–400 individuals (4-28, 4-29). Several informants noted that the public forums in the provinces were an important means of
reaching people in the rural areas and served to keep the issues in the spotlight.
Another observer noted that the higher frequency of meetings allowed a greater
chance for visiting foreign correspondents such as *New York Times* journalist Seth
Mydans to publish stories based on visits to the forums (4-26). Indeed, on January 10, following the forum in Rokar Khnong Commune, Takeo Province, a story
appeared first in the *International Herald Tribune* (January 24) and then in the *New
York Times* (January 30).[6]

Te Chanmono, the wife of Kem Sokha, was received by at least eight ambassadors following the arrest of her husband.[7] One human rights activist reported that
following Te Chanmono's meeting with the Japanese ambassador, she was very
optimistic that something would soon be done to secure her husband's release
(4-2). Japan was then Cambodia's largest bilateral donor. At the time, Te Chanmono was received by the German ambassador who held, on behalf of Austria,
the presidency of the European Union in Cambodia. She was also received by two

regional ambassadors, from Thailand and Singapore. Although the actual impact of these visits on the diplomatic community is not known, the fact that Te Chanmono was given appointments indicates the gravity of the arrests.

Statements were issued by national and international organizations following the arrests of Kem Sokha and Yeng Virak. A number of these were jointly released, such as the January 12, 2006, Joint Statement on the Arrest of Human Rights Activists that was signed by 37 Cambodian organizations, associations, and coalitions; 37 international civil society organizations (CSOs) and coalitions; and 157 staff of Cambodian or international organizations. On January 9, a World Bank Statement issued by Ian Porter, country director for Cambodia, addressed the arrests of prominent human rights activists. It read in part, "We are deeply concerned by the recent arrests and prosecutions and urge the Government to consider very carefully the compatibility of such actions with the commitments it has made towards building a more open, democratic and just society" (World Bank 2006b). Following the release of the activists on January 17, a letter from major garment buyers was sent privately to several senior government officials, including the prime minister, on January 20 that called for dropping the defamation charges (4-9, 4-30). On January 24, 2006, the prime minister announced that charges had been dropped, though he subsequently clarified that because the courts had begun investigating, the matter was now out of his hands. The investigation could in theory continue until a three-year statute of limitations expired;[8] even if activists were convicted, they could subsequently be pardoned (4-2).

Whether and how the various statements and letters in support of the detained activists affected political decision making is unknown. Some prominent Ministry of Interior officials, Ministry of Foreign Affairs and International Cooperation officials, and even advisors to the prime minister were said to have been privately displeased with the arrests because these actions were hard for them to defend (4-13, 4-27, 4-31).

The extent to which the events of 2005–2006 were a "national" movement of protest is difficult to assess. True, more than 180,000 thumbprints were collected (using the 2003 national election voter total of 5,168,837, this represents a nontrivial 3.5 percent of voters) in a protest campaign for freedom of expression over the course of one month, February 2006. But this was the peak of the campaign's effectiveness. The same month, the Alliance for Freedom of Expression in Cambodia also organized a march for freedom of expression that resulted in Prime Minister Hun Sen promising to decriminalize defamation. To date, however, this has not happened. On April 23, 2008, Sam Rainsy Party member of parliament (MP) Mu Sochua announced her intention to sue Prime Minister Hun Sen on the basis of remarks he made referring to the "unbuttoning of her blouse" and a comment of a "sexual nature" according to Rupert Colville, a spokesperson for the UN High Commissioner for Human Rights (qtd. in Schlein 2010). The day after Mu Sochua brought her lawsuit, the prime minister countersued "on the basis that publicly announcing the intension to sue him was defamatory" (Schlein 2010). Mu Sochua's case was dismissed, and her parliamentary immunity was lifted; she was found guilty of defaming the prime minister and ordered to pay about $4,000, which she refused to do. Instead, the fine was garnered from her wages against her will. Journalist Hang Chakra was jailed nearly ten months as punishment for publishing a series of articles that suggested corruption in the cabinet of a deputy prime minister in 2009 and was released only after receiving a royal pardon prior to the Khmer New Year in April 2010. Regardless of these sobering cases and the murder in April 2012 of renowned environmental activist Chut Wutty, followed by the killing of a fourteen year old girl in Kratie province by soldiers evicting her family, this freedom of expression movement itself (whether urban or rural, local, national, or even international) did contribute to the release of those activists incarcerated in 2005.

International Involvement

The UN secretary-general's special representative for human rights in Cambodia, Yash Ghai, visited Mom Sonando and Rong Chhun at Prey Sar along with Cheam Chany, a Sam Rainsy Party MP who had earlier been arrested, in military prison on December 3, 2005, during his first mission to Cambodia. Ghai met with the minister of foreign affairs on December 1, 2005. According to the ministry's Web site, Mr. Ghai "raised his concern about the freedom of expression and noted the development of the implementation of human rights and democracy in Cambodia," to which the minister reportedly asserted, "the issue relat[ed] to the detention of a number of critics who [were] involved with the defamation charges and made social disorder" and "was not the [sic] intimidation" (MoFAIC 2005).[9]

On January 5, 2006, the German ambassador (representing the European Union [EU] presidency), the French ambassador, and the European Commission delegate to Cambodia met with the minister of foreign affairs and international cooperation to make an official diplomatic representation or protest (known as a démarche) to the Royal Government of Cambodia. The meeting had been earlier scheduled on another topic, but the purpose was changed following the December 31, 2005, arrests. The German ambassador expressed concern "about the evolution of Human Rights and Democracy in Cambodia" and pointed to "the removal of immunity of some opposition party lawmakers" as well as the arrest of the director of the Cambodian

Center for Human Rights. He noted, "It looked like a campaign against the critics of the Government" (MoFAIC 2006). The minister's response denied that the case involved "a human rights problem" or restrictions on the "freedom of expression"; rather, it was a case of "defamation," and "The allegation aimed at making chaos and social instability" (MoFAIC 2005). International response to the arrests of Kem Sokha, Yeng Virak, and Pa Nguon Teang was considerably more vociferous than that which followed the arrests of Mom Sonando and Rong Chhun (4-11, 4-32), though the British ambassador had issued an EU démarche to the RGC following the October arrests, a press statement about which was released only on November 11, 2005.

On January 13, 2006, Swedish minister of justice Thomas Bodstrom visited Kem Sokha at Prey Sar prison. He relayed to the press that the Swedish government was worried about the arrest of peaceful activists for expressing their opinions. A meeting with human rights NGOs was arranged, and discussions centered on the detained human rights activists (4-18). According to a senior diplomat, Bodstrom and Hun Sen discovered during their discussions that Bodstrom's father had been the first international diplomat to welcome Hun Sen when the latter made an official visit to Sweden during his tenure as foreign minister of the People's Republic of Kampuchea. This historical coincidence helped build rapport (4-6).

On January 17, 2006, U.S. assistant secretary of state Christopher Hill met with prime minister Hun Sen. An advisor to the royal government surmised that Hill needed only to say, "70 percent of your exports go to the U.S.," for the prime minister to use the opportunity of the dedication of the new U.S. embassy in Phnom Penh that same day to grant the freedom of the human rights and civil rights activists (4-33). And indeed, the prime minister did release the activists that day. In the U.S. ambassador's speech dedicating the new U.S. embassy, the ambassador quoted Benjamin Franklin, saying, "Those who would give up essential liberty to purchase a little temporary safety, deserve neither liberty nor safety." He added: "And if that is true, then the opposite is also true. That is, when political leaders are willing to risk a little temporary instability in order to preserve an essential liberty they ought to be commended. It takes courage to take risks for freedom whether you are a human rights activist or a prime minister, and so today I would like to praise them both" (Mussomeli 2006). A Cambodian secretary of state speculated that Hill gave the prime minister an ultimatum (4-31). One senior diplomat said: "There must have been some kind of deal struck with carrots or sticks involved. If not, then perhaps the idea could have been planted to prime minister Hun Sen that he could be magnanimous and improve his image by taking the appropriate action," adding, "I believe that Cambodia's reliance on donor support and the upcoming Consultative Group meeting had some part to play toward the . . . decision to release Kem Sokha and allow Rainsy's return" (4-34).

An advisor to the prime minister characterized the release of Mom Sonando, Rong Chhun, Kem Sokha, and Pa Nguon Teang as a "gift" to Hill on the occasion of the U.S. embassy's dedication (Cheang 2006). In the neopatrimonial Cambodian cultural context, another informant agreed that the release of the activists was the epitome of exercising *kun* (debt of gratitude; 4-35). Another informant said that the timing of the release could not have been more political; had the prime minister offered the gift to Swedish minister of justice Bodstrom instead, it would have garnered no political capital but would have symbolically raised the gesture above politics and made it truly one for human rights (4-15). A senior diplomat said that the use of the word *gift* was meant to indicate that no strings were attached and that it was purely voluntary and done under no pressure whatsoever (4-6). Several informants credited Hill's visit as being the most important factor in the release of the activists.

This is a cautionary tale about international involvement in Cambodia, which ended happily but was misperceived considerably by external actors as having been the first stage of a Ukrainian-style Orange Revolution. In Ukraine from late November 2004 to January 2005, protests rocked Kiev due to election fraud that led to a Supreme Court-ordered revote, handing the opposition its stolen victory. Some of the USAID grantees' personnel in Cambodia came from postings in Central Eastern Europe and were eager to see a repeat. I found myself shocked to hear their complaints about how, in fact, prison conditions in Cambodia were not that bad, and that the fear of being sent to prison—exacerbated by Cambodians' memories of living under the Khmer Rouge—had prevented heroism from taking hold. This was lunacy—here were foreigners complaining about how Cambodians did not have the courage to head into jail cells because of unhelpful memories.[10] The foreigners had passports and, at the first sign of trouble, would have been on the next plane out of Cambodia.

Regional Involvement

The countries of the Association of Southeast Asian Nations (ASEAN) practice a policy of consensus in decision making and noninterference in one another's affairs. Thus, the official role of ASEAN in the events from December 2005 to January 2006 was limited. Few ASEAN dignitaries visited Cambodia in this period. On December 6, Nguyen Dy Nien, minister of foreign affairs of the Socialist Republic of Vietnam, made an official visit to exchange the Instruments of Ratification of the border treaty, and paid a courtesy call on the prime minister. Given the reason for Nguyen's visit, it is doubtful that the arrests of Mom Sonando and Rong Chhun were raised as an issue.

In contrast, George Yeo, foreign minister of the Republic of Singapore, led an official delegation to Cambodia on January 23–25, 2006. The prime minister used the opportunity of a press conference on January 24 following his meeting with Yeo to tell the media that "[The human rights activists'] letters were enough for me to end the case. . . . But I have to ask my lawyers and legal experts how to drop the charges against them after this compromise. . . . I do not want to challenge with any one. I would prefer to strike a compromise rather than challenge . . . I am calm now" (qtd. in Reuters 2006). Prime Minister Hun Sen referred to letters of apology penned by each of the jailed activists (with the lone exception of Yeng Virak, who had already been released before all the others). One informant suggested that an intervention made by an ASEAN diplomat may have had the strong effect of reminding the prime minister of the importance of his stance toward the United States. Following this intervention, the prime minister granted a meeting to a U.S. Senate staffer who had long been critical of him; it lasted an hour and a half. The staffer would typically have been seen by the deputy prime minister and Minister of Interior Sar Kheng.

Two members of the (nongovernmental) Working Group for an ASEAN Human Rights Mechanism came on a mission to Cambodia to address an unfolding human rights situation for the first time since the Working Group's founding (4-21). Kem Sokha was affiliated with this organization as chair of the Cambodian Working Group for an ASEAN Human Rights Mechanism (AHRM 2006). On January 1, the umbrella organization issued a statement affirming "the international community's call for the release of Kem Sokha and others" (AHRM 2006).

Although there is no evidence that at the time ASEAN diplomats adopted any particular strategy to put pressure on the RGC to release the activists, ASEAN members have considerable demonstrative influence on Cambodia, and it is probable that at least one of the interventions may have had some impact on the final release of the detainees, if only indirectly.

Lessons Learned

Among key strengths brought to life by the events of 2005–2006, the first was that civil society could collaborate and coordinate activities. Representatives of human rights, youth, and labor organizations all noted that different elements of civil society had worked together in an organized manner toward freeing the detained activists (4-18, 4-5, 4-23). One NGO senior staff member told me that every activity came under the umbrella of the Alliance for Freedom of Expression in Cambodia in the service of an agenda dedicated to the release of the human rights activists. To keep the momentum going, the issues were kept in the spotlight; participants focused on these issues rather than on the fear of being arrested themselves, something that "could have happened at any time" (4-20).

Other strengths included the use of innovative communications, such as text messaging, and generally improved relations with the media and the international community. The thumbprint campaign was seen as successful, and notwithstanding criticism of its publicity campaign, many felt that the yellow ribbon itself became a powerful symbol. In examining the role of communications, a youth association senior staff member told the story behind the innovative use of text messaging by mobile phone (4-28). The system evolved from a staffer's request for updates on the petition count in the provinces that led to a tally being sent back by text message every evening. Also, core group members—individuals who came from civil society but did not necessarily represent their organizations—used coded messages referencing different types of cuisine to convey secret venues for meetings (4-1, 4-23, 4-20). Web sites such as freesokha. com, which was registered as a domain name on January 6, 2006, added to the momentum for the precious few with Internet access.

The organizing extended to public relations with garment buyers and resulted in a private letter to the authorities being dispatched on January 20 , 2006 (4-30). Abroad, an advisor referred to the increasing press coverage during the weekend of January 14–16, just prior to the January 17 release of activists, as evidence of the increasingly effective use of media (4-26, 4-12). Summarizing this view, an NGO senior staff member said that working with the international community was very important, as "We needed to build a bridge to the outside world . . . and the media was key" (4-20).

At coordinating meetings, participants considered strategies to influence those elements that would speak loudest to the authorities, such as major donors or garment buyers or star power for the new U.S. embassy dedication (4-8). There was a conscious effort to strategically piggyback on the visit of Christopher Hill for the embassy's dedication in an effort to secure the release of the activists. Indeed, the U.S. embassy's perennial challenge remains how to get Cambodia on the radar screen of Foggy Bottom (U.S. State Department headquarters).

Views on the thumbprint campaign were overwhelmingly positive, as such a large number of signatures (more than 180,000) were collected in a short period of time (about one month). The message of the campaign was clear, and Cambodians were used to this method of using a thumbprint to signal their opinions. Individual motivations are not known, but I was told that popular opinion centered on authorities having gone too far by arresting Kem Sokha and Yeng Virak. This thumbprint campaign is a graphic example of the new networks and coalitions that came into being during this period, as well as their newfound ability to work together in a cohesive way.

The yellow ribbon emerged as a symbol of "our aspirations," according to a youth association head and a labor association head (4-2, 4-5). An NGO senior staffer added that the yellow ribbon sent a message that activists support nonviolence (4-20), as it presumably reminds Cambodians, who are overwhelmingly Buddhist, of the orange saffron robes of monks. A labor-linked NGO representative pointed out that advocacy efforts did not take a confrontational stance and as such were a reflection of Cambodia's newly achieved quiet maturity in politics (4-7).

Informants described at least three significant weaknesses of the civil society campaign. First, the role of information and disinformation was particularly important because of how it fashioned and circumscribed the behavior of citizen advocates and civil society. During a crisis, accurate and timely information is crucial, while disinformation can have serious repercussions. Some informants suggested that rumors about who might be arrested had nearly the same repercussions as the arrests themselves (4-11, 4-20). This was the case in the lead-up to the December 10, 2005, International Human Rights Day, in which some organizations declined to be involved. Given that the IHRD banner incident became the basis for the December 31 arrests, their fears were not unwarranted.

Youth group representatives complained that the core group, or organizing committee, did not have clear discussions (4-28, 4-29). An advisor based abroad noted how easily the group could be sidetracked by personalities (4-36). Human rights, labor, and youth group activists also pointed to the weak participation of NGO heads. Several informants noted that the goals and strategies for various campaigns were not clear. With respect to communications between civil society and the diplomatic community, one human rights activist complained that certain embassies did not reveal the findings of their bilateral meetings with the authorities (4-18). Although diplomats cannot and should not divulge confidential information, as we know all too well in the age of WikiLeaks, better exchanges of information between diplomats and activists could perhaps have alleviated some of the misconceptions.

Second, informants spoke of difficulties that grew out of the absence of one international voice. Informants across the diplomatic community, the government, development partners, and the private sector complained that despite the appearance of a consensus, the international community's statements were "very weak" or "disappointingly weak" and that at least some of Cambodia's most important donors felt that the arrests were legally reasonable (4-33, 4-30, 4-37, 4-38). One informant explained that because oil and gas revenues are expected in Cambodia's future, and because China is gaining influence as a nontraditional donor, the traditional donor community is losing influence (4-39). An entrepreneur claimed, "Many businesspeople were even happy to have the rights people arrested since it enhanced the sense of central control and stability" (4-40). Of course, it is not clear precisely how many businesspeople felt this way. Other business leaders declined to comment.[11]

Lack of leadership was the third weakness identified by informants. As previously noted, the first wave of arrests in October 2005 prompted a number of human rights leaders to leave the country temporarily; the second wave of arrests led to a pervasive sense of fear among activists and individuals involved in the organizing of International Human Rights Day. A number of human rights leaders were absent from the country or were imprisoned, leading to a power vacuum in some weak organizations.

Leaders' absence had a silver lining, however, as it permitted junior management of CSOs the opportunity to gain exposure and allowed the unprecedented emergence of an ad hoc core group that caused labor, human rights, and other sectors to come together and meet on a daily basis to plan activities (4-28, 4-20, 4-29). Because many of the core group members were junior managers, partnerships were forged more easily, as personalities and egos were subdued. Although trust levels had increased through the process of organizing these freedom of expression events and the newly emerging coalitions and networks, a number of informants made little effort to hide deep-seated animosity toward and lack of trust in one another. As with any hierarchical society or bureaucracy, when a meeting of leaders is arranged but some leaders are absent or send emissaries, this can poison working relationships.

New Coalitions and Pathways

The coalitions that forged new relationships and networks were of particular importance in achieving the civil society response to the human rights and freedom of expression events. Although many networks already existed, the new networks were an important addition.

Among examples, Yeng Virak's Community Legal Education Center's partnership with the Ministry of the Interior on the draft Freedom of Assembly Law showed constructive engagement and partnership between civil society and the RGC. In addition, the Cambodian Development Research Institute's many years of promoting dialogue through the Conflict Prevention in Cambodian Elections program has also been considered a success by many. In the context of the emergence of the Alliance for Freedom of Expression in Cambodia, a human rights activist pointed out that networks and coalitions such as the Cambodian Human Rights Action Committee (CHRAC), a membership organization of 18 human rights organizations; the Committee for Free and Fair Elections in Cambodia; the Cambodian Committee for Women; and the NGO Forum are but a handful of umbrella organizations that have existed for some time to advance relationships and networks with like-minded organizations (4-18). Thus, the entities created in the wake of the events considered here were entering an already crowded field. However, the new coalitions, linking groups that were not traditionally connected, were able to be quite effective in that highly charged environment.

The major coalition phenomenon that arose was among labor, human rights, and development-oriented NGOs and the wider civil society, including youth associations. While labor has dues-paying union members, human rights NGOs for the most part do not work on a paying membership basis. And while human rights NGOs have a decade of experience in advocacy, labor unions and federations are less experienced (4-7). Each brought a comparative advantage to the table that the other did not have, and their cooperation grew naturally with the help of individuals who straddled both worlds. Individuals who helped build the capacity of unions and federations to organize also contributed to the process of labor–human rights coalition building as they recognized that civil-political rights and socioeconomic rights could be sought together. The integration of these two issues encouraged dialogue between labor and human rights organizations, building a bridge between them.

While a few activists chose to go into hiding or left the country, others made conscious decisions to go public. One union leader who was believed to be under the threat of arrest came out to Prey Sar prison on a Saturday to release birds and balloons and to make a speech. Moreover, while no international NGO based in Cambodia condemned the arrests of Mom Sonando and Rong Chhun (4-11), Yeng Virak's arrest attracted the attention of NGOs involved with issues other than human rights. (Virak was known outside human rights circles for being an effective bridge builder with the authorities through his Community Legal Education Center.) The principled stands taken by particular activists played an important role. The courage shown by these activists also brought new partners into the process despite the previously described attitude displayed by some members of the foreign assistance community who could not understand why jail in Cambodia was a problem.

One network of NGOs in Cambodia that had rarely signed on to support human rights issues in the past got involved. Indeed, certain international NGOs complained that they should have been better informed during this time, as they wished to sign petitions in support of the activists—as, for example, when twenty-seven organizations signed a petition in favor of Yeng Virak's release (4-41, 4-42). It is believed that because International Human Rights Day was so innocuous—as one participant noted, "no one even saw that banner or even went near that booth"—and a large number of NGOs had participated in it, the wave of arrests that followed was perceived as excessive (4-9).

A labor leader whose organization normally takes a low-key approach when dealing with the authorities agreed, "The 31 December arrest showed that the government had crossed the line" (4-30). As a result, the organization issued a public statement; it had sent only private letters up to that point. A senior diplomat confirmed that in early December, major garment buyers meeting in Phnom Penh were told by the minister of commerce that Mom Sonando and Rong Chhun would be released by Christmas after letters of apology were arranged (4-6). When the release failed to materialize and more arrests instead rang in the new year, there was a sense of betrayal (4-30). Certainly, for those who consider the release of the activists from pretrial detention to have been a success, the adage "success has many fathers" applies. Members of civil society who were involved in activities were taking credit and were proud, regardless of whether or not the advocacy itself was at times more events-based than issue-based.

Meanwhile, a rising chorus from the international community expressing dismay with Cambodian authorities grew louder. Indeed, though the second wave of arrests took place on New Year's Eve, when many diplomats and donors were away from Phnom Penh, several ambassadors came to the Cambodian Center for Human Rights to witness the arrest of Kem Sokha. Prior to this, both the Canadian ambassador and the U.S. deputy chief of mission had attended the Conference on Freedom of Expression on October 24, 2005. Germany was represented in the audience (4-21). Following the arrest of Sokha, the German ambassador was interviewed by the *Cambodia Daily* for a story that appeared on January 3, in which he spoke "very frankly," according to another senior diplomat (4-27). As mentioned earlier, these remarks were then referenced by the USAID mission director in his January 4, 2006, CCHR public forum appearance in Siem Reap, and they were followed up on January 5, 2006, with the EU troika démarche to the minister of foreign affairs and international cooperation. Succeeding statements from the International Labour Organization and the World Bank—organizations that do not traditionally make public statements about politically sensitive matters—signaled a growing concern in the international community. These interventions were important because they established a relationship of positive reinforcement between civil society and members of the international community, so that it could not be said that the international community was going out on a limb or that civil society was crying wolf (4-10, 4-43, 4-39).

The Interplay Between Domestic and International Interventions

Few informants ventured to argue that the domestic human rights and freedom of expression events directly influenced the authorities to order the release of the human rights activists. Indeed, a few diplomats described the domestic agitation as little more than an irritant to the authorities (4-43, 4-34), and others argued that the government released the detainees when it "had got what it wanted" and calculated it could gain more from their release than it would lose (4-40, 4-44). Yet several informants across the diplomatic and development community and labor, human rights, and youth groups described a symbiotic relationship between civil society and the international community, stating that the latter acted as an intermediary in dialogue with the government (4-16, 4-39, 4-10, 4-27, 4-17). Such informants reiterated that the strength and conviction of civil society prompts members of the international community to speak up.

In order to understand the relationship between the international community and civil society, it is important to assess how effectively civil society can act as a counterweight to government weakness. While the events of 2005–2006 were a success for civil society, in that the activists were released, the victory was short-lived. At the time of this writing in June 2012, all the problems that the activists reacted against have once again reared their ugly heads. Sam Rainsy has had his parliamentary immunity stripped for the second time and is in exile. Members of his eponymous Sam Rainsy Party have had defamation lawsuits filed against them, the most prominent among them MP Mu Sochua, who was ordered to pay a fine of 16.5 million riels (approximately $4,000), which she has to date refused to pay but was garnered from her wages anyway.

In the second half of 2011, the Cambodian government introduced a draft Law on Associations and NGOs that would, according to an August 23 statement signed by ten international human rights organizations, "allow the Royal Government of Cambodia to intimidate and potentially shut down local, national and foreign NGOs, associations, and informal groups that criticize the government or government officials." The law does not adequately define terms or set guidelines for NGO registration, thereby inviting "arbitrary decision-making by officials." It's one more step toward a government-orchestrated "tightening of space for civil society, freedom of speech, and peaceful political opposition" (Adams et al. 2011).

All of this suggests that as tempting as it is to portray the events of 2005–2006 as a sign of the strength of Cambodian civil society, it is more realistic to echo Harold Kerbo's assessment in *The Persistence of Cambodian Poverty* that in Cambodia, civil society remains "very weak" (2011:183)—in no small part due to immense government pressure on NGOs and associations.

Aid Dependence and Cambodian Civil Society

CSOs include NGOs, trade unions, faith-based organizations, indigenous people's movements, and foundations, among other entities. It is not an understatement to say that the underpinnings of most of Cambodia's CSOs go back to sources external to Cambodia. Indeed, whether one looks at NGOs (some of which started arriving in-country in the early 1980s), trade unions (American trade unions have international nonprofit branches in Cambodia), faith-based organizations (which are primarily Christian), and so on, they are all connected in some fashion to outside funding sources.

In 2000, Kao Kim Hourn, who became a secretary of state of foreign affairs and international cooperation in 2004, addressed the question of the sustainability of CSOs in Cambodia: "We have to understand that in the past 10 years funding has been driven from outside. And I think we should expect that there will be a decline in the coming years," adding, "And if this is to be the increasing trend . . . the funding situation will affect not only the effectiveness of the civil-society organizations, but more importantly the future sustainability of the movement and the development of civil-society organizations in Cambodia" (Kao 2000).

The international community's lack of resolve on democratic transformation in Cambodia laid the groundwork for the tepid performance observed in civil society. Just as Kao Kim Hourn predicted in 2000, the drop in NGO funding (from bilateral, multilateral, and core/own resources) is troubling. This is especially true among Cambodian NGOs, whose funding dropped from $19.3 million in 2002 to $8.3 million in 2004—which approached 1997 levels (see figure 4.1). Such a drop cannot help but damage these organizations' ability to continue operating effectively.

Indeed, when adjusted for inflation, local NGOs likely received less in 2001 than they did in 1996. Their dependence on external funding makes them vulnerable to shifts in policy or funding priorities.

The funding picture for international NGOs is somewhat different. While this funding increased dramatically between 2002 and 2004, from $76.9 million to $115.5 million, it languished from 1998 through 2002 in the low-to-mid-$70 million range. A recent shift in USAID policy from encouraging multiparty political

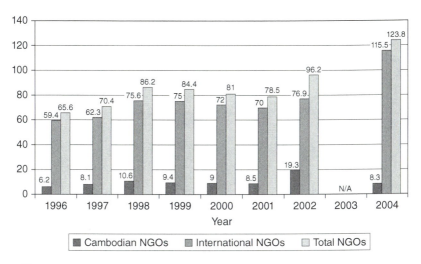

Figure 4.1 NGO BILATERAL, MULTILATERAL, AND CORE/OWN RESOURCES ($ MILLIONS).

[*Source*: Based on NGO Forum (2006).]

competitiveness to strengthening the accountability of the current one-party system is a case in point. This decision is understandable given the intractability of the ruling Cambodian People's Party. It is questionable, however, whether accountability can be achieved without competitiveness, and why those things should be mutually exclusive.

The funding data on NGOs, if representative of CSOs in general, suggest that they will require far more financial support than has thus far been invested. Without such support, CSOs will not be able to realize their full potential. Instead of shifting spending from international NGOs to local NGOs as an indication of localization, the 2004 increase in international NGO funding suggests that an opposite process is occurring. Local NGOs received an infusion in 2002 but then lost all their gains two years later, while international NGOs were given a $40 million increase in their funding envelope. If nothing else, the signs point to hard times ahead for local NGOs and for CSOs in general. NGOs' core funds, i.e., funding that excludes the financial resources delegated to them by other development partners—typically funds that are the NGOs' own resources as distinguished from NGO contributions—languished in the mid-2000s and began to increase in 2007, crossing the $100 million mark in 2008 (see figure 4.2).

They are projected to remain steady in 2009 and to increase in 2010. Projections for 2011 again show a precipitous decline, however, with a successive drop in

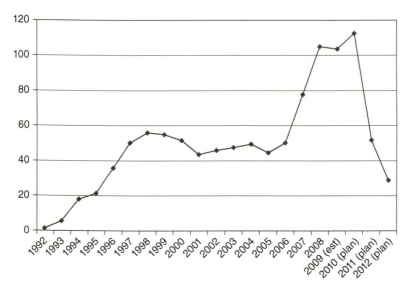

Figure 4.2 NGO CORE/OWN FUNDS (1992–2012) ($ MILLIONS).
[*Source:* Based on RGC (2010).]

2012. Such feast-or-famine cyclicality prevents successful long-term planning and is detrimental to the overall health of Cambodian civil society.

The Way Forward

Many who were interviewed spoke about the need to broaden civic engagement and put more emphasis on freedom of assembly. From February 11–13, 2006, a three-day march from Phnom Penh to Oudong for "Freedom of Expression and Non-Violence in Cambodia" was organized by the Alliance for Freedom of Expression; 100 participants (including all five human rights activists who had been imprisoned) took part. The march was intended to demonstrate support for freedom of expression in Cambodia. Participants demanded that the defamation lawsuits against activists be dropped and defamation decriminalized. The circumstances leading up to the march were criticized by some because the prime minister reportedly personally approved the event, thus reinforcing the "Rule of Man" as opposed to the "Rule of Law" (4-11). Similarly, when Cheam Channy's release was brokered with the help of Kem Sokha, some participants were highly critical of the process. The imprisoned person was handed Kem Sokha's mobile phone with the prime minister on the other end. Indeed, as has been remarked of the entire episode, just as the human rights activists were arrested with impunity, they were also released with impunity.

As part of its constructive engagement with the Ministry of Interior, the Community Legal Education Center went beyond the call for the decriminalization of defamation, organizing a workshop on the Law on Freedom of Assembly on February 9–10, 2006, at which the U.S. ambassador was invited to speak. The center's collaboration with the Ministry of Interior signaled promise for future institutional dialogue between activists and the authorities. A Memorandum of Understanding between the East-West Management Institute, a USAID grantee, and the Ministry of Justice was signed in the same period (4-8). A labor leader observed that freedom of assembly is linked with freedom of expression, given that assembly without expression is pointless (4-30).

One issue that merits attention is the need for advocacy in Cambodia to remain historically and culturally sensitive. Cambodia has only recently emerged from decades of violent conflict, and caution must be exercised in promoting activities that might endanger local citizen advocates. Considering the hierarchical nature of Cambodian society and the trauma caused by nearly 2 million deaths during the Khmer Rouge period, techniques such as mass protests leading to mass arrests— or confrontation—may not be culturally palatable. One youth association head pointed out that generational cleavages based on Cambodian tradition discourage younger people from learning about civil society issues and becoming activists (4-25). A Cambodian development worker said that "provocation will not work," because "especially in Cambodian culture, just [a] word can spark a conflict," while another called for "minimizing clashes between power groups and the liberal expression ideas group" (4-45, 4-46). Conflict avoidance in Asian culture has been well documented (see Takagi 2002:5, 10).

Demonstrating a clear conflict of vision between national and international advocates, a Cambodian NGO head complained that international colleagues expressed a desire to see larger rallies—rallies that implicitly had more potential for social change but also the potential for spinning out of control (4-20). As this informant recalled, the Prey Sar Saturday events were modestly attended on January 7 and 14, 2006, by a few dozen people at each, which, in his view, was perfectly fine by Cambodian standards.[12] In an interview with Woodsome (2006), Chea Vannath, then director of the Center for Social Development, said that most Cambodians are not ready for the democracy that rights groups are calling for and that Cambodian citizens want political reform, but because many of them are still traumatized by the brutalities of the Khmer Rouge period, they prefer to avoid conflict.

Efforts to directly improve democracy have failed in Cambodia, and many have begun to hope that civil society will help to reform the situation by consolidating democracy and strengthening human rights, freedom of expression, and so forth, through an emphasis on individual rights and human security. The events of 2005–2006 suggest that CSOs in Cambodia have great potential to work together in this vein and to act symbiotically with the international community to put pressure on the state in the desired direction. They also suggest that without *either* the CSO actions or the international support, these rights will not be protected. But the aftermath of the 2005–2006 events is not promising. The government hasn't fulfilled any of the promises it made—Sam Rainsy, as of this writing (June 2012), is back in self-exile with a prison sentence hanging over his head. Defamation and disinformation remain crimes, and the threat of lawsuits continues to constrain freedom of expression more than six years after the 2005–2006 events. While CSOs are weakening due to the vagaries of funding, this suggests that aid dependence is as much a problem for civil society as it is for government. What might help? As with government and foreign aid the lack of taxes means no representation accountability trap; if aid to CSOs encouraged the development of local funding sources, a culture of ownership would prevail.

CONCLUSION

AID DEPENDENCE, POOR governance, growth without development, weak health infrastructure and surveillance, and shallow democracy are five new types of metaphorical hungers felt by Cambodia. The Khmer Rouge maxim that hunger is the most effective disease applies. It is hunger for national ownership instead of aid dependence; hunger for good, or at least good enough, governance instead of misgovernance or malgovernance; hunger for human development instead of merely macroeconomic growth; hunger for livelihoods when emerging and reemerging infectious diseases arise and make lives expendable; and finally, hunger for democracy instead of elections as window dressing. These hungers promise to be a lethal mix not just for Cambodia's people but for the international community (however that term is defined). Just as Michael Lewis has described America's subprime mess in unvarnished terms, noting that loans were made to unqualified buyers who were "one broken refrigerator away from default" (2011:169), countries like Cambodia are one broken government away from disaster. For a global surveillance system that relies on the weakest link, there are no second acts. If the disease is lack of accountability, then the proof will be in a forthcoming pandemic.

According to Chea Vannath, former president of the Center for Social Development, democracy has been "fading away little by little" since the United Nations Transitional Authority in Cambodia left the country. She says this is the case "because there's nothing there": "It's just an illusion of democracy. The mirage of democracy. And the mirage disappeared. . . . So the natural forms come out." Vannath sees Cambodia "at the crossroads to have its own self-reliance, self-motivation," and the time is coming, she says, for the government to say, "Enough is enough, we don't care about your aid" (qtd. in Woodsome 2006). Madame Vannath's statement is aspirational, in the sense that she hopes to see Cambodia reject aid from a desire for national ownership. What is happening is far worse: Cambodia is on the cusp of proclaiming "We don't care about your aid" to Western donors as it falls under the influence of China and other lenders who have no interest in upholding human rights or democratic values. China's strategy has been to influence Cambodian decision makers and to obtain resources for China's own development (Burgos and Ear 2010).

The Khmer Rouge Tribunal

While I have not delved into the deeply troubled UN-backed Khmer Rouge Tribunal now taking place in Cambodia—another book unto itself—it is today on the verge of collapse. Back in mid-February 2002, the UN pulled out of talks with the Cambodian government because the latter had failed to enact legislation that would protect UN oversight and guarantee that prosecutors could pursue suspects despite previously granted amnesties. On February 21, 2002, the *New York Times* published my letter to its editor as follows:

> In 1976, my father died of dysentery under the care of Khmer Rouge "medicine." Although he, along with more than a million other dead Cambodians, deserves justice, I applaud the United Nations for its refusal to be taken down the Mekong by the Phnom Penh authorities.
>
> What surprised me most was that it took four and a half years for the international body to realize what was happening, slightly longer than the Khmer Rouge's own reign of terror, and another missed opportunity for global action.
>
> A tribunal governed solely under Cambodian law with a United Nations side agreement reduced to the status of a technical and administrative document would have been a disservice to the Cambodian people. All the United Nations did was to call a spade a spade.

(Ear 2002)

Unfortunately, within a year, the UN was forced back to the altar (despite the repeated warnings of its then Under-Secretary-General for Legal Affairs, Hans Corell, who had advised Kofi Annan to break off negotiations), courtesy of a UN General Assembly resolution orchestrated by the Cambodian government, with the United States and Germany playing matchmakers. A decade later, the chickens have come home to roost. Just as I predicted, having been taken down the Mekong, the UN now finds itself floating in the middle of the South China Sea with a jilted lover who has corrupted and politicized the tribunal beyond recognition. In the words of Albert Hirschman's classic 1970 treatise *Exit, Voice, and Loyalty*, the UN must decide to either leave ("exit"), speak up ("voice"), or buy in ("loyalty"). While it should speak up and ultimately exit (as did the two international investigating judges who resigned in succession claiming government pressure and obstruction, respectively), I predict that, as with foreign assistance undermining democracy and the rule of law in much of the developing world, the UN will simply buy in. In 2008, I joined the tribunal as a civil party—willing at the time to give it a chance—but as I now see it, it is only a matter of time before I make my own exit from the process, having spoken up repeatedly in the pages of the *Wall Street Journal* (Asia) and the global edition of the *New York Times*, respectively, about corruption, mismanagement, and political interference in the judicial process. What I, as one among millions of victims (a label I find oppressively confining and static), do matters little, but what the UN and the international community do matters a lot.

Aid and Its Discontents

The dismal quality of Cambodia's governance is, of course, largely the result of the government's own lack of political will and poor leadership. Yet donors also bear some responsibility for this outcome, given their deep commitments, financial and programmatic, to Cambodian institutions. Certainly, with respect to control of corruption and rule of law, Cambodia may be further now from progress than it was a decade ago. It is also apparent that official development assistance has made it more feasible, through fungibility, to divert resources and to enable corruption. This shows how hard it is for donors to be tough on a country that is genuinely aid dependent for the survival of much of its population. The challenge, then, is to decrease aid dependence while improving livelihoods. As experience in the garment sector has shown, one type of dependence (aid) has been replaced by another (garments). But the difference is immediately apparent—350,000 jobs were created in the garment sector, while the aid business, though an industrial complex in its own right, employs only tens of thousands whose success would also mean the industry's demise.

A difficult institutional environment is created by a combination of weak state capacity and poor governance. These in turn limit the scope for reform. Everywhere in Cambodia, civil servant salaries are abysmally low (barely above the poverty line) for both political economy and patronage reasons. In the livestock sector, illegal taxation is very costly and pervasive, especially in regard to the transport of cattle within the country and the informal payments associated with it. There are numerous reasons for this, but three are of particular note: the legacy of the Khmer Rouge and its implications for the country's human resources; patron-client relations within an embedded culture of corruption that prevents pro-poor policies from being implemented; and a donor-government nexus that has produced too many strategies and plans and too few funded mandates and feasible policies.

The case of Cambodia echoes the experience of other, more typical developing countries insofar as democracy, governance, and aid are concerned; we see here the ventriloquism that Nicolas van de Walle (2005:69) identified in the rise of the Poverty Reduction Strategy Papers (PRSPs), which the World Bank and the IMF required client countries to write as a condition for receiving aid. The game did not begin with PRSPs; they are simply one in a long chain of exercises devised by donors to create the illusion of ownership. Governments of developing countries parrot back what donors want to hear. Projects are formally proposed by the governments, but they are written by the donors.

In chapter 1 I addressed the illusion of ownership from a global standpoint and found that aid dependence is not, generally speaking, good for governance. I also showed that the effects of aid dependence on governance may not be, on the whole, as bad as some critics have suggested. Aside from political stability and, to a lesser extent, voice and accountability, donors cannot be said to have enjoyed success in improving governance worldwide, and certainly not in Cambodia. The lone exception in Cambodia's case is the effect of political stability, which is a by-product of a peace dividend sowed by Cambodian stakeholders and nurtured by the international community. Donors and the government were aligned on this issue; consider the political bargain made in Paris in 1991 to move Cambodia from a state of war to one of peace.

Cambodia's experience suggests that political stability alone is far from sufficient for sustainable development. Policies for which there is political will, such as a stable foreign exchange rate and control of inflation, have the best chance of succeeding. Policies that negatively affect patronage politics, such as efforts to control corruption and promote judicial independence, have the least likelihood of success. Judicial independence remains a serious problem in the developing world, and donors like the World Bank have already recognized that alternative justice mechanisms for the poor are needed. Alternatives have been implemented in Cambodia, with mixed success. As Un (2009) has argued, a weak judicial system is kept for political patronage reasons—the better to prevent checks and balances.

On the basis of what has been accomplished to date, however, foreign aid seems unlikely to deliver large improvements in governance and may even contribute to its further deterioration. The evidence is not hard to obtain. In Afghanistan, an increasingly detached president is pressured to increase the accountability of his government while echoes of 1970s Vietnam reverberate. The problems observed in Cambodia are not necessarily even those of heavily aid-dependent countries; for example, in today's Vietnam, problems of accountability—despite a centralized state—make it very difficult to stamp out corruption. In Indonesia, which coined the acronym KKN for *korupsi, kolusi, dan nepotisme* (corruption, collusion, and nepotism), a lack of confidence in the country's newfound democracy has made some long for the days of Soeharto's leadership. Decentralization, in Indonesia's case, has made it difficult to control what have become fiefdoms of power in the provinces. Governors don't listen, even when an epidemic is at hand; the central government has become powerless to do much more than coax and plead. In many ways, as one of my diplomat friends loves to say, "Cambodia is slowly becoming a normal country"—with all the attendant problems this status brings.

The arrival of China on the donor stage makes solutions even harder to come by. Globally, Knack suggests, "a larger fraction of aid could be tied or dedicated to improvements in the quality of governance, for example, in the form of programs to establish meritocratic bureaucracies and strong, independent court systems" (2001:326). This has been increasingly practiced in the annual allocations of World Bank aid. China's involvement in much of the developing world suggests, however, that any attempt to moderate flows to countries with poor governance can easily be offset by Chinese aid (Ear 2005; Burgos and Ear 2010). This is happening not just in China's neighborhood but also in Africa (Burgos and Ear 2012b), Latin America (Burgos and Ear 2011), and globally (Burgos and Ear 2012a). China's deep pockets have made it impossible for any threat of a reduction in aid to mean much. While there are few obvious strings attached to the aid, and certainly no demand for an improvement in human rights, it has been well recognized that Chinese companies—often linked with the government—are benefitting from the largesse of their central government. Despite this bleak picture, the Cambodian case does suggest some avenues for improving aid effectiveness.

How Do We Target Aid to Economic Development?

As I argued in chapter 2, targeting aid to economic development means removing—as much as possible—gatekeepers who stand between a country's national economy and the international system. Thus, aid must foster information, transparency, consultation, and participation in order to increase the demand for good governance.

Moore (2008) has summarized three main elements of governance from Paul Collier's book *Bottom Billion*:

1. The relationship between the quality of governance and national economic performance is highly dependent on circumstances. When the conditions are right, economies can grow fast despite poor governance (e.g., Bangladesh). But poor governance is generally bad for the economy, and really bad governance can destroy economies (e.g., Zimbabwe).

2. Governance is often bad in poor countries because their leaders, many of whom are among the "global superrich," benefit enormously from their role as gatekeepers between their national economies and the international system, so "it pays to keep their citizens uneducated and ill-informed" (Collier 2007:66).

3. The citizens, civic organizations, and governments of the rich world (the North) can best help improve governance in the poor world (the South) by reforming and better regulating the way the North interacts with the South in international arenas, especially in economic situations.

In Cambodia's experience, the presence of a private-sector organization, the Garment Manufacturers Association of Cambodia (GMAC), enabled collective action to lobby authorities for negotiated industrywide rent-seeking wage rates. This suggests that supporting associational activities will help countries achieve sufficient governance, at least within a given sector, although not necessarily beyond that sector. The exceptional relationship that evolved between GMAC and the Ministry of Commerce qualifies as what Miesel and Ould Aoudia call a "governance focal monopoly," in which "certain public governance institutions" acquire "the capacity for co-ordinating private interests by positioning themselves as the unavoidable focal point of governance relations" (2008:38). Institutions in this position "foster dialogue and coordination among public and private elites in which confidence is inextricably created on a basis that is *simultaneously* interpersonal, process-based and institutionalised" (38). Miesel and Ould Aoudia point to France in the three decades after World War II, Taiwan (1949 onward), Singapore under Lee Kuan Yew (1959 onward), South Korea under Park Chong Hee (1961 onward), and China starting in 1978. Of course, these were preponderantly authoritarian regimes that severely cracked down on civil rights and even human rights, but the lesson is that a focal point for matters of governance can be a key to adequate government breakthroughs if donors support its formation through sponsorship of champions inside ministries.

How Do We Target Aid to Solve Particular Problems in a Crisis Such as the Avian Influenza Threat?

Aid dependence has proven an effective and successful strategy for Cambodian authorities, as I explored in chapter 3. Not only do authorities vociferously clamor for a share of development funds to propel their nation into the global trading commons while acting as gatekeepers, but they also have managed to cleverly handle multilateral donors, international technical agencies, and private organizations to capture a nontrivial portion of—for example—animal and human influenza prevention and treatment funds. As long as Western powers arrive with wads of money to pay, Cambodian authorities will be more than happy to play (Ear and Burgos 2009:638).

But what of the peasants? Livelihood issues were overlooked in Cambodia owing to the low priority assigned to agriculture, aid dependence combined with low tax revenues, government manipulation of the media, a historic disregard for people's livelihoods, societal conformism, an upcoming election in which bad publicity from highly pathogenic avian influenza (HPAI) would erode confidence in the ruling party, lack of mechanisms to voice rural concerns, weak social cohesion, and an overall lack of purposeful guidance. To begin to address these problems, two policy actions are needed. First, greater government-donor coordination and oversight are necessary to align national and international interests. Second, making the protection of livelihoods a priority must be made explicit in the form of "pro-poor" HPAI risk reduction. Because 90 percent of poultry is raised in backyard villages, almost anything achieved with poultry (or livestock) can be considered pro-poor. The high cost of targeting the poor (to prevent leaks to the nonpoor) is often raised as an issue in the developing world and elsewhere. Focusing assistance and development programs on owners of livestock (including poultry) in Cambodia is a win-win proposition for poverty reduction and the protection of livelihoods.

Ultimate responsibility for the success or failure of policies must rest with Cambodian authorities, however; ownership of national development plans cannot be in the hands of donors. Effective responses and effective governance must go hand in hand. Poor governance and pervasive institutional failures have hindered disease mitigation responses in Cambodia. A rushed, emergency-oriented response to HPAI may indeed have undermined already weak governance capacity, fueling patronage networks and encouraging rent-seeking behaviors. Whether such funds have increased the ability of Cambodia—and the world—to prevent a future pandemic remains uncertain.

In chapter 4 I examined the "freedom of expression events" that occurred in 2005 and 2006. Civil society came together in some new and innovative coalitions and networks, and a few individuals took some strong, public, principled stands. Cambodians worked in new ways with the international community, and traditional networks were expanded. A number of lessons were learned during this process of advocating for the release of several human rights and civil society activists who had been imprisoned for expressing their views, and for allowing others to express theirs.

The first lesson learned was that acting together and trusting one another helped to produce one voice in civil society: "united we stand, divided we fall." Second, the need for a long-term strategy evaluated against what may be short-term "events-based" advocacy was made apparent. Third, there was a consensus that the law and justice can sometimes conflict and that international best practice and the Cambodian context need to be considered. Finally, better rapport with government both from an international and civil society perspective is needed—dialogue in which there is speaking *and* listening.

After all, the authorities used a law dating back to 1992, when the United Nations Transitional Authority in Cambodia was in the country, against defamation, applying criminal penalties to accuse these activists and, even more importantly, many more unnamed and powerless activists in the provinces. In that sense, well-intentioned foreign assistance undermined democracy, albeit thirteen years later.

What Should Policy Makers or Donors Be Doing Differently?

1. *Impose stronger consequences for corruption so that government is encouraged to tackle it.* In a simple cost-benefit model, punishments for corruption should become harsher, and the probability of detecting corruption should increase. When international financial institutions offer credible signals to member governments that aid will be taken away if corruption is uncovered, this will act as a deterrent.

2. *Recognize the importance of collective action to overcoming sectoral problems and find ways to encourage such action.* The lesson of collective action applies to garments,

livestock, and rice in Cambodia, as I elaborated upon in chapter 2. But, as I explored in chapter 3, it also applies to HPAI and other emerging infectious diseases, when collective action can literally mean the difference between life and death. And collective action in civil society to fight arrests of human rights and labor rights activists can produce results, especially when combined with international condemnation, as I discussed in chapter 4.

In business, collective action on the part of economic actors based outside of Cambodia has the potential to influence the government's human rights record. Hitting where it hurts—the pocketbook—is needed. This would require organizations such as Business for Social Responsibility (BSR)—which is based in San Francisco and represents marquee brands such as the Gap, Eddie Bauer, and Liz Claiborne—to cry foul not only when labor abuses take place but also in cases of human rights abuses, including arrests and murders of prominent labor and rights advocates. "We are quite concerned about what appears to be a pattern of violence against union leaders in the country. . . . It is of upmost importance to us as buyers that rule of law be swift, just and transparent. . . . This . . . ensures a stable business environment for us to continue to source our products," said a BSR letter dated April 25, 2007, addressed to Prime Minister Hun Sen and other senior government officials.

Donors can promote collective action by creating incentives through programs that require it. The cost of collective action must be decreased wherever possible. For example, a secretariat to fund the activities of a trade association concerned with corrupt practices undermining competitiveness could be significant, as was suggested by a major business leader in Cambodia. The same could be said not just of trade associations but of umbrella civil society organizations. Cambodia's lack of human resources means that the cost of talent in Cambodia can be significant. This is where donors have both helped and hurt, by bidding wages up and by providing incentives for such talent to join donor ranks. Yet this is also where donors might make a difference by providing the human resources to encourage collective action through the formation of sustainable local CSOs.

3. *Strengthen civil society as a counterweight to corruption.* The role of civil society is still limited and weak in Cambodia, as was made clear in chapter 4. Some new and innovative coalitions and networks have come together, and a few individuals have taken strong, public, principled stands. Cambodians have worked in new ways with the international community, and traditional networks have been expanded. But maintaining these successes depends on complementary international intervention. Together, domestic and international forces have managed to force the leadership's hand, especially when combined with buyer complaints cum threats. However, the strength of the garment sector is waning, and the buyers who once

commanded attention may not be so important when Korean banks and construction projects dot the skyline of Phnom Penh. The role of China in Cambodian affairs is enormous. This bodes ill for the protection of human rights in Cambodia. The diminishing and inconsistent aid to civil society organizations (CSOs) is an exacerbating factor; domestic civil society forces are all the more needed as China's influence increases and Western donors' decreases. But inadequate funding makes it difficult for CSOs to be effective. To illustrate this point, as of this writing the sensational Kony 2012 video about Joseph Kony and his Lord's Resistance Army in Africa has been viewed more than eighty-five million times on YouTube in twenty days. It implores viewers to make a difference. But as we have seen throughout this book, the path to disaster is indeed paved with good intentions. As Teju Cole has eloquently argued, "[T]here is much more to doing good work than 'making a difference.' There is the principle of first do no harm. There is the idea that those who are being helped ought to be consulted over the matters that concern them" (Cole 2012). A Hippocratic oath to development undergirded by a commitment to genuine participation would be a start.

Looking Forward

The case study approach taken in this book grew from analyzing a global data set that encompassed hundreds of countries and territories over many years that did not "select on" the dependent variable—fancy talk for bias in selecting cases to show a predetermined outcome. This protects the overall findings. Only case studies can explain the mechanisms by which specific outcomes are observed. Are more cases needed? Absolutely. Will they explain everything? Unlikely. Can generalizations be made as a result at this point? Probably not. But can existing research shed light on important political economy drivers? Certainly.

This study of the Cambodian case suggests quite strongly that thirty more years of aid will hurt Cambodia. The nation needs to fundamentally alter the relationship between its people and their government through taxation, which will bring accountability. As of now taxation is minimal, and foreign aid substitutes for missing taxes. Corruption makes up the difference between what Cambodia ought to collect and what it does in fact collect in terms of domestic revenues. If only for that difference, Cambodia could soon become a "normal country." The problem is that while Cambodia has shown remarkable growth over the past decade, it consistently ranks at or near the bottom in terms of corruption. Corruption costs Cambodia an estimated $300 million to $500 million per year. Corruption is far more burdensome—as a share of income—on the poor than on the rich, leading to increasing income inequality despite growth—a combustible combination. As a development expert once said, businessmen "only want rule of law when it suits them, when things have gone wrong for them." On the other hand, domestic revenues, driven primarily by tax revenues, matter as a credible commitment to nationally owned development. When revenues are too low (12 percent of gross domestic product, for example), the link between taxes and accountability is broken. Governments can ignore voters who don't pay taxes (except bribe taxes, which are unofficial). The real challenge is this: How can countries own their development when foreign aid disrupts this critical link? They can't. For accountable growth to take hold, foreign aid has to be tied to improved domestic and tax revenue performance. Until that happens, Cambodia's growth, while impressive, falls short. What Cambodia and other developing countries need is sustainable growth that, in John F. Kennedy's words, "lifts all boats."

The Roman poet Juvenal coined the phrase "bread and circuses" when he described Rome's situation nearly 2,000 years ago: "Already long ago, from when we sold our vote to no man, the People have abdicated our duties; for the People who once upon a time handed out military command, high civil office, legions—everything, now restrains itself and anxiously hopes for just two things: bread and circuses" (*Satire* 10.77–81). The first decade of the twenty-first century saw a remarkable transformation in Cambodia: GDP growth, higher property values, international investment, and development of educational institutions. People got their bread and circuses in the 2000s, but what of the next ten years and beyond? Under the Great Recession, Cambodia already faces hard times; the garment industry and tourism are hurting, and they have been the twin engines of Cambodia's recent economic transformation. Garments could be decimated if nothing is done. If sufficient governance is not achieved, the coming decades promise further challenges to Cambodia's economy and civil society.

When I think of what's next for Cambodia, I think of my mother's courage in escaping the Khmer Rouge in 1976, using the Vietnamese language as her passport. I think of her perseverance, taking her five children not just to Vietnam but to France in 1978 and then to America in 1985. What would she do? Now I am a father of two and, like all parents, I want a better future for my children. I understand what drove my mother. As I consider the hope that my children and their thirteen cousins represent, I remember the Cambodian proverb that my mom taught me when she was alive: *knowledge comes from learning; wealth comes from searching.*

APPENDIX

Table A.1 Chapter 1 elite survey respondent codes

Code	Years of experience	Category	Type	Employer
1-1	12	FX	M (7 yrs.) O (5 yrs.)	Membership organization for local and international NGOs
1-2	5	FX	M, A	INGO and LNGO
1-3	6	FX	M, A, teacher, researcher	Donor and LNGO
1-4	10	FX	M, A, research, advocacy	Donor, LNGO, and INGO (for several different employers)
1-5	11	FX	M	INGO
1-6	3.3	FX	M	Donor
1-7	7	FX	M, A	INGO
1-8	4	C	M	Donor
1-9	4	FX	A	Donor
1-10	6	FX	Donor official	Donor
1-11	4	FX	M, A	Donor and INGO
1-12	10	CX	M	Declined to state
1-13	7	CX	M	INGO and national institution
1-14	5	FX	M, A	Donor

Note: A, advisor; C, Cambodian only; CX, Cambodian expatriate; FX, foreign expatriate; INGO, international nongovernmental organization; LNGO, local nongovernmental organization; M, management.

Table A.2   Chapter 2 interview codes

Code	Descriptor
2-1	Member of parliament
2-2	Management of domestic conglomerate
2-3	Money changer
2-4	NGO representative
2-5	Garment factory owner
2-6	Ambassador
2-7	Garment factory owner
2-8	Entrepreneur and former secretary of state
2-9	Head of a government department
2-10	Banker
2-11	Rice miller
2-12	Rice buyer
2-13	Rice miller
2-14	Rice miller
2-15	Agricultural adviser
2-16	Adviser
2-17	Economic researcher
2-18	Banker
2-19	Embassy official
2-20	NGO rice expert
2-21	Livestock official
2-22	Livestock professional
2-23	Livestock NGO head
2-24	Private sector manager
2-25	Manager of international conglomerate
2-26	NGO livestock representative
2-27	Livestock NGO representative
2-28	Agricultural and livestock expert
2-29	Head of a government department
2-30	Agricultural advisor to minister
2-31	Veterinarian and livestock advisor
2-32	Livestock expert

Note: The titles listed in this table have been generalized to prevent identification of informants. For example, several informants were heads of trade associations, which would make their identities obvious. In addition, government officials do not have their ministries listed for the same reason.

Table A.3 Chapter 3 interview and elite survey respondent codes

Code	Descriptor
3-1	Government official
3-2	Donor staff
3-3	AI expert
3-4	IO veterinarian
3-5	AI expert
3-6	Farmer
3-7	Postconflict reconstruction expert
3-8	AI expert
3-9	NGO and IO doctor
3-10	Health expert
3-11	Donor staff and doctor
3-12	Donor staff
3-13	Veterinarian and consultant
3-14	Donor management
3-15	AI expert (e-mail)
3-16	AI expert
3-17	Vice president, agribusiness
3-18	Economist
3-19	Livestock expert
3-20	Donor staff
3-21	IO senior officer

Note: The titles listed in this table have been generalized to prevent identification of informants. For example, several informants were heads of trade associations, which would make their identities obvious. In addition, government officials do not have their ministries listed for the same reason. AI, avian influenza; IO, international organization; NGO, nongovernmental organization.

Table A.4   Chapter 4 interview codes

Code	Descriptor
4-1	International NGO staff
4-2	Human rights activist
4-3	International NGO staff
4-4	Youth NGO staff
4-5	Youth association head
4-6	Senior diplomat
4-7	International NGO head
4-8	Development partner
4-9	NGO advisor
4-10	Senior official, development partner
4-11	Human rights activist
4-12	Journalist
4-13	Senior diplomat
4-14	International NGO senior official
4-15	Human rights activist
4-16	NGO head
4-17	Journalist
4-18	Human rights activist
4-19	Labor association staff
4-20	NGO senior staff
4-21	Human rights activist
4-22	Labor leader
4-23	Union leader
4-24	Labor leader
4-25	Labor association head
4-26	International NGO head
4-27	Senior diplomat
4-28	Youth association senior staff
4-29	Youth association staff
4-30	Labor leader
4-31	Secretary of state
4-32	Human rights activist
4-33	RGC advisor
4-34	Senior diplomat
4-35	Development partner

Code	Descriptor
4-36	Advisor (based abroad)
4-37	Development partner
4-38	Diplomat
4-39	Senior diplomat
4-40	Entrepreneur
4-41	Attorney
4-42	Program manager
4-43	Senior diplomat
4-44	Researcher
4-45	Development partner
4-46	Development partner

Note: Development partners are donors who participate in the pledging session of the consultative group meetings; senior diplomats are ambassadors or deputy chiefs of mission; diplomats are third to first secretaries. NGO, nongovernmental organization.

NOTES

Introduction

1. The precise memo, bearing President Reagan's signature, was National Security Study Directive 2-84, "United States Policy in Southeast Asia [The Kampuchean Problem]," April 4, 1984.

2. http://www.un.org/en/peacekeeping/missions/past/untacbackgr2.html.

3. He also added, "They spent $2 billion, but when they left, the Cambodian factions were still fighting each others [sic]" (quoted in Everyday.com.kh 2008).

4. http://www.un.org/en/peacekeeping/missions/past/untacbackgr2.html.

5. According to Aschmoneit (1998:5), Achar (Abbot) Chun Chin of Wat Botum explained with some bitterness that in former times it had not been difficult to mobilize villagers to repair roads and ponds after the rainy season. But since the UN World Food Programme had been remunerating all community work with rice on a food-for-work basis, people had been asking the achar, "How much rice will you pay for that?" They were no longer willing to perform unpaid labor as before. Many achars have had similar experiences in their own villages.

6. My quixotically argued plea for this book's original title, along with a far more humdrum subtitle of "Aid Dependence and Democracy in Cambodia."

7. David Rieff (2002) argues in *A Bed for the Night* that the idea of an international community, with its mix of human rights abusers and defenders as one, is a sham.

1. Aid Dependence and Quality of Governance

1. These three reasons are inspired by and adapted from Knack (2004), which asked, "Does foreign aid promote democracy?"
2. I use "ODA" and "aid" interchangeably.
3. For an excellent survey of the macroeconomic effects of foreign aid, see Harms and Lutz (2004).
4. Donors might adjust their aid flows based on the quality of governance in the recipient country by either rewarding a well-performing country with additional aid or reducing aid in a poorly performing recipient country in order to encourage improvement.
5. In turn, Burnside and Dollar (1997) reference Boone (1994; 1996) for these instruments.
6. Regime theorists like Krasner define "regimes" as "principles, norms, rules, and decision-making procedures around which actors' expectations converge in a given issue area" (1982:135), and indeed many find terms like "political instability" overly broad, especially when compared to hegemonic stability theory—the idea that one hegemon or dominant state can make the international system more stable—which regime theorists like Kindleberger (1973), Keohane (1984), and Gilpin (1987) have developed.
7. The Khmer Rouge did print their own currency but never used it.
8. This was in essence the Council for Mutual Economic Assistance/Comecon.
9. This 1994 estimate was subsequently revised downward. The figure is used here to denote the severity of the situation with what was then the best available information.
10. Indeed, a perusal of the titles of World Bank reports published in the period 1994–1997 tells the story of transition: *From Rehabilitation to Reconstruction* (World Bank 1994); *Rehabilitation Program* (World Bank 1995); *From Recovery to Sustained Development* (World Bank 1996); and *Progress in Recovery and Reform* (World Bank 1997).
11. Four years after UNTAC, the so-called events of July 5 and 6, 1997, threw the economy into chaos, further highlighting the country's dependence on aid. The factional fighting saddled the economy with at least $100 million in damage. Foreign direct investment steeply declined in the aftermath of the events of July 1997 and has only in recent years recovered thanks to China, South Korea, and Vietnam. The January 29, 2003, anti-Thai riots, which resulted in the burning of the Thai Embassy along with the Royal Phnom Penh Hotel and other Thai business interests, were the main setback of the early postmillennium period, costing the country millions of dollars in damage. Foreign observers of the self-inflicted mayhem at the time were angered by some rioters' attitude that destroyed property would simply be rebuilt with other people's money.

12. http://www.dai.com/about/index.php.
13. http://www.worldvision.org.kh/whatwestandfor.aspx.
14. To compare apples to apples, the bank from 1993 to 1994 ascribed the original 39 percent national poverty rate to the accessible part of the country and derived a 28 percent poverty rate for the same area in 2004.
15. Unusable responses included four that did not contain any answers and one that did not meet the three-year criteria. (The informant reported 1.5 years' experience as a foreign expatriate advisor working for the RGC.) One informant declined to rate donor success numerically.
16. More than 200 e-mails were sent asking recipients to respond or to refer the author to individuals they might know who met the three-year criteria. Responses online were completely anonymous save for an optional question at the end of the survey requesting an e-mail address for follow-up.
17. This is akin to a snowball sample.
18. This includes references to RGC, "Parliament," and "National Institution."
19. Some informants indicated, for instance, that they worked for a national institution, the parliament, a university, and an international organization.
20. Informants described, among other professions, "political appointee" and "donor official," for example.
21. The governance indicators presented here aggregate the views on the quality of governance provided by a large number of enterprise, citizen, and expert survey respondents in industrial and developing countries. These data are gathered from a number of survey institutes, think tanks, nongovernmental organizations, and international organizations.
22. Whether there are differences in views among individuals who worked in management, as advisors, in education/research, or in some other capacity is difficult to determine because so many informants cross-listed themselves as functioning in one, two, or more capacities. The same is true across government, donors, and NGOs (whether local or international), where quite a few informants had worked for more than one type of organization over the years.
23. Others have argued that elections must come *before* the democratic process: "It is a common opinion that free and fair elections represent the culmination of the democratic process. However, for fledgling democracies and countries recovering from crisis, elections are not an end, but rather a beginning, a critical but nonetheless preliminary step in the transition to democratic governance. Realizing the promise of elections—and minimizing the risk of public disillusionment with the democratic process—requires investments in long-term democratic development, in particular the consolidation of governing institutions like parliaments" (UNDP n.d.).

24. Prior to 1996, when the "c-word" (*corruption*)—as it was known—was seen as off-limits and political, the bank's approach to corruption was ridiculed as the three-monkeys policy: see no evil, hear no evil, speak no evil (see BWP 2003).

2. Growth Without Development

1. This chapter draws on two visits to Cambodia in 2008 during which more than 50 formal interviews were conducted with government officials, donor and NGO representatives, the private sector, and civil society representatives. It brings together qualitative input from these informants. Naturally, there is no scientific basis to the sampling other than to seek relevant informants. Interviews took place without interpreters in the language in which the interviewee felt most comfortable (English, Khmer, or French). The work was carried out during May and June 2008. Information from informants used is coded numerically to protect identities, and a complete list is shown in the Works Cited.
2. This section is drawn from Pak (2008) with permission. The *Oknha* portion is based on an essay by Doung (2008).
3. The interest rate used in determining the present value of future cash flows.
4. As compared in World Bank and ADB (2003:ix).
5. This section is drawn from the contribution of Verena Fritz to the World Bank mission's scoping note, for which I was a team member.
6. The ILO monitoring system is currently being rolled out on a voluntary basis to several other countries: Vietnam, Jordan, and Lesotho.
7. See http://www.gmac-cambodia.org.
8. Cambodian Federation of Employers and Business Associations, http://www.camfeba.com.
9. http://www.gmac-cambodia.org.
10. See http://www.ftuwkc.org.
11. http://www.irri.org/science/ricestat/data/may2008/WRS2008-Table12-USDA.pdf.
12. http://www.gmac-cambodia.org.
13. http://www.fao.org/es/ESC/en/15/70/highlight_533.html.
14. I am particularly grateful to Don Jameson, a former U.S. foreign service officer in Cambodia and subsequent deputy chief of mission in Burma, for an e-mail exchange he and I had on precisely this topic on May 9, 2010.
15. http://stats.oecd.org/glossary/detail.asp?ID=6043.
16. The Fly America Act, 49 U.S.C. App. 1517, as implemented in the U.S. Comptroller General's guidelines, Decision B-138942, March 31, 1981, requires federal employees and their dependents, consultants, contractors, grantees, and others

performing U.S. government-financed foreign air travel to travel by U.S. flag air carriers. Some exceptions are allowed as a matter of necessity or unavailability.

17. Guimbert (2010:back cover).

3. An International Problem

1. The U.S. government is supporting the RGC's effort to reduce human exposure to HPAI through the technical expertise of USAID, the U.S. Centers for Disease Control and Prevention, the U.S. Department of Agriculture, and the U.S. Naval Medical Research Unit No. 2.

2. Like the previous chapter, this chapter relies upon more than forty semistructured interviews with government officials, donor and NGO representatives, the private sector (including conglomerates, farmers, and wet market stallholders), and civil society representatives. These interviews were conducted in Khmer, French, and English over the course of three visits to Cambodia, primarily in Phnom Penh and the environs, but with one site visit to the province of Kampong Som. A visit to Psah Orussey's wet market in Phnom Penh was also made to gain an appreciation for conditions on the ground. Interviews lasted anywhere from forty-five minutes to two hours. The first was a preliminary visit in February 2008 (one week), the second was in May 2008 (two weeks), and the third was in June 2008 (one week).

3. This was needed because five departments (the Department of Communication and Relations, the Department of Emergency Preparedness and Training, the Department of Emergency Response and Rehabilitation, the Department of Search and Rescue, and the Department of Administration and Finance) across several ministries have official roles and responsibilities. See UNSIC (n.d.).

4. Not identified to protect informant.

5. Statistics found in this section are from Ear (2009b).

6. The e-mail asked recipients to respond or to refer the author to individuals who worked on HPAI in Cambodia. Responses online were completely anonymous save for an optional question at the end of the survey requesting an e-mail address if follow-up was desired.

7. The online portion of the survey was open for respondents for a period of ten days. Of these, forty-four visited the survey Web site, and seventeen completed responses were received. The survey contained fourteen questions, requesting that respondents rate the effectiveness of government and donors, respectively, on a Likert scale, as well as provide written responses where appropriate.

8. Of the respondents, 59 percent (10) had one to three years' experience, 24 percent (4) had four to six months' experience, and 18 percent (3) had less than three

months' experience working on HPAI in Cambodia. The area in which these individuals worked on HPAI ranged widely, because cross-listing was permitted: human health (24 percent), animal health (16 percent), disaster management (24 percent), livelihoods (4 percent), wildlife (8 percent), and other (24 percent). This other category included six written responses: risk reduction and capacity building at the village level (animal and human health); combining animal health and livelihoods impacts; UN agency; communication for transmission risk reduction; communication; and AHI coordination incorporating all of the above. Respondents worked in a wide variety of areas related to HPAI control activities, including wildlife. Overwhelmingly, respondents were "Donor Agency or Foreign Government (Bilat/Multi/UN, etc.)" (65 percent), to a much lesser extent the international NGO community (24 percent), For-Profit Private Corporation (6 percent), and "Other, Please specify" (12 percent). The survey focused on perceptions of effectiveness of the HPAI response.

4. Shallow Democracy

1. This chapter draws on qualitative input from seventy-three informants in NGOs, labor unions, youth associations, the media, government, the international community, and the private sector. Of these, forty-two were of Cambodian origin. There is no scientific basis to the sampling other than that these individuals had some involvement or stake in the events. The interviews took place without interpreters in the language in which the interviewee felt most comfortable (English, Khmer, or French). They were guided by open-ended questions and allowed for a wide range of free-flowing responses. Interviews lasted approximately one hour, although some were considerably longer. A significant number of in-person interviews were completed, while written input was also solicited and received from informants based outside Cambodia or unable to meet in person.

2. This timeline is based on CCHR (2006).

3. The group included labor and human rights activists. Almost all of the members are believed to have been interviewed for this chapter; however, only a handful actually referred to the group (presumably the four or five core group members).

4. The description of the event is adapted from Licadho (2006b).

5. One union leader reported 30 in attendance, while a foreign participant reported 130 (4-22, 4-8).

6. The stories were "Free Speech Gains Voice in Cambodia's Villages" (*International Herald Tribune*) and "Haunted by Past Horrors, Cambodians Speak Out" (*New York Times*), respectively.

7. CHRAC also met with ambassadors, as did the Alliance for Freedom of Expression in Cambodia and other groups, but no precise details are available.

8. A human rights activist (4-11) maintains that the three-year stipulation is inaccurate and that it should in fact be six months (the maximum detention period). Of course, respect for this would mean that countless individuals currently in indefinite detention should have been freed long ago (indeed, many years ago).

9. According to Berthiaume (2005), a meeting with the prime minister was reportedly canceled because the latter was ill.

10. For example, one foreigner wanted to publicize jailed human rights activist Kem Sokha's particular cell conditions. The latter happened to be sharing his cell with a notorious sex trafficker who had somehow bribed the guards to let him have a television. The presence of a television made the cell decent in these foreigners' view.

11. The chairman of the International Business Club, which includes a number of the most important foreign investors, published a letter entitled "Free speech not for the irresponsible" in the *Phnom Penh Post* (January 13–26, 2006). Signed only with his name, the letter read in part: "The protection of free speech when that speech is irresponsibly exercised has the potential to unleash passions and prejudices held by many people. Twice in recent years, in 1998 and 2003, demagogues have incited violence and death through the abuse of free speech." He added, "This possibility worries potential investors far more than the employment of laws which are an unfortunate residue of the UNTAC era" (Sciaroni 2006).

12. This account differs from the count given by a labor participant (4-22) and in Licadho (2006b).

WORKS CITED

ActionAid. 2005. *Real Aid: An Agenda for Making Aid Work*. ActionAid International. http://www.actionaid.org.uk/doc_lib/69_1_real_aid.pdf (accessed June 7, 2012)

ADB. 2005. "Overview of Civil Society: Cambodia." Civil Society Briefs, July. Manila: Asian Development Bank.

Adams, B., S. Belhassen, A. Callamard, B. Edman, E. Eguren, D. Kramer, M. Lawlor, E. Sottas, S. Taylor, and G. Venkiteswaran. 2011. "Re: New Law Threatening the Operation of NGOs and Associations in Cambodia" Joint Open Letter, August 23. Signed by Brad Adams, Asia Director, Human Rights Watch; Souhayr Belhassen, President, International Federation for Human Rights (FIDH); Agnes Callamard, Executive Director, ARTICLE 19; Brittis Edman, Program Director, Southeast Asia, Civil Rights Defenders; Enrique Eguren, Program Director, Protection International; David J. Kramer, President, Freedom House; Mary Lawlor, Director, Front Line Defenders; Eric Sottas, Secretary General, World Organization Against Torture (OMCT); Simon Taylor, Founding Director, Global Witness; Gayathry Venkiteswaran, Executive Director, Southeast Asian Press Alliance (SEAPA). http://www.hrw.org/news/2011/09/12/cambodia-letter-undp-regarding-new-draft-ngo-law (accessed June 7, 2012)

AED. 2007. "'SuperHero' Chicken Emerges in Fight Against Avian Influenza." Press Release, Academy for Educational Development, January 10. http://www.prnewswire.

com/news-releases/superhero-chicken-emerges-in-fight-against-avian-influenza-53390147.html (accessed June 7, 2012).

AFP. 2004. "Outbreak of Bird Flu Confirmed in Chickens in Cambodia: FAO." Agence France Presse, January 23.

AHRM. 2006. "International Community Calls for Kem Sokha's Release." Working Group for an ASEAN Human Rights Mechanism, January 1.

AKP. 2008. "Guinea to Import Rice from Cambodia." Phnom Penh: Agence Khmer de Presse, July 3.

Albritton, R. B. 2004. "Cambodia in 2003: On the Road to Democratic Consolidation," *Asian Survey* 44(1):102–109.

Amnesty International. 1997. "Cambodia: Escaping the Killing Fields?" ASA 23/038/1997, News Service 178/97, October 23. http://www.amnesty.org/en/library/asset/ASA23/038/1997/en/c6bef862-e981-11dd-8224-a709898295f2/asa230381997en.html (accessed June 7, 2012)

AP. 2005a. "Cambodian Man Confirmed to Have Died from Severe Strain of Bird Flu, Deputy Minister Says." Associated Press, March 25.

AP. 2005b. "Cambodia Says It Will Repay Aid Funds." Associated Press, January 19.

AP. 2006a. "Cambodia Gives Garment Cos. Tax Holiday." Associated Press, June 16.

AP. 2006b. "Cambodians Need Incentives to Report Sick Birds." Associated Press, April 10.

AP. 2006c. "Cambodia Promised US$601 Million in International Aid." Associated Press, March 4.

Aristide, J.-B. 2000. *Eyes of the Heart: Seeking a Path for the Poor in the Age of Globalization.* Monroe, ME: Common Courage Press.

Arulpragasam, J., F. Goletti, T. M. Atinc, and V. Songwe. 2004. "Trade in Sectors Important to the Poor: Rice in Cambodia and Vietnam and Cashmere in Mongolia." In *East Asia Integrates: A Trade Policy Agenda for Shared Growth*, eds. K. Krumm and H. Kharas. Washington, DC: World Bank; Oxford: Oxford University Press.

Aschmoneit, W. 1998. "Traditional Self-Help Associations in Cambodia. How to Identify and Cooperate with Them." Poverty Reduction Project, GTZ.

AusAID. 2004. "Options for an Australian-Cambodian Agricultural Market Oriented Program." Volume 2, Detailed Options Description. Phnom Penh, October 29.

Bennett, S. and J. Gale. 2008. "'Flu Fatigue' Poses Public Health Threat, WHO Says." Bloomberg, September 15. http://www.bloomberg.com/apps/news?pid=20601124&sid=atooOdQTLVEo&refer=home (accessed June 7, 2012)

Beresford, M. 2004. "Cambodia in 2004: An Artificial Democratization Process." *Asian Survey* 45(1):134–139.

Bernama. 2007. "Australia Commits Funds for Bird Flu-Related Projects." Bernama Malaysian National News Agency, August 1.

Berthiaume, L. 2005. "New UN Envoy Calls for Gov't Critics' Release." *The Cambodia Daily*, December 6.

Berthiaume, L. and C. T. Prak. 2006. "Arrests Could Hurt Economy." *The Cambodia Daily*, January 3.

Better Factories. 2008. "Twentieth Synthesis Report on Working Conditions in Cambodia's Garment Sector." April 30. http://www.betterfactories.org/content/documents/1/20th%20Synthesis%20Report%20Final%20(EN).pdf (accessed June 7, 2012)

Better Factories. 2012. "Twenty-Seventh Synthesis Report on Working Conditions in Cambodia's Garment Sector." January 30. http://www.betterfactories.org/content/documents/1/Synthesis%20Report%2027th%20(En).pdf (accessed June 7, 2012)

BIC. 2010. "World Bank Investigates Cambodian Land Titling Project." June 3. http://www.bicusa.org/en/Article.11897.aspx (accessed June 7, 2012)

Boone, P. 1994. "The Impact of Foreign Aid on Saving and Growth." London School of Economics, mimeo.

Boone, P. 1996. "Politics and the Effectiveness of Foreign Aid." *European Economic Review* 402:289–329.

Bräutigam, D. and K. Botchwey. 1999. "The Institutional Impact of Aid Dependence on Recipients in Africa." Working Paper WP1999:1. Bergen: Chr. Michelsen Institute.

Burgos, S. and Ear, S. 2010. "China's Strategic Interests in Cambodia: Interests and Resources." *Asian Survey* 3(50) (May–June):615–639.

Burgos, S. and S. Ear. 2011. "China's Natural Resource Appetite in Brazil." *Asian Journal of Latin American Studies* 24(2):69–89.

Burgos, S. and S. Ear. 2012a. "The Geopolitics of China's Global Resource Quest." *Geopolitics* 17(1):47–79.

Burgos, S. and S. Ear. 2012b. "China's Oil Hunger in Angola." *Journal of Contemporary China* 21(74):1-17.

Burnside, C. and D. Dollar. 1997. "Aid, Policies, and Growth." Policy Research Working Paper 1777. Washington, DC: World Bank. http://documents.worldbank.org/curated/en/1997/06/438824/aid-policies-growth (accessed June 7, 2012)

Burnside, C. and D. Dollar. 2000. "Aid, Policies, and Growth." *American Economic Review* 90(4) (September):847–868.

BWP. 2003. "Inside the Institutions: How the World Bank Deals with Fraud and Corruption in Its Projects." Bretton Woods Project, July 21.

Calavan, M., S. Briquets, and J. O'Brien. 2004. "Cambodia Corruption Assessment." Prepared for USAID Cambodia by United States Agency for International Development and Casals & Associates, August 19.

Carothers, T. 2009. "Democracy Assistance: Political vs. Developmental?" *Journal of Democracy* 20(1):5–19.

CCHR. 2006. "Arrest of CCHR President Mr. Kem Sokha and CLEC Director Mr. Yeng Virak." Fact Sheet, Cambodian Center for Human Rights, January 2.

CEDAC. 2007. "Gender and Socio-Economic Impacts of HPAI and Its Control on Rural Livelihood and Bio-Security of Smallholder Poultry Producers and Poultry Value Chain in Cambodia." *Executive Summary*, Centre d'Etude et de Développement Agricole Cambodgien, Phnom Penh: CEDAC.

Cereno, T. 2008. "An Update on the Training Programme for Village Animal Health Workers and Village Chiefs." Building Capacity at the Grassroots Level to Control Avian Influenza, GCP/CMB/027/GER, Food and Agriculture Organization, March.

Chandler, D. 1991. *The Tragedy of Cambodian History: Politics, War and Revolution since 1945*. New Haven, CT: Yale University Press.

Cheang, S. 2006. "Cambodia Releases Four Government Critics." Associated Press, January 17.

Chun, S. and K. May. 2010. "PM Scraps Rice-Export Licences to Boost Trade." *Phnom Penh Post*, April 28.

Cochrane, L. 2005. "Rice Fraud Deal Struck." *Phnom Penh Post*, 14/08, April 22–May 5.

Cole, T. 2012. "The White Savior Industrial Complex." *The Atlantic*, March 21. http://www.theatlantic.com/international/archive/2012/03/the-white-savior-industrial-complex/254843/ (accessed June 7, 2012).

Collier, P. 2007. *The Bottom Billion*. Oxford, UK: Oxford University Press.

Collier, P. 2009. *Wars, Guns, and Votes*. New York: HarperCollins.

Collier, P. and D. Dollar. 2004. "Development Effectiveness: What Have We Learnt?" *Economic Journal* 114(96):F244–71.

Coren, M. 2003. "Riot Bill Grows as Government Hunts for Cash." *Phnom Penh Post*, January 31–February 14.

DAI. 2008. "Cambodia SME Development in Selected Agri-Sectors/ Value Chains: Final Scoping and Design Report." Development Alternatives Inc.

Dietz, R. D. 2002. "The Estimation of Neighbourhood Effects in the Social Sciences: An Interdisciplinary Approach." *Social Science Research* 31(4):539–575.

Doyle, K. 2003. "Developing Democracy." *The Cambodia Daily* 277, June 14–15. http://www.camnet.com.kh/cambodia.daily/selected_features/un_story.htm (accessed June 7, 2012)

Doyle, M. and N. Sambanis. 2006. *Making War and Building Peace: United Nations Peace Operations*. Princeton, NJ: Princeton University Press.

DPA. 2002. "Despite Criticism of Reform, Cambodian Donors Pledge Record Windfall." Deutsche Presse-Agentur, July 21.

DPA. 2008. "Cattle Rustling May Cripple Cambodian Rice Harvest Say Farmers." Deutsche-Presse-Agentur, June 20.

Duong, S. 2008. "Le prix à payer pour entrer dans la caste des oknhas." Ka-Set.info, April 14. http://ka-set.info/actualites/pouvoirs/cambodge-information-oknha-business-politique-080414.html (accessed June 7, 2012)

Dy, C. 2008. "Bridging the Gap Between Awareness and Practice: Participatory Learning of Rural Beliefs and Practices on HPAI Prevention and Response in Cambodia." May 19 e-mail sent to the Communication Initiative and placed on the Communication Initiative site June 3. http://www.comminit.com/en/node/270744/36 (accessed June 7, 2012)

Ear, S. 2002. "Cambodia and the U.N." *The New York Times*, Letter to the Editor, February 21. http://www.nytimes.com/2002/02/21/opinion/l-cambodia-and-the-un-728799.html (accessed June 7, 2012)

Ear, S. 2005. "Governance and Economic Performance: Credibility, Political Will, and Reform." *Cambodian Economic Review* 1(1) (May):17–52. http://www.csua.berkeley.edu/~sophal/ear_cer.pdf (accessed June 7, 2012)

Ear, S. 2007a. "Does Aid Dependence Worsen Governance?" *International Public Management Journal* 10(3):259–286.

Ear, S. 2007b. "The Political Economy of Aid and Governance in Cambodia." *Asian Journal of Political Science* 15(1):68–96.

Ear, S. 2009a. "Cambodian 'Justice'." *The Wall Street Journal* (Asia ed.), Op-Ed, September 1. http://online.wsj.com/article/SB10001424052970203946904574301583107436174.html (accessed June 7, 2012)

Ear, S. 2009b. *Cambodia's Victim Zero: Global and National Responses to Highly Pathogenic Avian Influenza*, STEPS Working Paper 16, Brighton: STEPS Centre.

Ear, S. 2010. "Khmer Rouge Tribunal vs. Karmic Justice." *International Herald Tribune* (Global ed. of *The New York Times*), Op-Ed, March 17. http://www.nytimes.com/2010/03/18/opinion/18iht-edear.html (accessed June 7, 2012)

Ear, S. 2011a. "Avian Influenza: The Political Economy of Disease Control in Cambodia." *Politics and the Life Sciences*, 30(2):2–19.

Ear, S. 2011b. "The Political Economy of Highly Pathogenic Avian Influenza in Cambodia." *International Journal of Poultry Science* 10(1):71–75.

Ear, S. and S. Burgos. 2009. "Livelihoods and Highly Pathogenic Avian Influenza in Cambodia." *World's Poultry Science Journal* 65(4):633–640.

EIC. 2007. *Addressing the Impact of the Agreement on Textile and Clothing Expiration on Cambodia*. Economic Institute of Cambodia, June.

Ek, C. and H. Sok. 2008. "Aid Effectiveness in Cambodia." Wolfensohn Center for Development Working Paper 7, December, Washington, DC: Brookings Institute. http://www.brookings.edu/~/media/Files/rc/papers/2008/12_cambodia_aid_chanboreth/12_cambodia_aid_chanboreth.pdf (accessed June 7, 2012)

Ek, M. 2006. "Cambodian Ostracised for Reporting Bird Flu." Reuters, Wednesday, April 12. http://newsgroups.derkeiler.com/Archive/Soc/soc.culture.cambodia/2006-04/msg00087.html (accessed June 7, 2012)

Embassy of Cambodia. n.d. "Policies Towards FDI." Royal Embassy of Cambodia in New Zealand. http://www.embassyofcambodia.org.nz/investment.htm (accessed June 7, 2012)

FAO. 2007a. "Cambodia: FAO to Focus on Training in HPAI Surveillance." News & Features Archive, Food and Agriculture Organization of the United Nations, October 22. http://www.fao.org/avianflu/news/cambodia.htm (accessed June 7, 2012)

FAO. 2007b. "Evaluation of FAO Activities in Cambodia (2002–2007)." Final Report, Food and Agriculture Organization of the United Nations, Rome, December. http://typo3.fao.org/fileadmin/user_upload/oed/docs/Cambodia_FAO_Cooperation_2007_ER.pdf (accessed June 7, 2012)

FAO and WHO. 2005. "Update on the Avian Influenza Situation." *Bulletin on Avian Influenza in Cambodia*, 10, Food and Agriculture Organization and World Health Organization.

Feyzioglu, T., S. Vinaya, and M. Zhu. 1998. "A Panel Data Analysis of the Fungibility of Foreign Aid." *World Bank Economic Review* 121:29–58.

Frings, V. 1993. "The Failure of Agricultural Collectivization in the People's Republic of Kampuchea, 1979–1980." Working Paper no. 80, Center of Southeast Asian Studies. Clayton, Aus.: Monash University.

FRONTLINE. 2006. "The Age of Aids." Interview with Richard Holbrooke, FRONTLINE TV documentary. http://www.pbs.org/wgbh/pages/frontline/aids/interviews/holbrooke.html (accessed June 7, 2012)

Gibson, D. 1993. "Cambodian Reconstruction Still a Long Way Off." *Kyodo News*, March 31.

Gilpin, R. 1987. *The Political Economy of International Relations*. Princeton, NJ: Princeton University Press.

GMAC. 2010. "Garment Manufacturers Association in Cambodia Bulletin." http://www.gmac-cambodia.org/bulletin/2010.pdf (accessed June 7, 2012)

GMAC. n.d. "A member of GMAC: P.P.S Ltd. (Cambodia)." Garment Manufacturers Association of Cambodia Web page. http://www.gmac-cambodia.org/memberpop.asp?memberID=24 (accessed May 12, 2010)

Godfrey, M. 2003. "Youth Employment Policy in Developing and Transition Countries: Prevention as Well as Cure." Social Protection Discussion Paper Series no. 0320. Social Protection Unit, Human Development Network, World Bank. Washington, DC: World Bank, October. http://siteresources.worldbank.org/SOCIALPROTECTION/Resources/SP-Discussion-papers/Labor-Market-DP/0320.pdf (accessed June 7, 2012)

Godfrey, M., S. Chan, T. Kato, P. V. Long, D. Pon, S. Tep, S. Tia, and S. So. 2000. "Technical Assistance and Capacity Development in an Aid-Dependent Economy: The Experience of Cambodia." Working Paper 15. Phnom Penh: Cambodia Development Resource Institute, August.

Goldsmith, A. 2001. "Foreign Aid and Statehood in Africa." *International Organisation* 55(1):123–128.

Golub, S. 2003. "Beyond Rule of Law Orthodoxy: The Legal Empowerment Alternative." Rule of Law Series, Democracy and Rule of Law Project no. 41, Carnegie Endowment for International Peace, October. http://www.carnegieendowment. org/files/wp41.pdf (accessed June 7, 2012)

GPSF-ABAP. 2004. "The Issues and Recommendations." Draft survey report, August 1. Phnom Penh: Government–Private Sector Forum Agro Business and Agro Processing Working Group.

Guimbert, S. 2010. "Cambodia 1998–2008: An Episode of Rapid Growth." Policy Research Working Paper 5271, The World Bank, East Asia and Pacific Region, Poverty Reduction and Economic Management Department, April. http://www-wds.worldbank.org/external/default/WDSContentServer/WDSP/IB/2010/04/14/000158349_20100414084009/Rendered/PDF/WPS5271.pdf (accessed June 7, 2012)

Hall, J. A. 2000. Human Rights and the Garment Industry in Contemporary Cambodia. *Stanford Journal of International Law* 36:119.

Hammergren, L. 1998. "Political Will, Constituency Building, and Public Support in Rule of Law Programs." Working Paper PN-ACD-023, Center for Democracy and Governance, Bureau for Global Programs, Field Support, and Research, U.S. Agency for International Development, August. http://siteresources.worldbank. org/INTLAWJUSTINST/Resources/PoliticalWill.pdf (accessed June 7, 2012)

Hansen, H. and F. Tarp. 2000. "Aid Effectiveness Disputed." *Journal of International Development* 12:375–398.

Harms, P. and M. Lutz. 2004. "The Macroeconomic Effects of Foreign Aid: A Survey." Discussion Paper no. 2004-11, Department of Economics, University of St. Gallen. http://www.vwa.unisg.ch/RePEc/usg/dp2004/dp11_har.pdf (accessed June 7, 2012)

Headey, D. 2005. "Foreign Aid and Foreign Policy: How Donors Undermine the Effectiveness of Overseas Development Assistance." Working Paper Series no. 05/2005, Centre for Efficiency and Productivity Analysis, School of Economics, University of Queensland. http://www.uq.edu.au/economics/cepa/docs/WP/WP052005.pdf (accessed June 7, 2012)

Heckelman, J. and S. Knack. 2005. "Foreign Aid and Market-Liberalizing Reform." World Bank Policy Research Working Paper 3557. Washington, DC: World Bank. http://www.wds.worldbank.org/external/default/WDSContentServer/IW3P/IB/2005/04/11/000012009_20050411132948/Rendered/PDF/wps3557.pdf (accessed June 7, 2012)

Heritage Foundation. 2005. "Index of Economic Freedom: Cambodia." Washington, DC: Heritage Foundation.

Hickler, B. 2007. "Bridging the Gap Between HPAI 'Awareness' and Practice in Cambodia: Recommendations from an Anthropological Participatory Assessment." Mission from July 24 to August 31, 2007–Cambodia, Emergency Centre for Transboundary Animal Diseases (ECTAD), FAO Regional Office for Asia and the Pacific.

Hing, T. 2002. "Foreign Direct Investment: Opportunities and Challenges for Cambodia, Laos and Vietnam." Cambodia Country Report. Hanoi, August 16–17. http://www.imf.org/external/pubs/ft/seminar/2002/fdi/eng/pdf/thoraxy.pdf (accessed June 7, 2012)

Hirschman, A. 1970. *Exit, Voice, and Loyalty: Responses to Decline in Firms, Organizations, and States*. Cambridge, MA: Harvard University Press.

Hookway, J. 2005. "In Rural Cambodia, Dreaded Avian Influenza Finds a Weak Spot." *Wall Street Journal*, Saturday, March 5.

Hughes, C. 2001. "Transforming Oppositions in Cambodia." *Global Society* 15(3) (July):295–318.

Hughes, C. 2003. *The Political Economy of Cambodia's Transition, 1991–2001*. London: RoutledgeCurzon.

Hughes, C. 2005. "Candidate Debates and Equity News: International Support for Democratic Deliberation in Cambodia." *Pacific Affairs* 78(1):77–93.

Hughes, C. 2006. "The Politics of Gifts: Tradition and Regimentation in Contemporary Cambodia." *Journal of Southeast Asian Studies* 37:469–489.

Hunt, L. 2004. "Cattle Rustlers Herd up the Price of Meat." *Phnom Penh Post* 13/15, July 16–29.

Ieng, V. S. n.d. "Biography of Mr. Van Sou Ieng." Given to the author by World Bank Cambodia office via e-mail, November 9, 2008.

Ifft, J. 2005. "Survey of the East Asia Livestock Sector, Rural Development and Natural Resources Sector Unit of the East Asia and Pacific Region of the World Bank." Working Paper, September.

IMF. 2004. "Cambodia: 2004 Article IV Consultation." Country Report no. 04/328, October 22. Washington, DC: International Monetary Fund. http://www.imf.org/external/pubs/ft/scr/2004/cr04328.pdf (accessed June 7, 2012)

The Independent. 1994. "Profile: Bureaucrat at Large in the Balkans: Yasushi Akashi, Almost Painfully Diplomatic UN Envoy." *The Independent* (UK), April 30. http://www.independent.co.uk/opinion/profile-bureaucrat-at-large-in-the-balkans-yasushi-akashi-almost-painfully-diplomatic-un-envoy-1373287.htm (accessed June 7, 2012)

Japan Times. 2006. "Preventing a Flu Pandemic." January 26.

JEN. 2004a. "Asian Gov'ts Agree to Bird Flu Surveillance Network." *Japan Economic Newswire*, January 28.

JEN. 2004b. "Cambodia Culls Chickens to Prevent Bird Flu." *Japan Economic Newswire*, January 26.

JEN. 2005a. "Cambodia Bans Import of Live Birds, Poultry Eggs from Neighbours." *Japan Economic Newswire*, February 10.

JEN. 2005b. "Japan Donates Motorbikes, Cash to Fight Bird Flu in Cambodia." *Japan Economic Newswire*, March 31.

Jonas, O. 2008. "Update on Coordinated International Assistance." Olga Jonas, Avian and Human Influenza Global Program Coordinator, The World Bank, Sixth International Ministerial Conference on Avian and Pandemic Influenza, Sharm El-Sheikh, October 24–26.

Juvenal. 1992. *The Satires*. Trans. Niall Rudd. Oxford: Oxford University Press.

Kao, K. H. 2000. "Cambodian Civil Society: Challenges and Prospects." Remarks, December 14. http://www.asiasociety.org/countries-history/conflicts/cambodian-civil-society-challenges-and-prospects?page=0%2C3 (accessed June 7, 2012)

Kate, D. T. 2004. "Donor Aid Consumed in Mountain of Reports." *The Cambodia Daily*, August 19.

Kaufmann, D., A. Kraay, and M. Mastruzzi. 2005. "Governance Matters IV: Governance Indicators for 1996–2004." June. http://info.worldbank.org/governance/wgi/pdf/govmatters4.pdf (accessed June 7, 2012)

Kaufmann, D., A. Kraay, and P. Zoido-Lobatón. 1999. "Governance Matters." *Policy Research Working Paper* no. 2196. Washington, DC: World Bank. http://papers.ssrn.com/sol3/cf_dev/AbsByAuth.cfm?per_id=163813 (accessed June 7, 2012)

Kaufmann, D., A. Kraay, and M. Mastruzzi. 2006. "Governance Matters V: Governance Indicators for 1996–2005." Washington, DC: World Bank, September 15. http://www.govindicators.org (accessed June 7, 2012)

Kaufmann, D., A. Kraay, and M. Mastruzzi. 2009. "Governance Matters VIII: Aggregate and Individual Governance Indicators, 1996–2008." World Bank Policy Research Working Paper No. 4978, June 29. http://ssrn.com/abstract=1424591 (accessed June 7, 2012)

Keohane, R. 1984. *After Hegemony: Cooperation and Discord in the World Political Economy*. Princeton, NJ: Princeton University Press.

Kenjiro, Y. 2005. "Why Illness Causes More Serious Economic Damage Than Crop Failure in Rural Cambodia." *Development and Change* 36(4):759–783.

Kerbo, H. 2011. *The Persistence of Cambodian Poverty*. Jefferson, NC: McFarland.

Khan, M. 2006. "The State and Economic Development: What Role, What Risks?" An ODI Poverty and Public Policy Group Event, November 22. http://www.odi.org.uk/events/states_nov06/ODI%20State%20and%20Development.pdf http://www.odi.org.uk/events/presentations/135.pdf (accessed June 7, 2012)

Khoun, L. 2008. "Child Dengue Deaths Down but Mortality Rate up in 2008." *The Mekong Times*, June 25. http://ki-media.blogspot.com/2008/06/child-dengue-deaths-down-but-mortality.html (accessed January 27, 2009)

Kindleberger, C. 1973. *The World in Depression: 1929–1939*. Berkeley: University of California Press.

Knack, S. 2001. "Aid Dependence and the Quality of Governance: Cross-Country Empirical Tests." *Southern Economic Journal* 68(2):310–329.

Knack, S. 2004. "Does Foreign Aid Promote Democracy?" *International Studies Quarterly* 48(1):251–266.

Koma, Y. S. 2008. "Proposed Strategies to Utilize the Potential of Rice Production in Cambodia." CEDAC Agriculture and Rural Development Discussion Note, June. http:// ciifad.cornell.edu/sri/countries/cambodia/camARDricedisco608.pdf (accessed June 7, 2012)

Krasner, S. D. 1982. "Structural Causes and Regime Consequences: Regimes as Intervening Variables." *International Organization* 36(2):185–205.

Kyodo News. 2001. "Akashi Says U.N. Unfairly Blamed for Spread of AIDS in Cambodia." *Kyodo News*, July 11.

Lambourne, W. 2009. "Transitional Justice and Peacebuilding after Mass Violence." *International Journal of Transitional Justice* 3(1):28–48.

Land, A. and P. Morgan. 2008. "Technical Cooperation for Capacity Development in Cambodia: Making the System Work Better." Final Report, January, Cambodian Rehabilitation and Development Board of the Council for the Development of Cambodia (CRDB/CDC). http://www.cdc-crdb.gov.kh/cdc/aid_management/TC%20Cambodia%20report%20FINAL%20(Jan%202008).pdf (accessed June 7, 2012)

Larson, C. 2009. *As We Forgive: Stories of Reconciliation from Rwanda*. Grand Rapids, MI: Zondervan.

Leopard Cambodia Fund. 2009. "In the News." *Leopard Cambodia Fund Monthly Newsletter* 9, January.

LeVine, V. 1989. "Supportive Values of the Culture of Corruption in Ghana." In *Political Corruption: A Handbook*, eds. A. Heidenheimmer, M. Johnston, and V. LeVine. New Brunswick, NJ: Transaction Publishers.

Lewis, M. 2011. *The Big Short: Inside the Doomsday Machine*. New York: W. W. Norton & Company.

Licadho. 2006a. "Cambodia: Attacks on Freedom of Expression & Political Rights." Briefing Paper, Cambodian League for the Promotion and Defense of Human Rights, January.

Licadho. 2006b. "Civil Society Members Show Support for Detainees." Cambodian League for the Promotion and Defense of Human Rights, January 16.

Lizée, P. P. 2002. "Human Security in Vietnam, Laos, and Cambodia." *Contemporary Southeast Asia: A Journal of International and Strategic Affairs* 24(3):509–527.

Ly, S., M. Van Kerkhove, D. Holl, Y. Froehlich, and S. Vong. 2007. "Dispatches: Interaction Between Humans and Poultry, Rural Cambodia." *Emerging Infectious Diseases* 13(1):130–132. http://www.cdc.gov/ncidod/EID/13/1/130.htm (accessed June 7, 2012).

MacLean, L. 2006. *National Integrity Systems: Transparency International Country Study Report of Cambodia 2006.* Berlin: Transparency International.

Maguire, P. 2005. *Facing Death in Cambodia.* New York: Columbia University Press.

May, K. 2010. "Garment Industry Remains Wary Despite Export Growth." *Phnom Penh Post*, May 10.

May, T. 2008. "Illegal Cattle Exports to Vietnam on the Rise, Border Villagers Say." *Phnom Penh Post Online*, August 26.

MC&D. 2005. "Press Summary." Media Consulting & Development Co Ltd., December 1.

McCargo, D. 2005. "Cambodia: Getting Away with Authoritarianism?" *Journal of Democracy* 16(4):98–112.

McKenny, L. 2005. "WFP-Government Rice Fraud Talks Yield Nothing." *Phnom Penh Post* 14/02, January 28–February 10.

Miesel, N. and J. Ould Aoudia. 2008. "Is 'Good Governance' a Good Development Strategy?" Working Paper 58, Agence Française de Developpement, January.

Minder, R. 2008. "Cambodia Holds Land Deal Talks." *Financial Times*, November 20.

MLG and DFDL. 1999. "Mekong Law Report: Cambodia Investment Guide." Mekong Law Group and Dirksen Flipse Doran and Le, Phnom Penh.

MoC. 2008. "Estimated Cambodian Export Data Under GSP/MFN Scheme to the Main Markets." Ministry of Commerce, May.

MoC and MPDF. 2005. "Cambodia and the WTO: A Guide for Business." Ministry of Commerce and Mekong Project Development Facility, March.

MoC and JICA. 2001. "Rice Study: Post Harvesting and Marketing." Phnom Penh: Ministry of Commerce/Japan International Cooperation Agency.

MoFAIC. 2005. "Deputy Prime Minister HOR Namhong Meets with UN's envoy." Ministry of Foreign Affairs and International Cooperation Web site, December 1.

MoFAIC. 2006. "Deputy Prime Minister HOR Namhong Meets with EU Troika." Ministry of Foreign Affairs and International Cooperation Web site, January 5.

Moore, M. 2008. "Improving Governance in Bottom Billion Countries." *In Focus* 3. http://www.ids.ac.uk/files/New09-Governance-web.pdf (accessed June 7, 2012)

MPDF. 2004. *Business Bulletin Issues* 3. Phnom Penh, Mekong Project Development Facility.

MSNBC. 2008. "Were Bird Flu Fears Overblown? H5N1 Virus 'Extremely' Stable, Says Animal Health Chief." *MSNBC News Services*, January 10. http://www.msnbc.msn.com/id/22590623/ (accessed June 7, 2012)

Mukherjee, B. 2006. "Does Third-Party Enforcement or Domestic Institutions Promote Enduring Peace after Civil Wars? Policy Lessons from an Empirical Test." *Foreign Policy Analysis* 2(4):405–430.

Mussomeli, J. 2006. "Speech: Dedication of the New Embassy; Remarks by Ambassador Joseph A. Mussomeli." January 17.

NGO Forum on Cambodia. 2002. "NGO Statement to the 2002 Consultative Group Meeting on Cambodia." Phnom Penh, June 19–2. http://www.ngoforum.org.kh/docs/publications/DPP_ngo_2002.zip (accessed June 7, 2012)

NGO Forum. 2006. "NGO Statement to the 2006 Consultative Group Meeting on Cambodia." http://www.ngoforum.org.kh/docs/publications/DPP_CGFeb2006khmerandenglish.zip (accessed June 7, 2012)

OECD. 2011. "Statistics on Resource Flows to Developing Countries." http://www.oecd.org/dac/stats; http://www.oecd.org/dataoecd/1/15/1879774.gif (accessed June 7, 2012)

OHCHR. 2007. "Economic Land Concessions in Cambodia: A Human Rights Perspective." Office of the High Commissioner for Human Rights, June. http://cambodia.ohchr.org/WebDOCs/DocReports/2-Thematic-Reports/Thematic_CMB12062007E.pdf (accessed June 7, 2012)

OIE. 2008. "Comments on recent OIE Director General statements on the avian influenza situation." Press release. World Organisation for Animal Health, January 16, 2008. http://www.oie.int/for-the-media/press-releases/detail/article/comments-on-recent-oie-director-general-statements-on-the-avian-influenza-situation-1 (accessed June 7, 2012)

Öjendal, J. and K. Sedara. 2006. "Korob, Kaud, Klach: In Search of Agency in Rural Cambodia." *Journal of Southeast Asian Studies* 37(3):507–526.

Osborne, M. 1994. *Sihanouk: Prince of Light, Prince of Darkness*. Honolulu, HI: University of Hawaii Press.

Otte, J. and D. Roland-Holst. 2008. "RE: [Pro-Poor Risk Reduction Case studies] E-CONSULTATION DISCUSSION. . . . RISK," e-mail from Joachim Otte to author and other e-consultants, August 20, 9:37 P.M.

Oxfam GB. 2007. "Report on Land Holding in Cambodia." Land and Fishery Program, Oxfam GB Cambodia, March 12.

Pak, K. 2008. "Ok Nha and Advisors in Cambodia." Unpublished brief, June 11.

Pongsudhirak, T. 2008. "Thailand Since the Coup." *Journal of Democracy* 19(4): 140–153.

Post, L., C. Salmon, and A. Raile. 2008. "Using Public Will to Secure Political Will." In *Governance Reform Under Real World Conditions: Citizens, Stakeholders, and Voice*, eds. S. Odugbemi and T. Jacobson. Washington, DC: The World Bank.

Prak, C. T. 2005. "Minister Vows to Beat Graft or Leave Post." *The Cambodia Daily*, March 14.

Prescott, N. and M. Pradhan. 1997. *A Poverty Profile of Cambodia*. Report WDP 373. Washington, DC: World Bank, October 31. http://www-wds.worldbank.org/servlet/ WDSContentServer/WDSP/IB/1997/10/01/000009265_3971126124351/Rendered/ PDF/multi_page.pdf (accessed June 7, 2012)

Prud'homme, R. 1969. *L'économie du Cambodge*. Presses Universitaires de France, Paris.

REC. 1997. "European Union Appealed for Unconditional Aid to Cambodia." *Newsletter of the Royal Embassy of Cambodia*. Washington, DC: Royal Embassy of Cambodia.

Retired Diplomat. 2003. Chapters 1 and 2, "Memoirs of a Retired Diplomat in Cambodia." Posted to a forum in KhmerConnection.com, August 14. http://khmer.cc/ community/t.c?b=13&t=1331 (accessed June 7, 2012)

Reuters. 2006. "Cambodia PM Drops Defamation Suits Against Critics." Reuters News, January 24.

RGC. 2004a. "Address by Samdech Hun Sen on the 'Rectangular Strategy' for Growth, Employment, Equity and Efficiency: First Cabinet Meeting of the Third Legislature of the National Assembly at the Office of the Council of Ministers." Phnom Penh: Royal Government of Cambodia, July 16.

RGC. 2004b. "Implementing the Rectangular Strategy and Development Assistance Needs." Government Position Paper, Phnom Penh: Royal Government of Cambodia, November.

RGC. 2007. *Comprehensive Avian and Human Influenza National Plan: Part 1–Prevention and Preparedness*. Royal Government of Cambodia, July.

RGC. 2010. *The Cambodia Aid Effectiveness Report 2010*, Draft version, April 20, prepared by the Cambodian Rehabilitation and Development Board of the Council for the Development of Cambodia for Third Cambodia Development Cooperation Forum (CDCF) June 2–3.

Richner, B. 2007. "The Dengue Disaster: A Mirror of the Hypocrisy of the Health Policy for the Poor World." Advertisement, *The Cambodia Daily*, July 27. http://www.beat-richner.ch/images/CambiodiaDaily_Richner2777.jpg (accessed June 7, 2012)

Rieff, D. 2002. *A Bed for the Night: Humanitarianism in Crisis*. New York: Simon & Schuster.

Rodrik, D. 2007. *One Economics, Many Recipes: Globalization, Institutions, and Economic Growth*. Princeton, NJ: Princeton University Press.

Rodrik, D. 2008. "Spence Christens a New Washington Consensus." *Economists' Voice*, Berkeley Electronic Press/Project Syndicate, July.

Ros, S. 2008. "What the Parties Spend for the General Election." Trans. Tola Ek. *Cambodge Soir Hebdo*, May 22.

Ros, S. and P. Vireze. 2008. "Green Trade Plans Venture with Indonesian Firm." *The Cambodia Daily*, August 15.

Rose-Ackerman, S. 1999. *Corruption and Government: Causes, Consequences, and Reform.* Cambridge: Cambridge University Press.

Rushdy, S. 2009. "Achieving Cambodia's Millennium Development Goals: Gap Analysis." PriAct, 15 October. http://www.foodsecurity.gov.kh/sites/default/files/documents/CMDG_Gap_Analysis_FINAL.pdf (accessed June 7, 2012)

Sanders, A. 2006. "The Evil Within: Genocide, Memory and Mythmaking in Cambodia," MA thesis, Radboud University Nijmegen, Nijmegen, the Netherlands. http://www.ikvpaxchristi.nl/files/Documenten/Jongeren/Aafke%20Sanders%20hele%20scriptie.pdf (accessed June 7, 2012)

Schlein, L. 2010. "UN Denounces Defamation Case against Politician in Cambodia." *Voice of America*, July 13.

Sciaroni, B. 2004. "The State of the Private Sector." Remarks made at the Consultative Group Meeting, December 5–7. http://www.cdc-crdb.gov.kh/cdc/7cg_meeting/7cg_document/the_state_private_sector.htm (accessed June 7, 2012)

Sciaroni, B. 2006. "Free Speech Not for the Irresponsible." Letter to the Editor, *Phnom Penh Post*, 15/01, January 13–26.

Scoones, I. and P. Forster. 2008. *The International Response to Highly Pathogenic Avian Influenza: Science, Policy and Politics*, STEPS Working Paper 10, Brighton: STEPS Centre.

Scott, J. C. 1976. *The Moral Economy of the Peasant: Rebellion and Subsistence in Southeast Asia.* New Haven, CT: Yale University Press.

Sen, H. 2011. "Address at the Groundbreaking Ceremony for the Construction of the Second ChrauyChangva Bridge." *Phnom Penh*, November 2. http://www.cnv.org.kh/2011_releases/02nov11_jruayjangva%20bridge%20ii%20groundbreaking.html (accessed June 7, 2012)

Sok, H. 2005. "The Political Economy of Development in Cambodia: How to Untie the Gordian Knot of Poverty?" Economic Institute of Cambodia, October-December.

Stiglitz, J. E. 2007. *Making Globalization Work*. New York: W. W. Norton.

St. John, R. B. 2005. "Democracy in Cambodia—One Decade, US$5 Billion Later: What Went Wrong?" *Contemporary Southeast Asia* 27(3):406–428.

Svensson, J. 2000. "Foreign Aid and Rent-Seeking." *Journal of International Economics* 51:437–461.

Takagi, K. 2002. "Relation of Culture to Motivational Orientations." University of California, Los Angeles, Fall. http://www.studentgroups.ucla.edu/upj/fall2002/kaoritakagi.pdf (accessed June 7, 2012)

Tavares, J. 2003. "Does Foreign Aid Corrupt?" *Economics Letters* 79:99–106.

Totten, S. and P. Bartrop. 2008. *Dictionary of Genocide*. Westport, CT: Greenwood Press.

UN. 1992. "The Secretary-General's Consolidated Appeal for Cambodia's Immediate Needs and National Rehabilitation." United Nations Transitional Authority in Cambodia, May.

UN. 2000. *United Nations Development Assistance Framework Cambodia: 2001–2005.* Phnom Penh: United Nations.

UNDP. n.d. "Global Programme for Parliamentary Strengthening." http://web.undp.org/eu/Global_Programme_for_Parliamentary_Strengthening.shtml (accessed June 7, 2012)

Un, K. 2005. "Patronage Politics and Hybrid Democracy: Political Change in Cambodia, 1993–2003." *Asian Perspective* 29(2):203–230.

Un, K. 2006. "State, Society, and Democratic Consolidation: The Case of Cambodia." *Pacific Affairs* 79(2):225–246.

Un, K. 2008. "Cambodia's 2008 Parliamentary Elections: Prospects for Opposition Politics." *Asia Pacific Bulletin*, East-West Center, August 22. http://www.eastwestcenter.org/sites/default/files/private/apb022_2.pdf (accessed June 7, 2012)

Un, K. 2009. "The Judicial System and Democratization in Post-Conflict Cambodia." In *Beyond Democracy in Cambodia: Political Reconstruction in a Post-Conflict Society*, eds. J. Ojendal and M. Lilja. Copenhagen, Denmark: NIAS Press.

UNRC. 2006. "Partnership Meeting on Avian and Pandemic Influenza." Official Minutes taken by United Nations Resident Coordinator's Office, UN Main Conference Room, UNRC, February 20, 2:30–4:20 P.M.

UNRC. 2008. "Avian Influenza and Pandemic Preparedness Funding Matrix Cambodia 2008–2009." Handout prepared by United Nations Resident Coordinator's Office, Phnom Penh, Cambodia.

UNSIC. n.d. "Role and Responsibilities of Ministries: Cambodia." UN System Coordinator for Avian and Human Influenza. http://www.un-influenza.org/regions/asia/role_and_responsibilities_of_ministries+++%09 (accessed June 7, 2012)

UN System. 2008. "Update on the Avian Influenza Situation." *Bulletin on Avian Influenza in Cambodia*, 151, May 16, UN System in Cambodia.

UPI. 1996. "Cambodian PM Jubilant over Donor Aid." United Press International, July 16.

USAID. 2007. "Factory-Level Value Chain Analysis of Cambodia's Apparel Industry." Report produced by Nathan Associates Inc. and Werner International for review by the United States Agency for International Development, September.

U.S. Department of State. 2005. "United States Promotes Bird Flu Prevention in Southeast Asia; Health Secretary Michael Leavitt Extends Aid to Cambodia, Laos." Department of State, October 13. http://usinfo.org/wf-archive/2005/051013/epf404.htm (accessed June 7, 2012)

U.S. Department of State. 2006. *Country Reports on Human Rights Practices, 2005: Cambodia.* Bureau of Democracy, Human Rights, and Labor. Washington, DC: U.S. Department of State.

U.S. Department of State. 2011. "Trafficking in Persons Report." http://www.state.gov/documents/organization/164452.pdf (accessed June 7, 2012)

van de Walle, N. 2005. *Overcoming Stagnation in Aid-Dependent Countries.* Center for Global Development. Washington, DC: Brookings Institution Press.

VSF. 2005. "Review of the poultry production and assessment of the socio-economic impact of the highly pathogenic avian influenza epidemic in Cambodia." Final Report, Vétérinaires Sans Frontières prepared under FAO's TCP/RAS/3010 "Emergency Regional Support for Post Avian Influenza Rehabilitation." http://www.apeiresearch.net/document_file/document_20070706103902-1.pdf (accessed June 7, 2012)

Walsh, N. P. 2009. "Cambodia Farm Land Sold to Wealthy Nations." Channel 4 News, January 29. http://editorials.cambodia.org/2009/01/cambodia-farm-land-sold-to-wealthy.html (accessed June 7, 2012)

Wasson, E. and K. Kimsong. 2006. "Tax Holiday Extended, Bond Market Approved." *The Cambodia Daily*, June 17–18.

Way, L. 2008. "The Real Causes of Color Revolutions." *Journal of Democracy* 19(3):55–69.

Wells, D. 2006. "'Best Practice' in the Regulation of International Labor Standards: Lessons of the U.S.-Cambodia Textile Agreement." *Comparative Labor Law and Policy Journal* 27:357–376.

Wescott, C., ed. 2001. *Key Governance Issues in Cambodia, Lao PDR, Thailand, and Viet Nam.* Asian Development Bank, Programs Department West, April. Manila: ADB.

WHO. 2004. "Summary of Probable SARS Cases with Onset of Illness from 1 November 2002 to 31 July 2003." April 21. http://www.who.int/csr/sars/country/table2004_04_21/en/index.html (accessed June 7, 2012)

Woodd, R. 2004a. "Government in $2 Million Rice Fraud." *Phnom Penh Post* 13/18, August 27–September 9.

Woodd, R. 2004b. "Action Swift Against Scamsters, Says WFP." *Phnom Penh Post* 13/19, September 10–23.

Woodsome, K. 2006. "Cambodian Activists Struggle to Mobilize Nervous Public to Demand Greater Human Rights." Voice of America, January 16.

World Bank. 1994. *Cambodia: From Rehabilitation to Reconstruction.* Report No. 12667. Washington, DC: World Bank, October 2. http://documents.worldbank.org/curated/en/1994/02/698604/cambodia-rehabilitation-reconstruction-economic-report (accessed June 7, 2012)

World Bank. 1998. *Assessing Aid: What Works, What Doesn't, and Why.* Washington, DC: World Bank. http://documents.worldbank.org/curated/en/1998/11/438890/assessing-aid-works-doesnt (accessed June 7, 2012)

World Bank. 1999. *Cambodia: Poverty Assessment*. Report 19858-KH. Washington, DC: World Bank, November 22. http://www-wds.worldbank.org/servlet/WDSContent-Server/WDSP/IB/1999/12/30/000094946_99122006055630/Rendered/PDF/multi_page.pdf (accessed June 7, 2012)

World Bank. 2000. *Cambodia, Governance and Corruption Diagnostic: Evidence from Citizen, Enterprise and Public Official Surveys*. Washington, DC: World Bank, May.

World Bank. 2004a. *Seizing the Global Opportunity: Investment Climate Assessment and Reform Strategy for Cambodia*. Report no. 27925-KH. Washington, DC: World Bank, August 12. http://siteresources.worldbank.org/INTCAMBODIA/Resources/Global-opportunity.pdf (accessed June 7, 2012)

World Bank. 2004b. *Cambodia at the Crossroads: Strengthening Accountability to Reduce Poverty*. Report No. 30636-KH. Washington, DC: World Bank, November 15. http://siteresources.worldbank.org/INTCAMBODIA/Resources/1-report.pdf (accessed June 7, 2012)

World Bank. 2005a. *World Development Indicators, 2005*. Washington, DC: World Bank.

World Bank. 2005b. "World Bank Group President James D. Wolfensohn Wraps up Visit to Cambodia, Urges: 'Seize The Opportunity.'" Press release. Phnom Penh: World Bank, February 11. http://go.worldbank.org/HG6QX3ZSH0 (accessed June 7, 2012)

World Bank. 2006a. *Halving Poverty by 2015: Poverty Assessment 2006*. Report No. 35213. Washington, DC: World Bank, February 7. http://www-wds.worldbank.org/servlet/WDSContentServer/WDSP/IB/2006/02/22/000012009_20060222102151/Rendered/PDF/352130REV0pdf.pdf (accessed June 7, 2012)

World Bank. 2006b. "International Pledging Conference on Avian and Human Influenza." Beijing, January 17–18. http://go.worldbank.org/WM53VJH7W0 (accessed June 7, 2012)

World Bank. 2006c. "World Bank Statement on Cambodia." World Bank Country Office Press Release, January 9. http://go.worldbank.org/OR2NGA0M40 (accessed June 7, 2012)

World Bank. 2008a. "Cambodia's Efforts to Fight Avian Flu Get World Bank, Multi-donor Support." World Bank, March 25. http://go.worldbank.org/O78GS5GIY0 (accessed June 7, 2012)

World Bank and ADB. 2003. "Cambodia: Enhancing Service Delivery Through Improved Resource Allocation and Institutional Reform; Integrated Fiduciary Assessment and Public Expenditure Review." World Bank and Asian Development Bank Report no. 25611 KH, September 8. http://www-wds.worldbank.org/servlet/WDS_IBank_Servlet?pcont=details&eid=000090341_20030924104425 (accessed June 7, 2012)

Xinhua. 2004. "Cambodia Bans Import of Birds from Neighboring Flu Nations." *Xinhua General News Service*, January 13.

Xinhua. 2007a. "Cambodia to Educate Remote Communities About Dangers of Avian Influenza." *Xinhua General News Service*, September 25.

Xinhua. 2007b. "FAO Helps Train Cambodian Veterinarians on Bird Flu Surveillance." *Xinhua General News Service*, July 13.

Xinhua. 2008a. "Cambodia Grants Sale of 6,000 Tons Broken Rice to Senegal." April 23. Chinaview.cn. http://news.xinhuanet.com/english/2008-04/23/content_8036128.htm (accessed June 7, 2012)

Xinhua. 2008b. "Dengue Death Rate Reaches 10% in Cambodia in 2007." *Xinhua General News Service*, January 4.

Xinhua. 2008c. "Donor Countries Pledge About $1 Bln to Cambodia for 2009." *People's Daily Online*, December 6. http://english.people.com.cn/90001/90777/90851/6548262.html (accessed June 7, 2012)

Zeeuw, J. 2005. "Projects Do Not Create Institutions: The Record of Democracy Assistance in Post-Conflict Societies." *Democratization* 12(4):481–504.

INDEX